I0901007

IMAGES of America

FARRELL

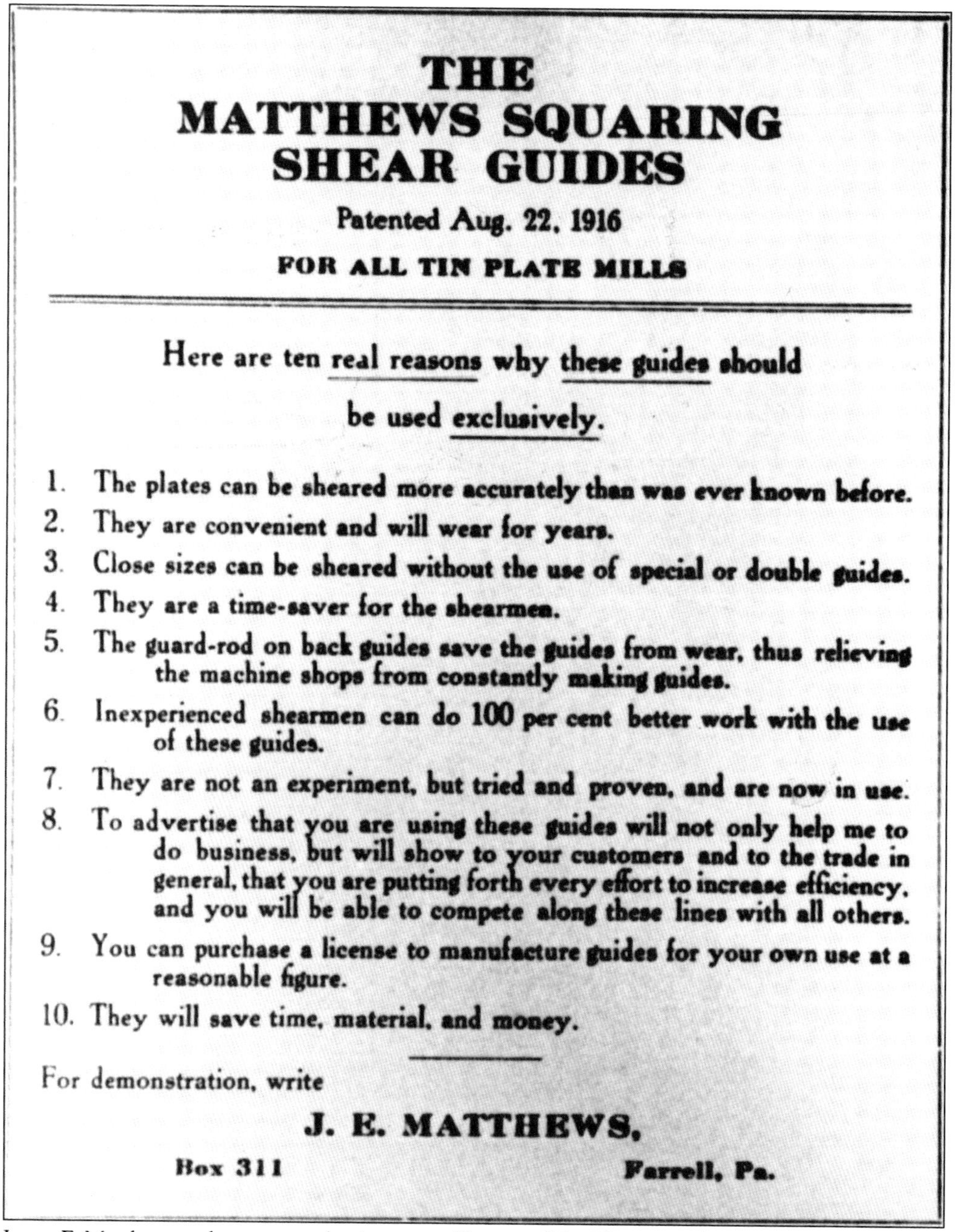

James E. Matthews, a shearman at the American Sheet and Tin Plate's South Sharon Works, invented a shear guide patented in 1916 and recognized as "the work of a genius." (Author's collection.)

On the Cover: After World War II, the congregation of St. Michael's Church participated in a Victory Day parade down Idaho Street. Myer Frank Furniture is in the background. Myer Frank, a Lithuanian Jewish immigrant, came to the area on the back of his father's peddler wagon. (Courtesy of the Stey-Nevant Public Library.)

IMAGES
of America

FARRELL

Roland Barksdale-Hall

ARCADIA
PUBLISHING

ISBN 978-0-7385-9230-5

Published by Arcadia Publishing
Charleston, South Carolina

Printed in the United States of America

Library of Congress Control Number: 2011945127

For all general information, please contact Arcadia Publishing:
Telephone 843-853-2070
Fax 843-853-0044
E-mail sales@arcadiapublishing.com
For customer service and orders:
Toll-Free 1-888-313-2665

Visit us on the Internet at www.arcadiapublishing.com

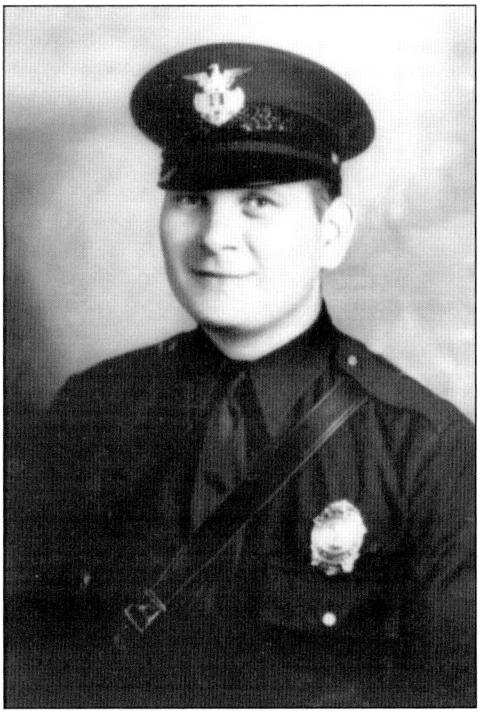

To Frank J. Egercic, whose love of Farrell and dedicated service helped to preserve the success stories from the past for those who followed

Contents

ACKNOWLEDGMENTS

The research libraries, archives, and photographic collections of the Stey-Nevant Public Library and Mercer County Historical Society have been of immeasurable help with this project. These collections provide a treasure of interesting images and stories that document the history of Farrell. The staff, who provide service, have earned my gratitude. Some images in this volume appear courtesy of the Mercer County Historical Society (MCHS); Library and Archives, Senator John Heinz Pittsburgh Regional History Center (SJHPRHC); and Stey-Nevant Public Library (SNPL).

It would be impossible to thank all the countless supporters who helped make this book possible. Please accept my humble appreciation to some who contributed to this endeavor, including Calumet Lodge No. 25, Prince Hall Affiliation; First National Bank; Greater Morris Chapel African Methodist Episcopal Church; Mercer County Historical Society; Msgr. Geno Monti School of Our Lady of Fatima; Shenango Valley Urban League; Southwest Gardens Economic Development Corporation; Stey-Nevant Public Library; Rev. Donald Berdis; Rev. Thomas Bolling; Alan Brandt; John Gallichio; Andrea Bohach Grega; Rudolph Hammond; William Jarrett; Dr. James Kollar; Kerry Lapcevich; Joanne Lloyd; James Mendez Matthews; Shirley Matthews; Russell Phillips; Joe C. Pulliam; Martha Richards; Debbie Matthews Walters; Ronald and Karen Weston; Rosella Vuich; Karen Vargo Wildman; Roger Winston; Michael Wright; and Ann Yazvac.

I would like to thank my editor at Arcadia Publishing, Abby Henry, for her expertise and ready response to inquiries; my neighbors Alan Brandt, Irene Johnson, Shirley Jean Matthews, Martha Richards, Ann Yazvac, Marcy Pedas Sigler, Ted Pedas, Tom Pedas, George Pedas, Karen Vargo Wildman, and Roger Winston for sharing countless family stories. For research assistance I am indebted to Art Louderback, Joanne Lloyd, Bill Philson, Margaret Orchard, Paulette Farkas, Charlene Kay, Toni Sheehan, and Cheryl Smoot.

Dr. Laurence Glasco, Dr. Joseph Rishel and Patricia Powers provided the early guidance and encouragement that fostered my interest in local history. Colleagues at Penn State Shenango and Farrell Area School District gave a friendly boost at the right time.

Long-serving policeman Frank J. Egercic (1913–1993), a 1931 Farrell High School alumnus, collected images that document the culture and life in Farrell. He meticulously covered events that span 80 years. His enterprising Egercic-Husnick-Yazvac family members, in particular Ann Yazvac and Fred and Rose Husnick, were gracious in providing access to the collection.

Michael Wright, executive director of the Shenango Valley Urban League, helped to solicit support. Colleagues at the Shenango Valley website shared their network of friends and neighbors with an interest in the welfare of Farrell. Marcy Pedas Sigler and the philanthropic Pedas family lovingly shared from their Farrell research database, family papers, and collective memories.

Mayor Ollie Brown McKeithan and the Farrell's head librarian Margaret Orchard, who approached me about researching and writing about Farrell, have provided encouragement and support. Fr. Donald Berdis and the congregation of St. Ann-Our Lady of Fatima have been a godsend in this and other life endeavors. May God continue to bless the city of Farrell. I count myself and family just one among the multitude of her thankful beneficiaries.

Finally, to my precious wife, Drusilla, and children, Rillis, Drew, Vonita, and Imanuel-Tiefing, thank you for your love and patience, not just with this endeavor, but in this wonderful life.

INTRODUCTION

At the turn of the 20th century, South Sharon emerged from undeveloped lands into an industrial center. Waves of job seekers and speculators came in search of opportunity. In 1901, Frank Buhl broke ground for an industrial development in a dense, woody, and swampy area south of Sharon. South Sharon, hailed as "The Magic City," saw rapid population growth and economic development. In 1912, South Sharon was incorporated as Farrell in recognition of James A. Farrell, then president of United States Steel. Carnegie Steel, American Sheet and Tin Plate, and American Steel and Wire spurred the population growth and development of the area. A business corridor arose on Idaho Street and Broadway Boulevard, attracting shoppers from outlying communities. The first decade witnessed the transformation of the frontier into a cosmopolitan center.

Collective family stories flesh out the achievement of the American dream. Among those attracted by the recruitment campaigns and monetary incentives of regional steel mills were the Steversons of Georgia. Etania Steverson was a sharecropper in rural Georgia. The boll weevil's destruction of the cotton crop prompted an exodus of African Americans from the rural South to the industrial North. During the Great Migration, natives of two black belt states, Georgia and Alabama, comprised the largest African American migrant population in western Pennsylvania. Around the same time, across the Atlantic Ocean, Steve Pedas (Efstathios Tsimpedas), a goat herder, faced dismal economic prospects in Greece and immigrated to America. He moved to Farrell and found employment in the mills. Both men benefited from expanded opportunity in the industrial center.

The first generation of eastern and southern European immigrants and southern migrants were courageous to pull up roots and come to Farrell. Transplants from across the world found the work difficult and dangerous and ample housing remained in short supply, yet they endured and relied on extended families and social networks from former villages. Multiethnic neighborhoods characterized by synagogues, churches, and social clubs formed. The first wave of settlers was mainly Irish, English, Welsh, and German, and they were followed by Italians, Slovaks, and Croatians. Others included Greeks, Serbians, Hungarians, Romanians, and Poles. Later, southern migrants followed Bulgarians and Macedonians. The first generation treasured the privilege of American citizenship.

During the prosperous 1920s, the majority of ethnic groups witnessed social tension. Elitist fraternal groups worked against African American unity by promoting classism. In Farrell, the local Knights of Pythias, with its rich endowment, attracted semiskilled workers, but their exorbitant fees and exclusionary practices worked against them. Prince Hall Masonry played an important role in the development of bourgeois values, although during the 1920s, it was no less susceptible to factional strife than other African American organizations. In 1920, there was a challenge to the status quo when a group of African American men moved to establish another Masonic Lodge in Farrell. Appeals for unity thwarted this drive, but a rift among the wives of those involved meant that two female auxiliaries operated until 1929, when attrition forced a merger. Around the same time, the existence of two synagogues in Farrell discouraged unity. The Orthodox B'Nai Zion, organized in 1902 by a majority of Hungarian Jews, met early on Greenfield Avenue. Russians, Romanians, and Lithuanians separated from the B'Nai Zion congregation in 1916 and organized the Orthodox Ahabath Achim congregation on Lee Avenue. The two synagogues merged in 1930.

In 1932, the borough of Farrell became a city. During the 1930s and 1940s, the social ethnic clubs raised money for nationalist churches, promoted gymnastics and other sporting activities, and taught how to become an American citizen. They also boosted ethnic interests and ethnic candidates. *Ripley's Believe It Or Not* listed Farrell as a town with one of the highest number of churches and bars per capita. The bars catered to many ethnic social clubs, providing working-class people an opportunity to preserve their cultural traditions, learn the English language, and find a sense of belonging. In 1940, the Croatian Civic League basketball team won an independent national basketball competition in Gary, Indiana. By 1944, the Twin City Elks Lodge owned a meeting facility and a bus and had won the National Elks Basketball Championship in New York City. The social ethnic clubs allowed the first and second generations to put down roots, and later generations felt more integrated into American society. While some viewed the loss of social ethnic clubs whimsically or at best with nostalgia, their decline proved an accomplishment of a mission—full American citizenship.

In the 1950s, Farrell staked its reputation as a title town. No matter if they were children of peasants, goat herders, or cotton pickers, everyone received the same quality education at Farrell High School. It remained up to the individual what they did with that quality education. With hard work and perseverance, later generations achieved success. In 1952, coach Edward McCluskey won the first of seven state basketball championships. Farrell had already established an enviable reputation as a championship basketball town almost a decade before the emergence of the famed McCluskey basketball dynasty. The Farrell High School Steelers established a state record for wins, having won more than 20 state titles: seven in basketball, two in football, one in girls' track, eight in girls' volleyball, and three in wrestling. Although the community was touched with racial unrest in the 1960s, hard work and winning was instilled in this new generation. After graduating from Farrell High School, locals distinguished themselves in business, sports, education, and civic service. Many also served in the military, and all residents fully participated in the American political process.

Beginning in the 1980s, the regional economy of western Pennsylvania, including Farrell's, suffered due to the decline of steel manufacturing, upon which the town had a historical dependence. Between 1980 and 1990, the workforce of Sharon Steel, based in Farrell, decreased from 4,500 to 2,500. Some were forced to leave in search of other opportunities and carried with them a spirit of enterprise forged in Farrell. The annual Farrell High School Alumni Banquet still calls them back home. This banquet has provided the opportunity to rekindle friendships, celebrate successes, and remember Farrell's golden past. As Larry Flint writes in his poem "Farrell," which appeared in the Farrell Boosters Club 1932 souvenir program, southern and eastern European immigrants and southern migrants selected Farrell as their chosen city.

They say my town's a city built of many kinds and creeds,
With tinge of many nations' blood and many brands and breeds.
But mine's a chosen city! Mine's a people born afar.
And, free to settle where they chose, they settle where they are.
There were a thousand cities, but they passed them all in line.
Is it to blame or praise it that they chose to come to mine?

My town's a melting pot, they say, a many-peopled place.
But my town finds its glory in a mixed and mingled race.
My town's a town of souls select, unleashed from bonds of birth,
Who chose my town to live in for its welcome and its worth.
My town is cosmopolitan, a city built of those
Who live and love and laugh within its wall—because they chose.

One

SOUTH SHARON

"MAGIC CITY"

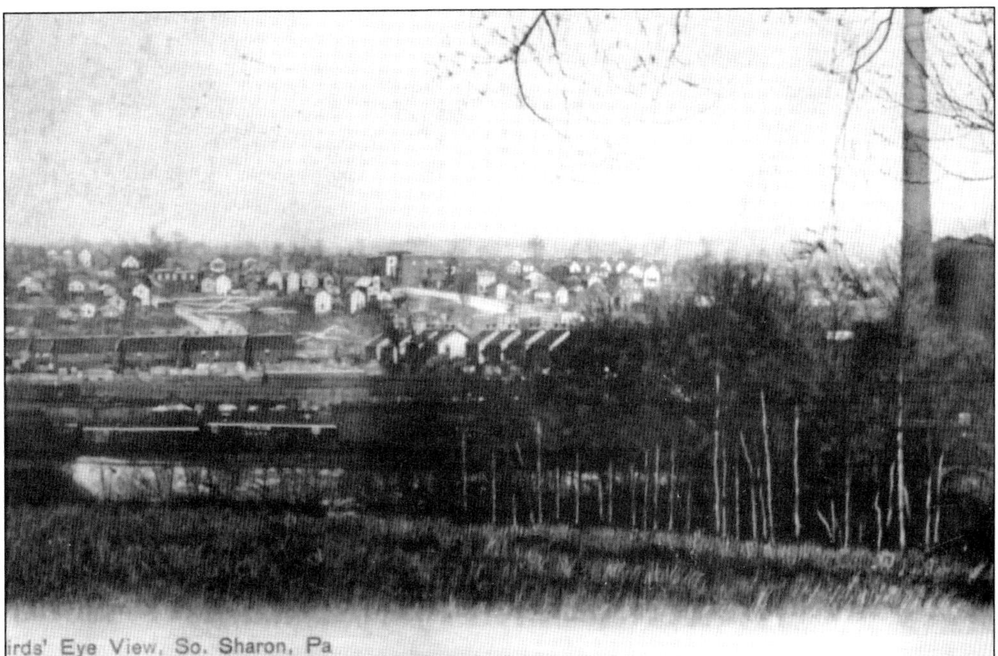

Hope of achieving the American dream attracted eastern and southern European immigrants and southern migrants to South Sharon. Directly behind this crop of trees on the bottomlands is the multiethnic enclave known as Little Italy. Residents lived near the mills for convenience. (Courtesy of MCHS.)

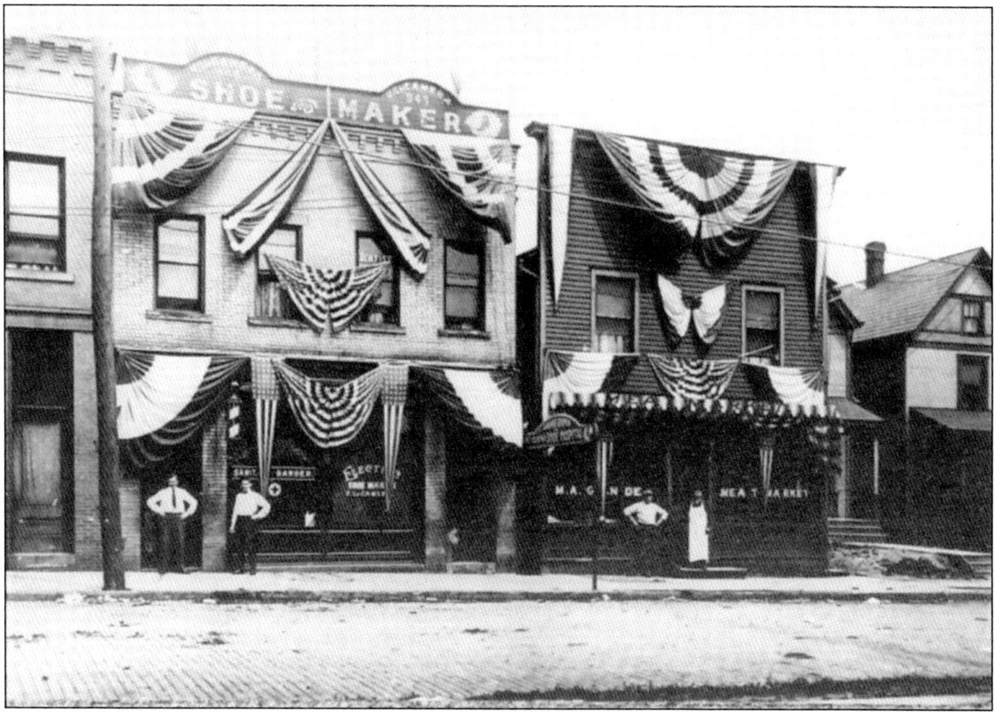

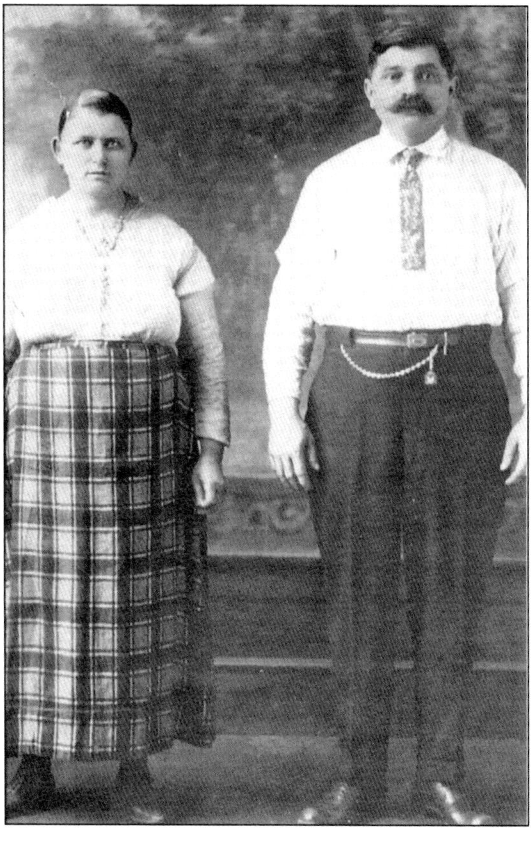

The Beechwood Improvement Company advertised 150- to 250-foot lots at a price range of $50 to $190 with 10 percent down. Boosters touted, sometimes embellished, the new city of South Sharon and its benefits. Chiccarino's Barber Shop, Vincent LaCamera's Shoe Market, and M.A. Grande Meat Market were located on Fruit Avenue in 1911. Vincent LaCamera (1877–1958), born in Altomonate, Italy, became a prominent realtor and insurance man. (Courtesy of Ann Yazvac)

Prominent Croatian immigrants owned grocery stores near Staunton and Greenfield. Grocer John Frankovitch was the European Hotel's proprietor in 1913. Anton Pintar was also a grocer as well as president of Croatian Fraternal Union, Lodge 187, in South Sharon. His son Anthony J. Pintar served on the first public library board and was a school principal. Fellow Croatian immigrants Tom Egercic (1879–1965) and Anna Valetich (1886–1938) met and married in South Sharon around 1909. (Courtesy of Ann Yazvac.)

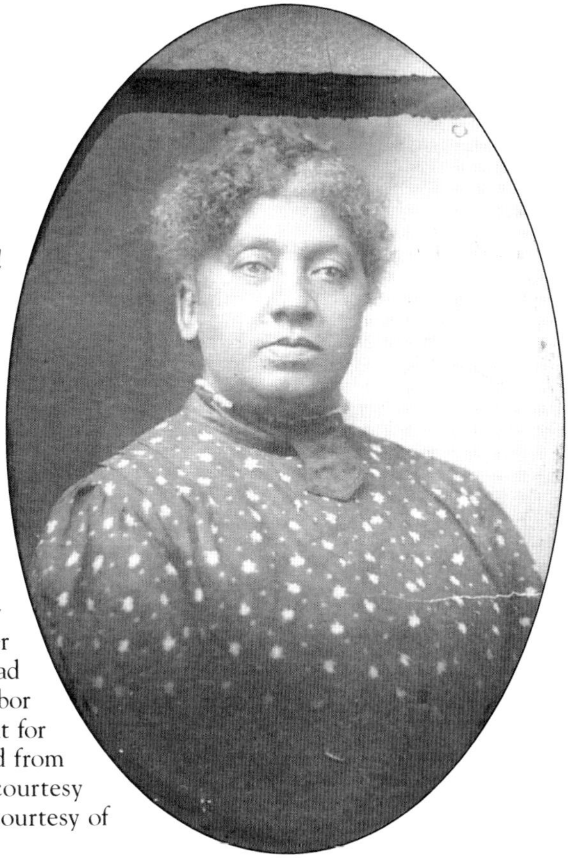

According to a story in the *Sharon Herald* on September 25, 1903, a 300-foot double lane bridge with sidewalks was constructed of iron and stone masonry and was scheduled for completion in four months. Settlers came to South Sharon from Pennsylvania, Ohio, and West Virginia. Hardworking Italian immigrants came from Venango County to settle in Little Italy. Earlier Italians worked laying pipes from the Titusville oilfields. In the pioneer days, firemen often could not reach Little Italy because of dirt roads made muddy by rain. Below, Scotty Wilson and his father exercise a team of fire horses. The Homestead Strike of 1892 disrupted families and the labor movement and was a life-changing event for Matilda Matthews (right), who migrated from Homestead to South Sharon. (Right, courtesy of Shirley Matthews Williams; below, courtesy of Ann Yazvac.)

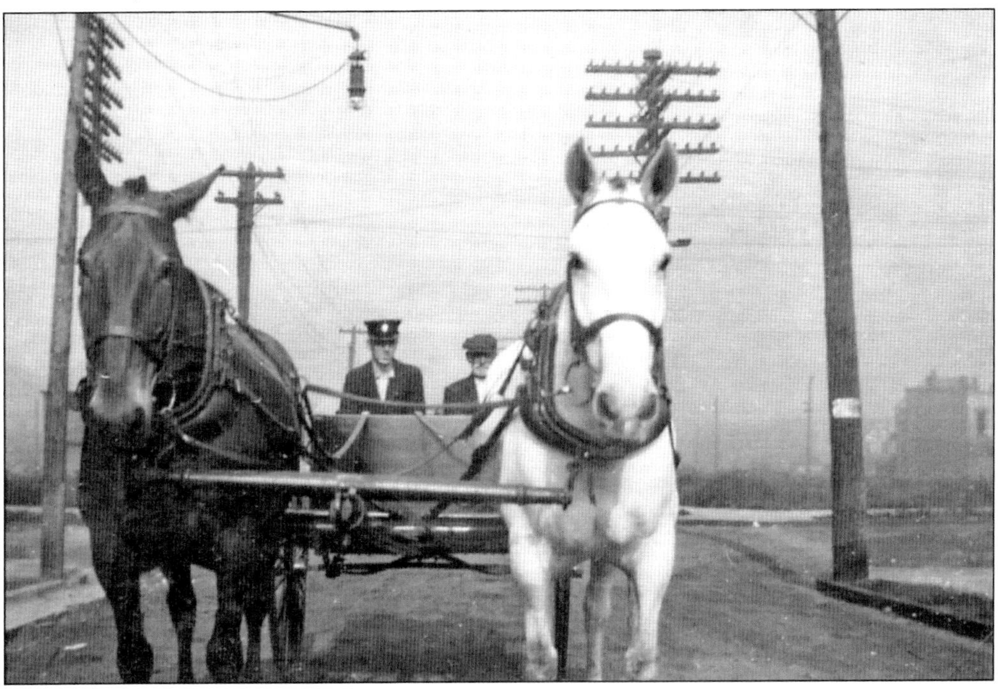

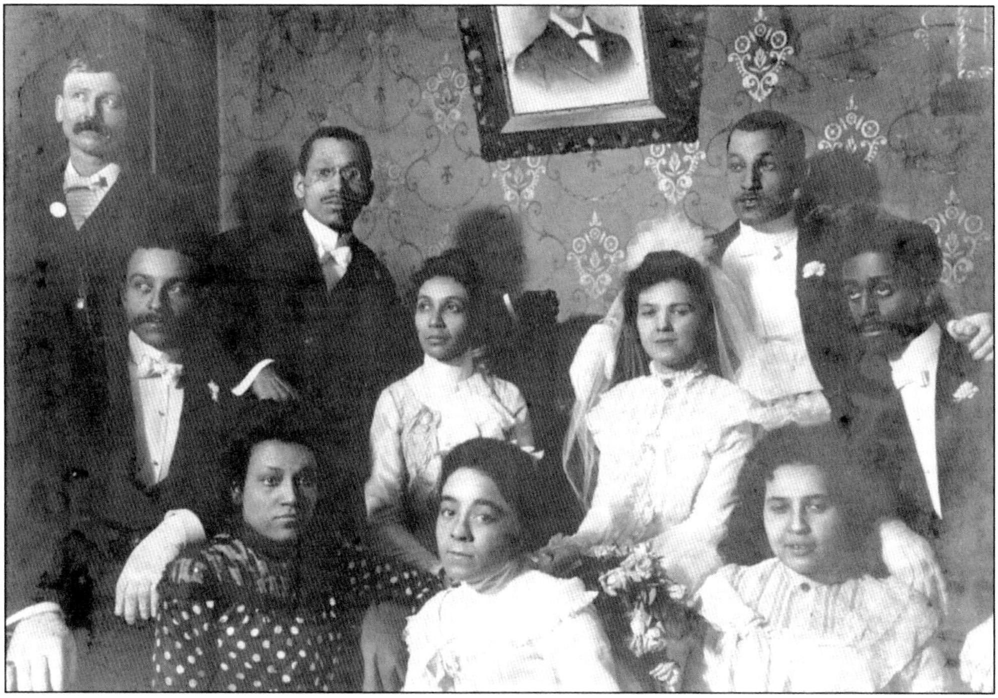

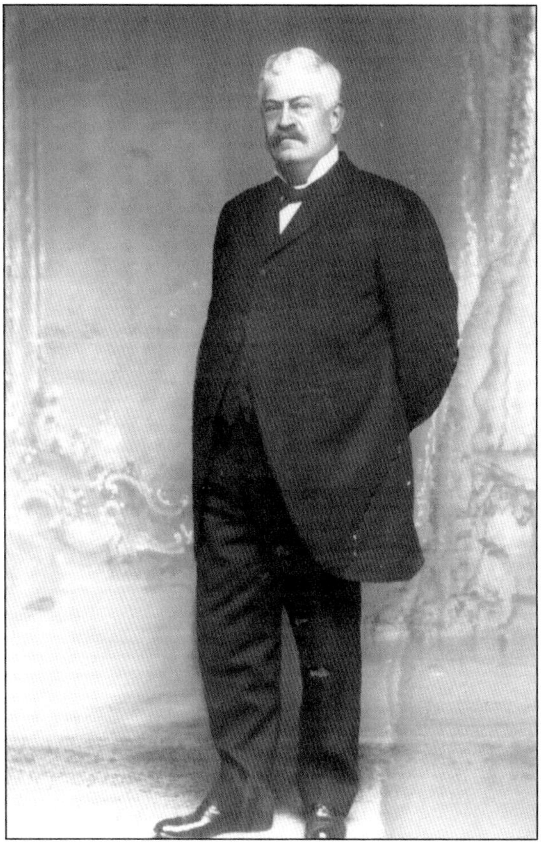

William Hunter Dammond, an African American inventor and engineer, worked as a draftsman, an exceptional feat at a time when skilled work was limited for African Americans in western Pennsylvania. The wedding party of Edna Dammond Richmond included, from left to right, (first row) Lula Dammond Thompson, unidentified, and Emma Dammond Thompson; (second row) Howard Dammond, Mable Dammond, Edna Dammond Richmond, and ? Thompson; (third row) unidentified, William Hunter Dammond, and Walter Dammond. (Author's collection.)

Frank H. Buhl (1848–1918), president of the Buhl Steel Company, was a primary developer of the iron and steel industry in the twin communities of Sharon and South Sharon. Recognized for his philanthropy, several sites bore Buhl's name. In the 1930s, a proposal to merge the two cities and name it Buhl City was circulated, but it was defeated at the polls. (Courtesy of MCHS.)

In 1940, the Buhl trustees established the Frank H. Buhl Center in Farrell, later known as the Carver Community Center. Buhl's status, coupled with his many philanthropic pursuits, made the kidnapping of Billy Whitla, Buhl's grand-nephew, a sensational national event. When it was rumored that Whitla was in Pittsburgh, thousands turned out to search for the boy. (Courtesy of MCHS.)

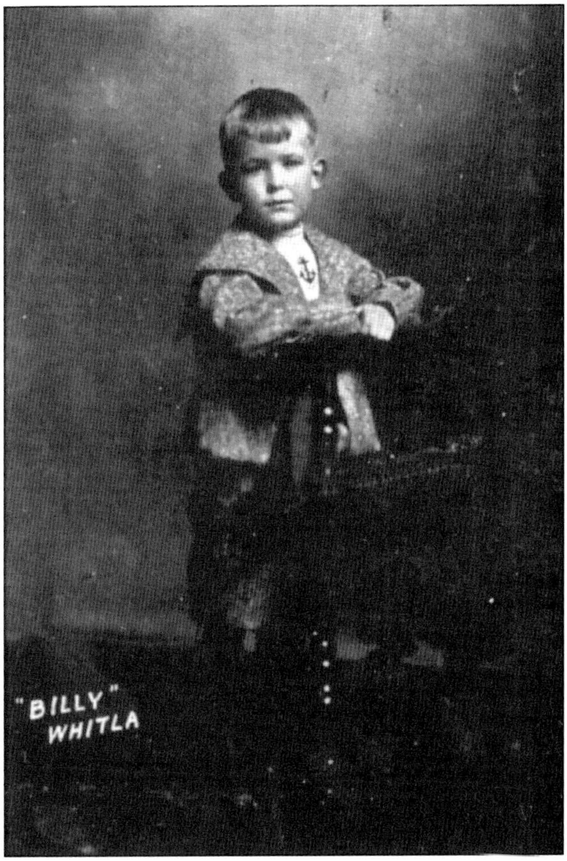

Buhl and John Stevenson spearheaded the expansion of the Buhl Steel Company. Stevenson later served on the board of directors of Farrell's Colonial Trust Company, seen here. The Buhl Steel Company, acquired by the Carnegie-Illinois Steel Company, became known as the Carnegie-Illinois Steel Farrell Works, and an industrial complex developed around its buildings. (Courtesy of MCHS.)

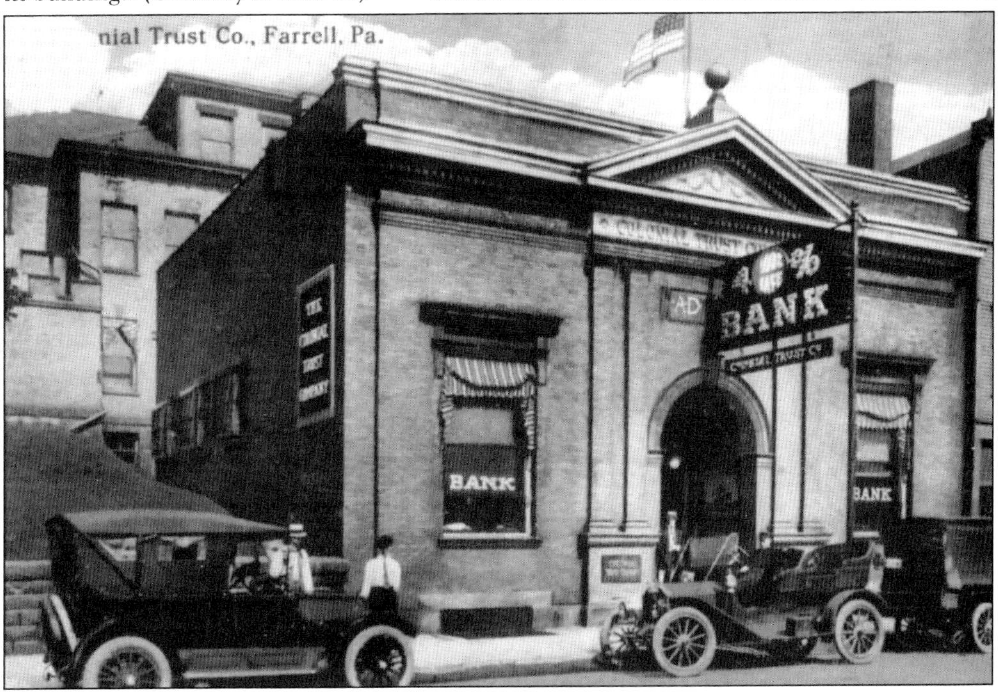

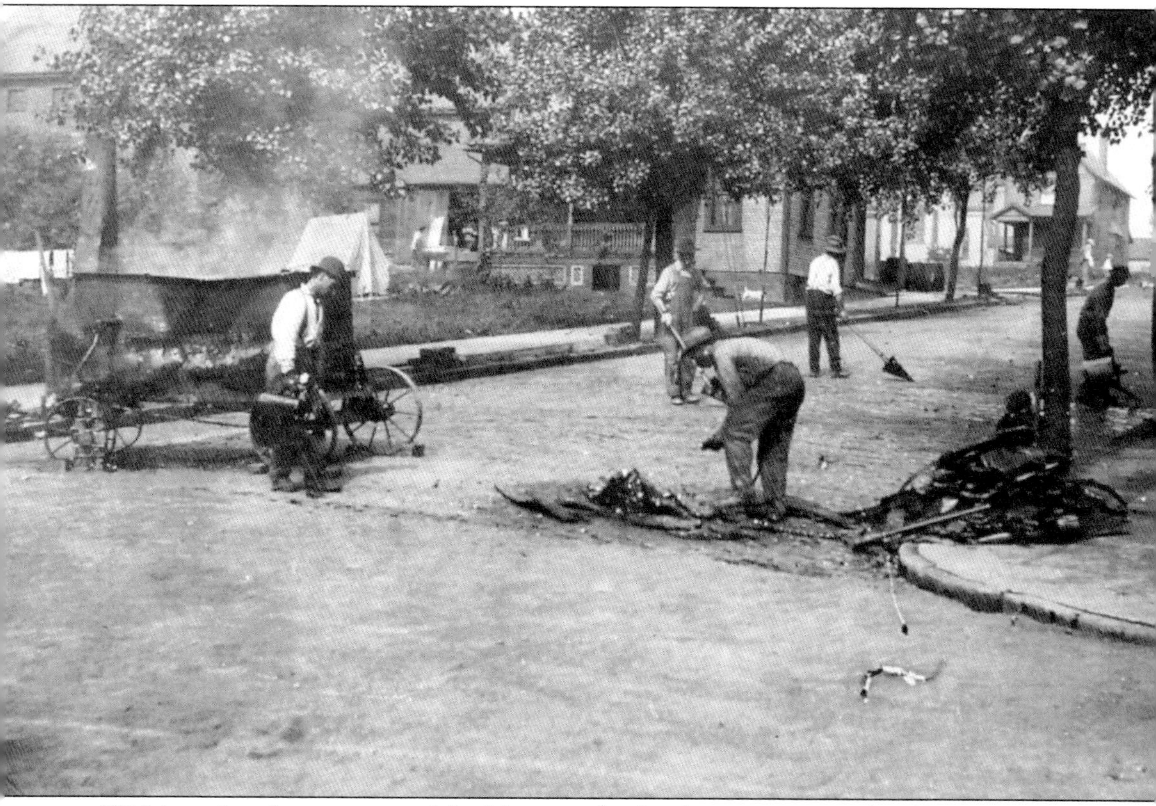

Within a decade, commercial buildings and schools sprang up and mills were on the horizon. Boardinghouses and hotels dotted the landscape. The bricklayers, who laid the redbrick streets that became South Sharon's trademark, were celebrated. The elimination of unpaved roads was in progress. Here, the corner of Darr Avenue and Adams Street in South Sharon gets paved. (Courtesy of Ann Yazvac.)

Two

Steel Heritage
American Made

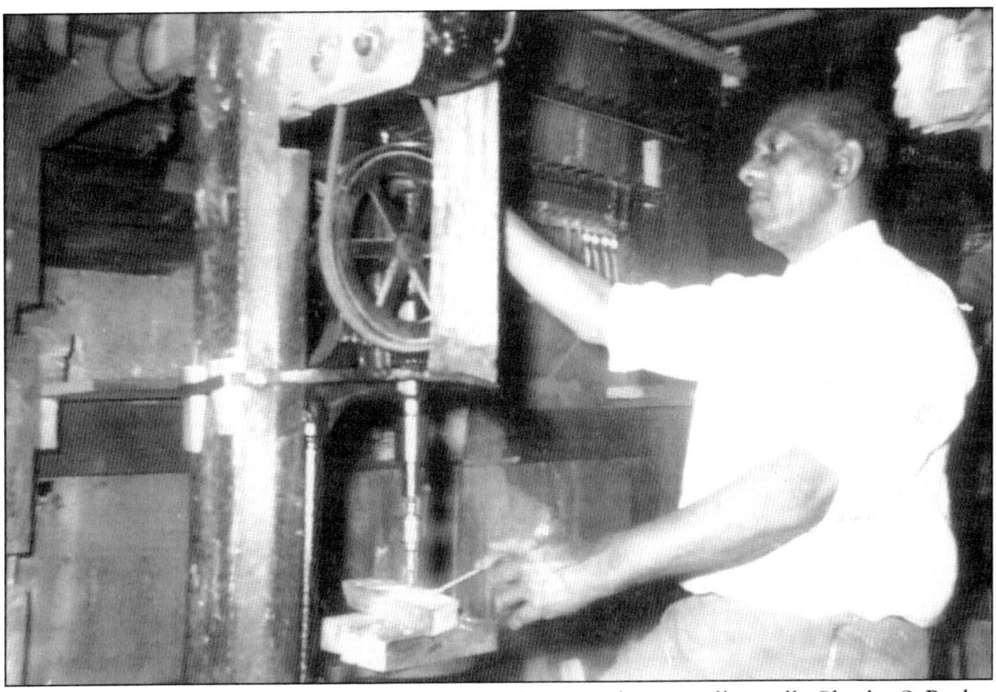

In 1916, "American Tin for Everything" was the slogan at the tin mill, recalls Charles S. Butler, a former tin worker. In 1916, James E. Matthews invented a shear guide used for snipping tin at the American Sheet and Tin Plate Company. (Courtesy of Shirley Matthews.)

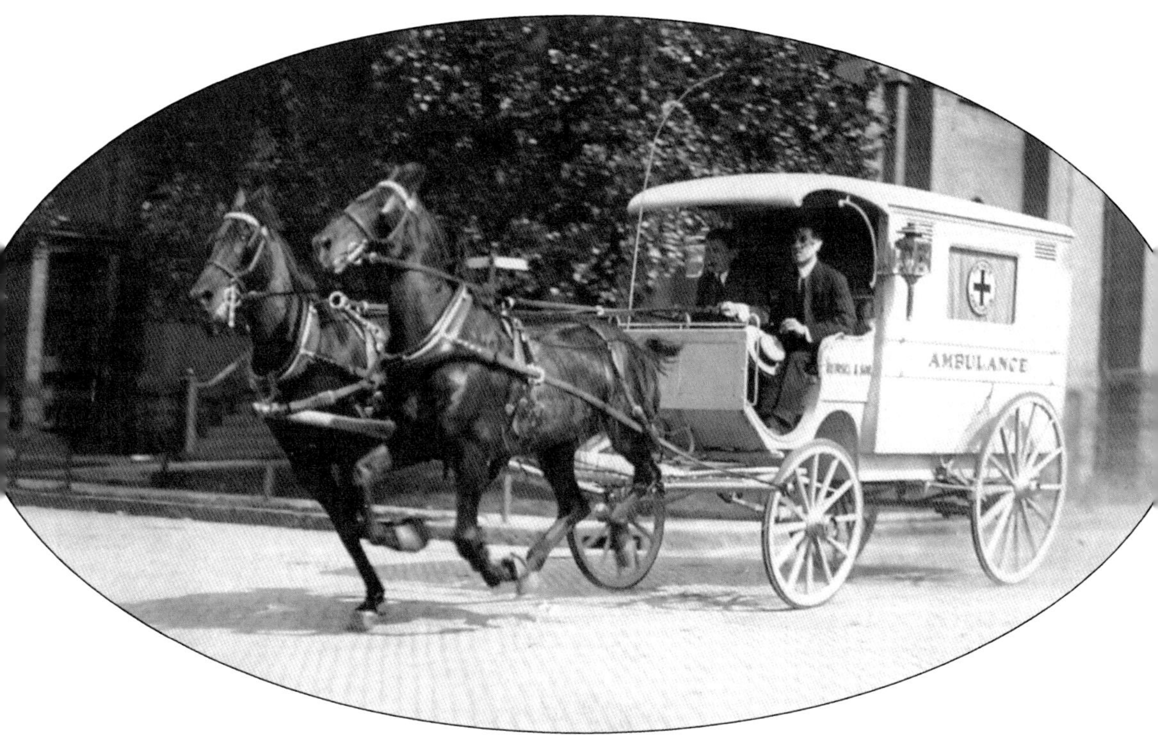

Opportunities for advancement opened with retirement. George Ray, a retired mill worker, recalled the old guard protecting positions in the mill. As late as the 1940s, Ray recalled how some crane operators with seniority refused to train an Italian who had been promoted to a crane man. The majority of skilled work favored those with prior mill experience, though unions supported preferential hiring practices at the same time. When the Amalgamated Association of Iron and Steelworkers called a strike in 1909, local company officials of the American Sheet and Tin Plate Company exploited racial antipathies and employed African Americans as skilled, nonunion workers. In 1919, union organizers addressed meetings in six different foreign languages, including Italian, Slovak, Polish, and Croatian. The workers had many legitimate concerns, such as hazards and pay; however, an outbreak of violence detracted from their concerns. The national 1919 strike took an unexpected turn in Farrell when a crowd of about 2,000 "strikers, spectators and many immigrant women" faced off with strikebreakers as they exited the gate of the American Steel and Wire Company near Staunton Avenue. Several strikebreakers were attacked and beaten badly. A bloody clash between state troopers called to the scene and area strikers followed. Ambulances, like the one seen above, had to rush to the scene. Over two days, a sweep of homes by state troopers in the multiethnic neighborhood around Staunton Avenue where alleged sharpshooters operated resulted in death and serious injury to both men and women, the bulk being immigrants. Kathryn Egercic Husnick recalled that policemen on horseback struck people on foot with billy clubs, and there was gunfire in residential areas, too. The innocent hurt included an immigrant, who was shot and killed in his garden. She never forgot the terror of those times. Paul Prat, a laborer at Sharon Steel Hoop, who resided at 1017 Greenfield Avenue, was actually the first person killed when he allegedly hurled a brick that struck an officer in the back of the head. A 33-year-old Romanian, Alex Russ, an employee at Sharon Steel Hoop, was also killed, and two state troopers were wounded. In the press, alleged Bolshevists were blamed for the disturbance in Farrell, although unfair labor practices partially contributed to the unrest. Finally, on September 23, 1919, the front-page headlines stated, "Farrell Quiet After Fatal Disorders." Samuel Malloy recounted, though, "The way families behaved during the 1919 strike was a curse which passed from generation to generation. Families just couldn't live it down." (Courtesy of Ann Yazvac.)

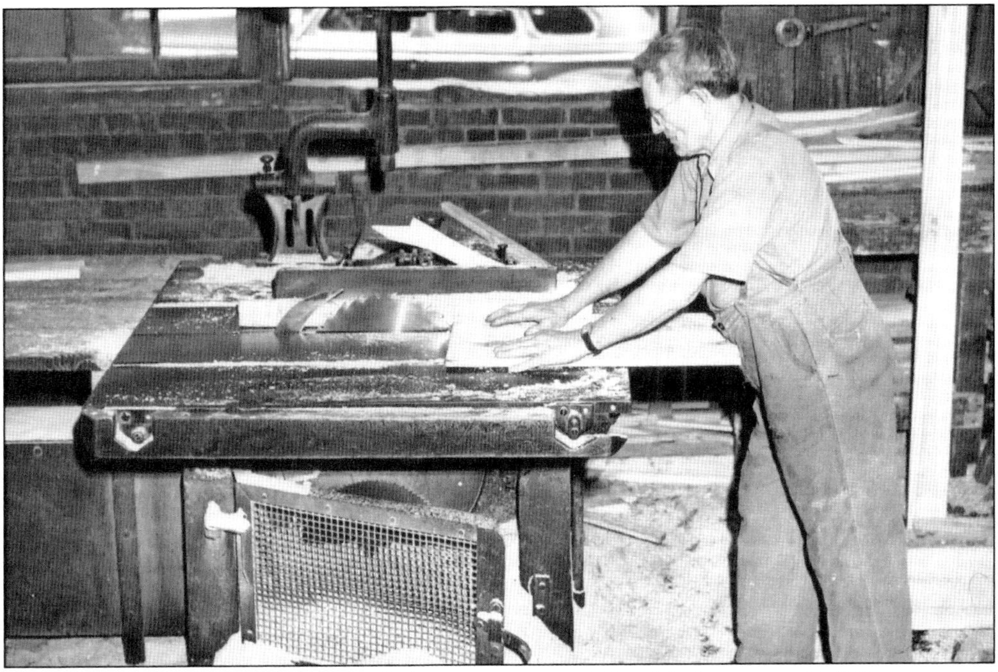

A *Farrell News* article, titled "Farrell Americanization School Is Largest in U.S.," announced that 500 employees from the American Sheet and Tin Plate Company (AMSTP) enrolled in the Americanization program in one evening; the total number enrolled was almost 1,000. It was conducted at the James A. Farrell school. In 1919, AMSTP manager J.T. Douhert and Rev. P.J. Bowen were prominent in promoting Americanization in Farrell. By the 1940s, the majority of steelworkers were American citizens. (Courtesy of Ann Yazvac.)

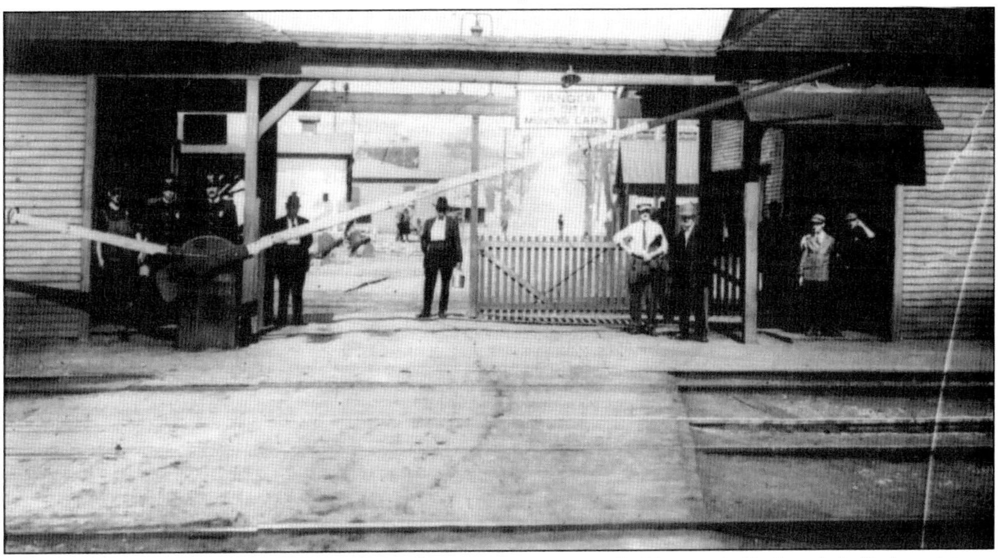

Millworkers of English, Welsh, Irish, and German ancestry held semiskilled and skilled positions early on. In 1909, James E. Matthews, a native of Homestead and a six-year veteran at the company's South Sharon Works accepted a shearer's job and went on to invent his famous shear guide. By 1919, eastern and southern European immigrants and southern migrants were positioning for advancement in the mills. (Courtesy of MCHS.)

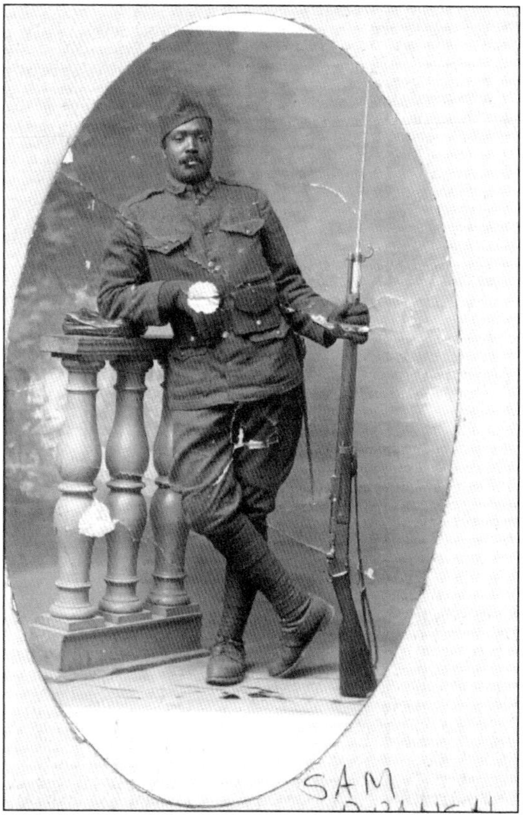

Daniel Phillips, Charles Wayne, and H. Russell Wayne were recognized as early African American rollers in the tin mill, an exceptional circumstance for an African American worker in western Pennsylvania. Following World War I, southern migrants became the second wave of African Americans attracted by employment to the Farrell mills. Pictured is Sam Branch, a veteran of World War I. (Courtesy of Shirley Jean Matthews.)

Some African American veterans of World War I, imported as strikebreakers, faced challenges. Samuel Malloy recounted a harrowing account about his grandfather, Gus McDowell, during the 1919 strike in Farrell. McDowell, an employee at the American Steel and Wire Company, was pinned down by sniper gunfire at Staunton Avenue. Malloy (below, seated at right) was an honoree at the first officer's banquet of Greater Morris Chapel African Methodist Episcopal Church. (Author's collection.)

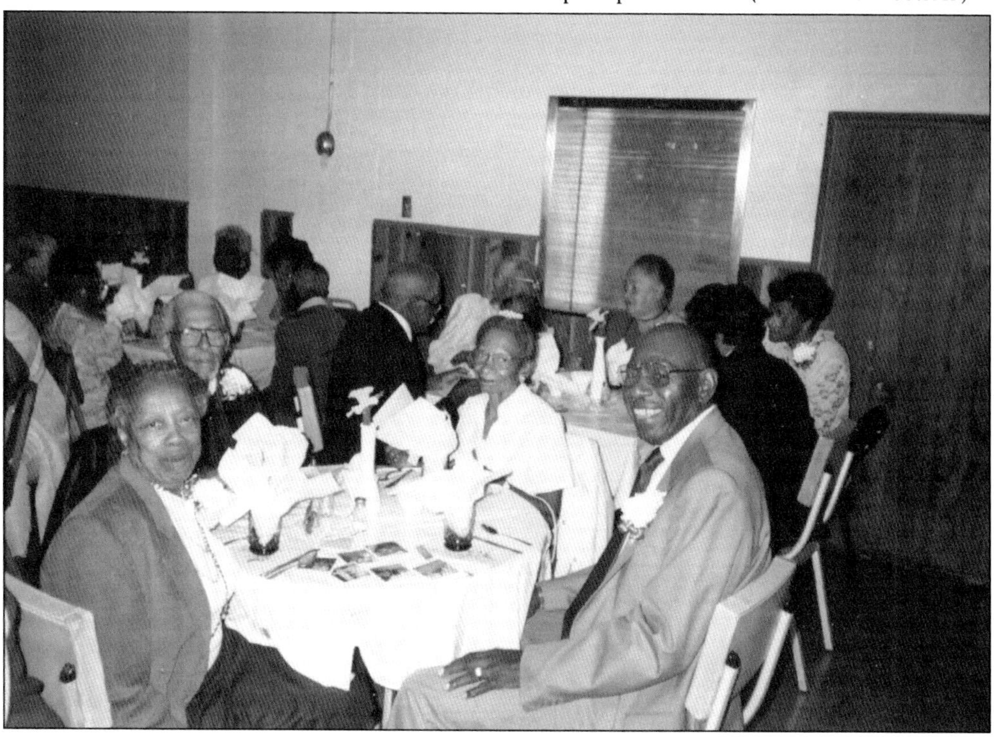

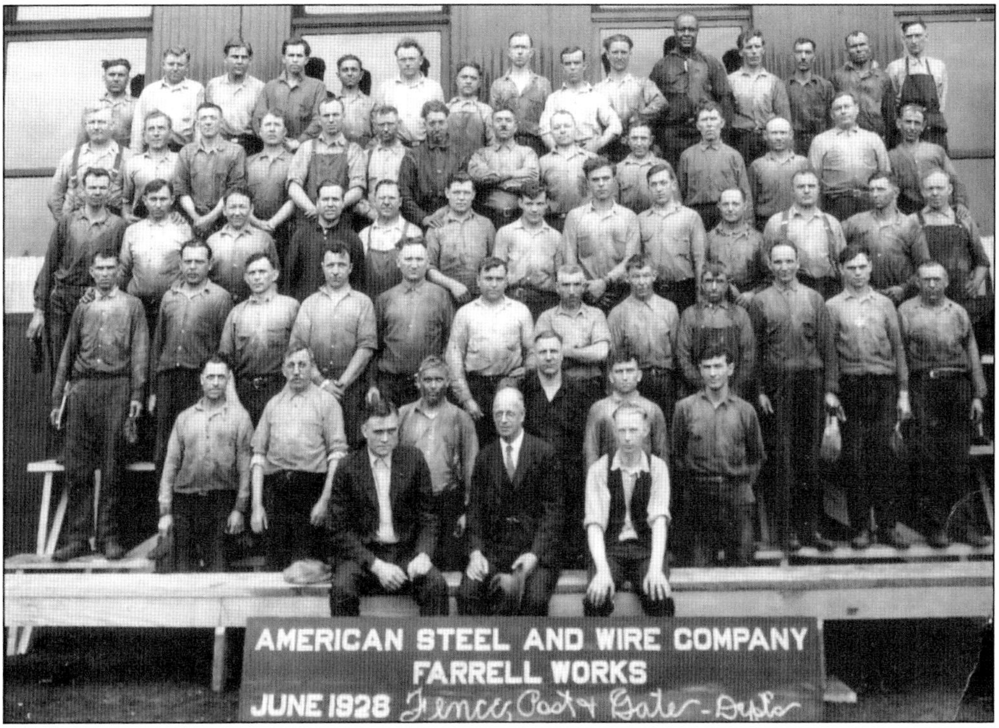

The American Steel and Wire Farrell Plant produced wire fences and nails. Thirty-year-old Fred Husnick Sr. (third row, fourth from left) and George Bedich (fourth row, eighth from left), who were second- and third-generation Croatian Americans, worked at the nail plant. Andrew Adams, an African American coworker, spoke Croatian, German, and 11 other languages and was popular within the Croatian community. (Courtesy of Ann Yazvac.)

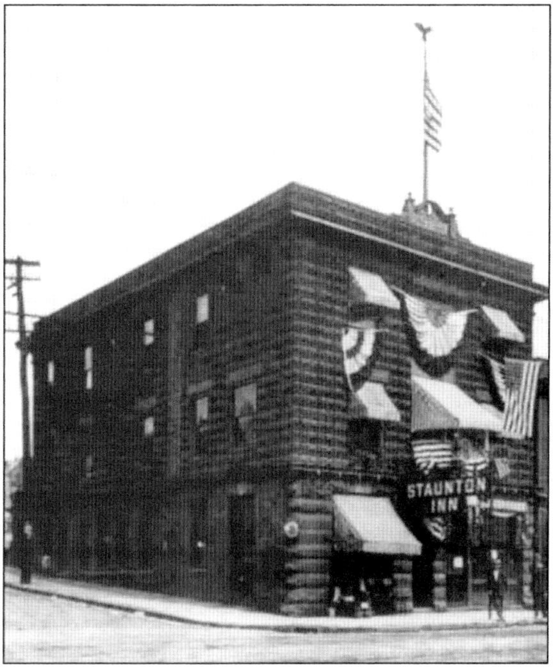

After getting pinned by sniper gunfire during the 1919 strike, Gus McDowell swam across the Shenango River to safety. He went home and did not return to the plant until the unrest died down. The Staunton Inn, pictured here, is where the unrest occurred. African Americans lived in mixed neighborhoods with Croatian Americans on Staunton and Greenfield Avenues, later Market Avenue. Newspaper accounts from the day corroborate the account of sniper fire. (Courtesy of Ann Yazvac.)

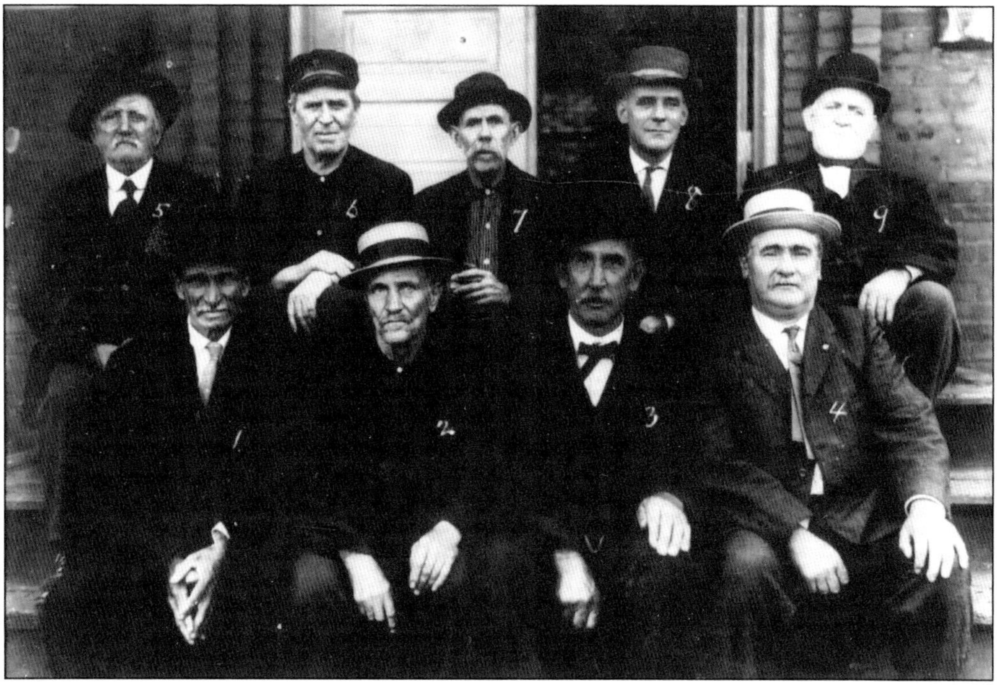

In 1901, Aaron Skuse, a native of Bristol, England, moved from New York to Farrell and started work as a roller at the tin mill. For more than 40 years, Skuse resided on Fruit Avenue. Carnegie Steel workers, all with 30 years of service, are, from left to right, (first row) George Richards, Nick Pits, Henry I. Davis, and John G. Lewis; (second row) John W. Jones, Patrick Carney, Thomas Hanrahan, W.T. May, and Evan Thomas. (Courtesy of MCHS.)

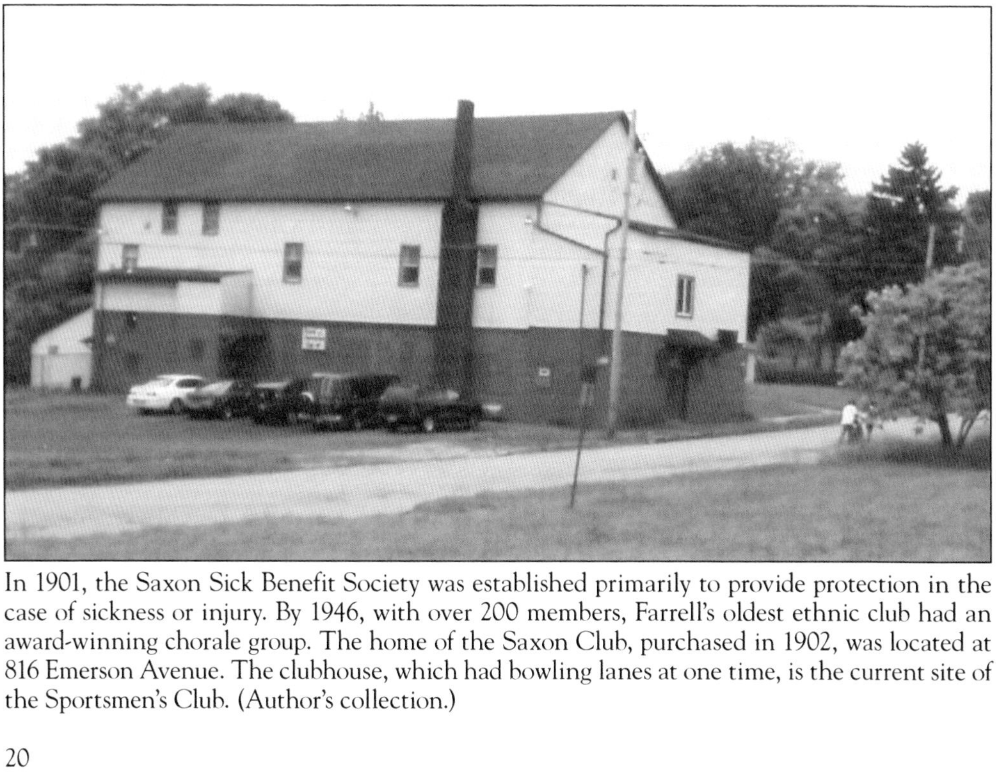

In 1901, the Saxon Sick Benefit Society was established primarily to provide protection in the case of sickness or injury. By 1946, with over 200 members, Farrell's oldest ethnic club had an award-winning chorale group. The home of the Saxon Club, purchased in 1902, was located at 816 Emerson Avenue. The clubhouse, which had bowling lanes at one time, is the current site of the Sportsmen's Club. (Author's collection.)

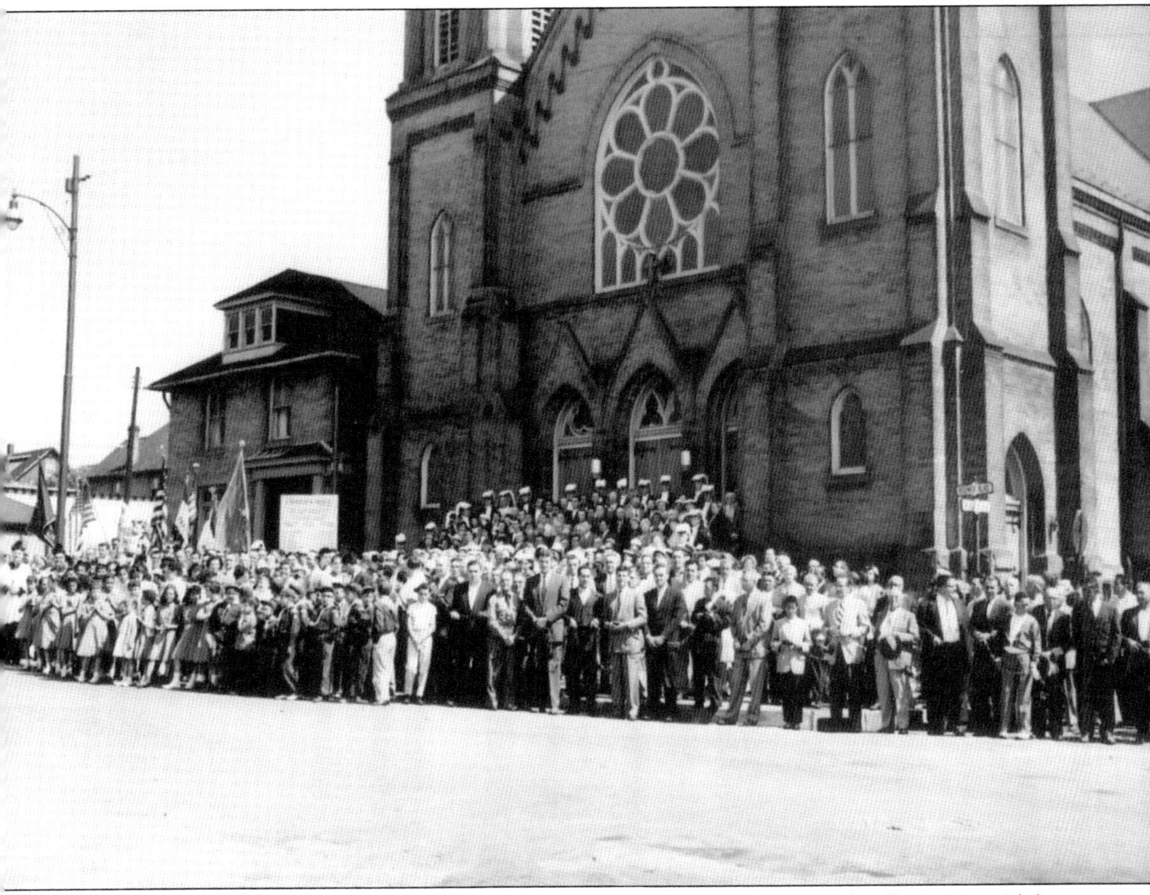

From the first church meeting of 100 faithful gathered in the "Little Red Schoolhouse" on Idaho Street, several congregations developed, including United Presbyterian Church, First Methodist Episcopal Church, First Congregational Church, and First Baptist Church. United Presbyterian was one of the first churches built in South Sharon, on Fruit Avenue. Due to its large number of churches, some locals called Fruit Avenue "Church Row." According to the *Farrell Press*, a Presbyterian pastor once broke away to organize a national Druid movement rooted in Welsh lore. By 1930, nationalist congregations included Holy Trinity Slovak Evangelical Lutheran Church, Holy Cross Romanian Orthodox Church, St. John the Baptist Romanian Byzantine Catholic Church, St. Adalbert's Polish Roman Catholic, St. Anthony Italian Catholic Church, and St. George's Serbian Orthodox Church. In 1909, German and Irish parishioners were in the majority at St. Elizabeth Roman Catholic Church. A gathering is seen here in front of the commanding Gothic structure. (Courtesy of Msgr. Geno Monti School of Our Lady of Fatima.)

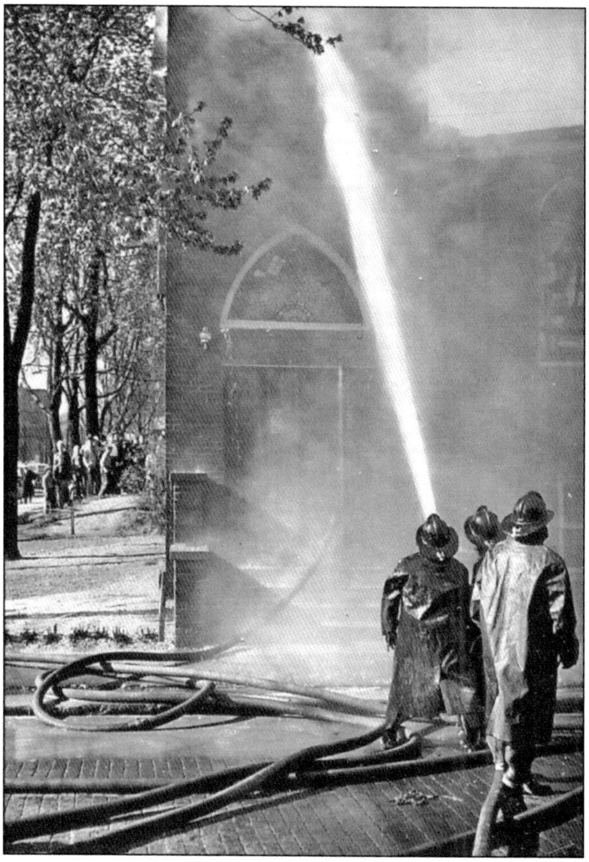

Grace Evangelical Lutheran Church was organized for the large German Lutheran population in the neighborhood and first met at Federal and Fruit Streets, when Farrell was still known as South Sharon. According to the December 29, 1939, issue of the *Farrell Press*, in 1902, Rev. John Adam Frischkorn, a native of Germany, became the first regular pastor. In 1947, the church caught fire. (Courtesy of Ann Yazvac.)

Germans were known for reliable craftsmanship and established a reputation for honesty and hard work. Within a year of burning down, Grace Evangelical Lutheran Church was rebuilt and actively served the community until 2000, when Jesus' Church Faith Christian Center Ministries, led by Ralph T. and JoAnn Newell, moved into the site at 901 Fruit Avenue. (Author's collection.)

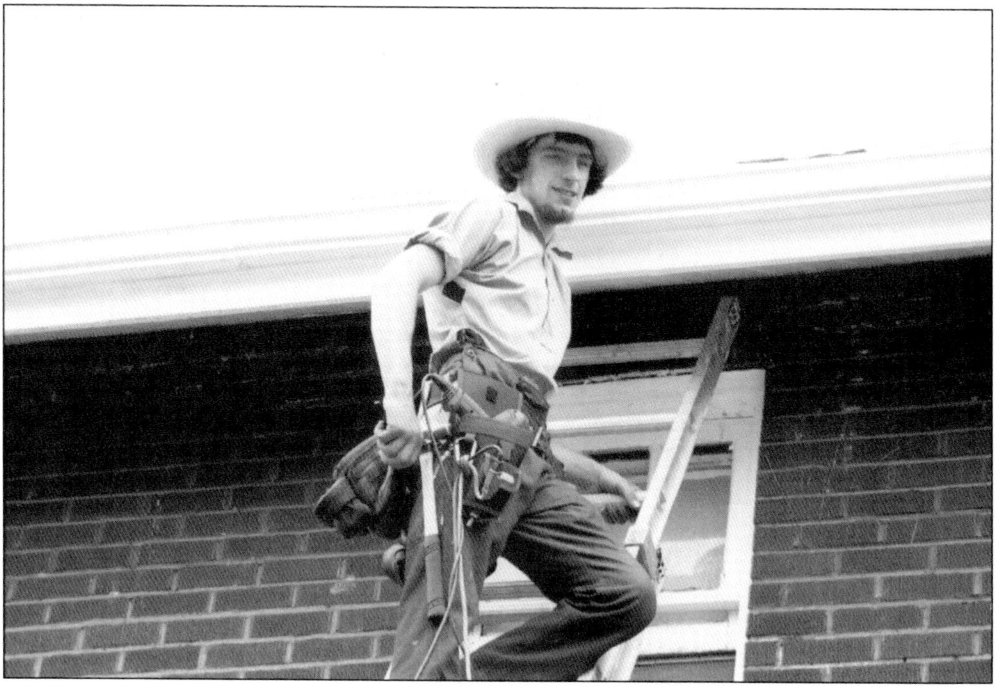

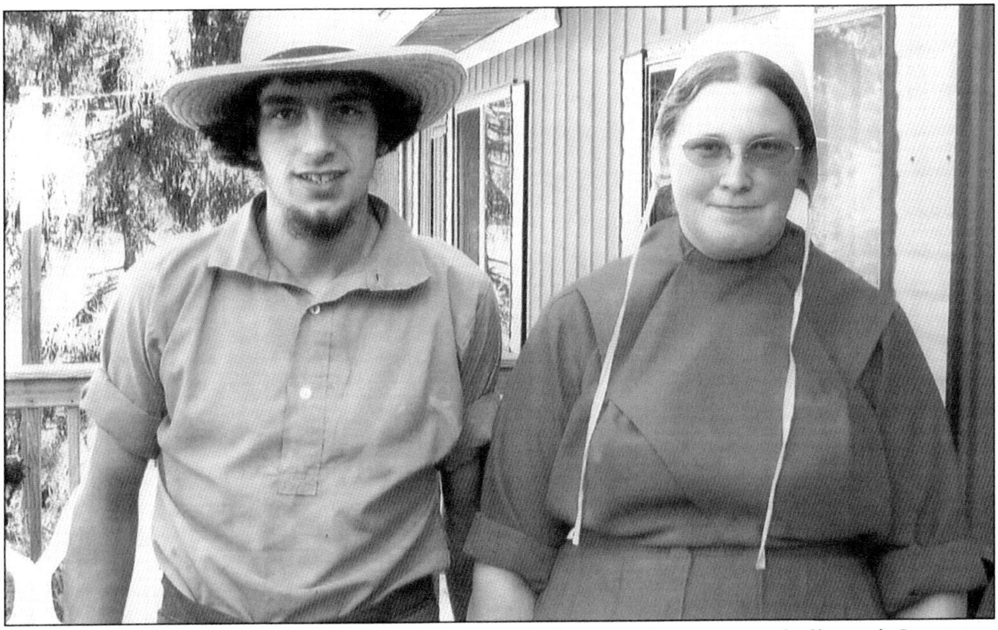

During World War I, the loyalty of Americans with German descent was challenged. Suspicion fell upon these law-abiding citizens for a season. Young people endured taunts of "Kaisers," and the German Home, located on Spearman Avenue, covered the "Deutsche Heim" on the front building with a large American flag during the day as a safety precaution. Good American citizens mistakenly were grouped together with wrongdoers. (Author's collection.)

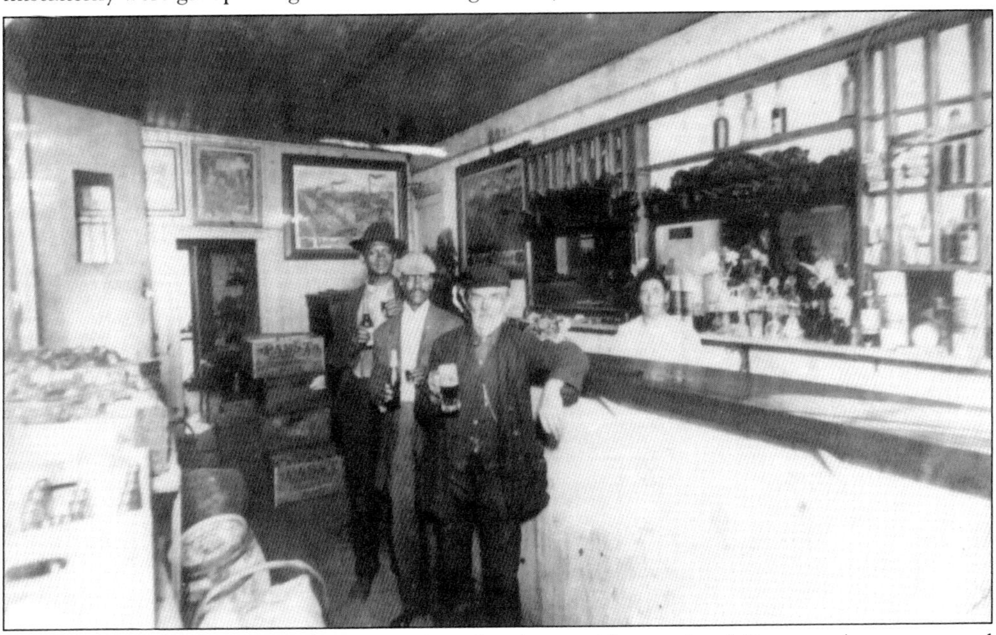

Relationships slowly returned to normal, and as honorable people of German descent proved their loyalty by enlisting in the military and buying Liberty Bonds, the social stigma lifted. A degree of social mixing occurred in Farrell, which would have been unheard of in the segregated South. Neighbors' willingness to share in an old-fashioned beer party with German friends was eventually regained. (Author's collection.)

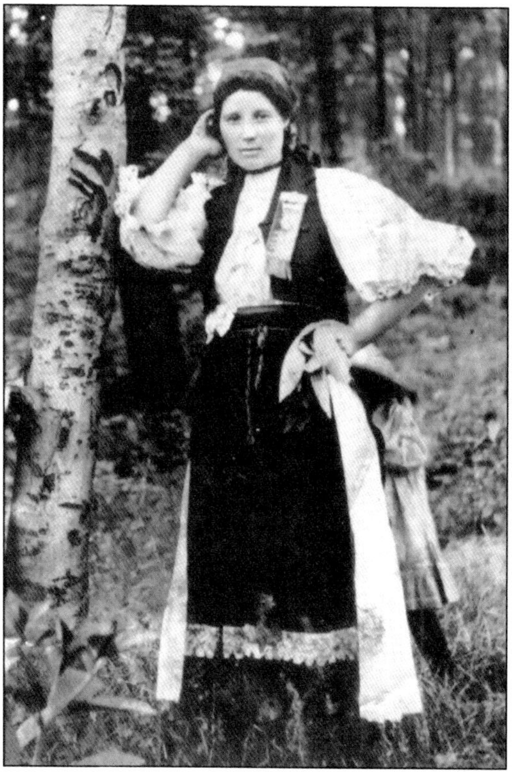

Before World War I, many Romanians settled in Farrell, and there were three Romanian societies in the area. However, after World War I, many returned to Romania and some moved on to Cleveland, Ohio, and other industrial cities. Two of the societies were affected by this mass immigration, and the remaining society members merged into one. This woman is dressed in traditional Romanian costume in 1902. (Courtesy of Alan Brandt.)

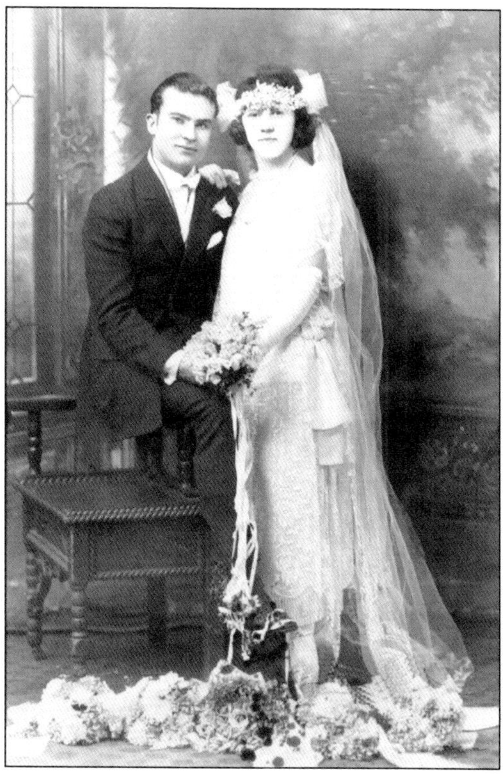

Disputes about crossing the picket line carried over to feuds at boardinghouses. Around 1912, the 33-year-old Russ emigrated from Romania to Farrell and became a chipper at the National Malleable Castings plant. Seven years later, he was bludgeoned to death at his boardinghouse at Darr Avenue and Federal Street, survived by his bride, who was still in Romania. (Courtesy of Alan Brandt.)

In 1902, Nicolae Schiau, known as Nick, was born in Transylvania, Romania. Here, he sits on his mother's lap with his older sisters, Anna and Maria, nearby. All are dressed in the traditional costume of Transylvania. He was about four years old when he first came with his parents and two sisters to the United States in 1906. Five years later, the whole family returned to Romania. (Courtesy of Alan Brandt.)

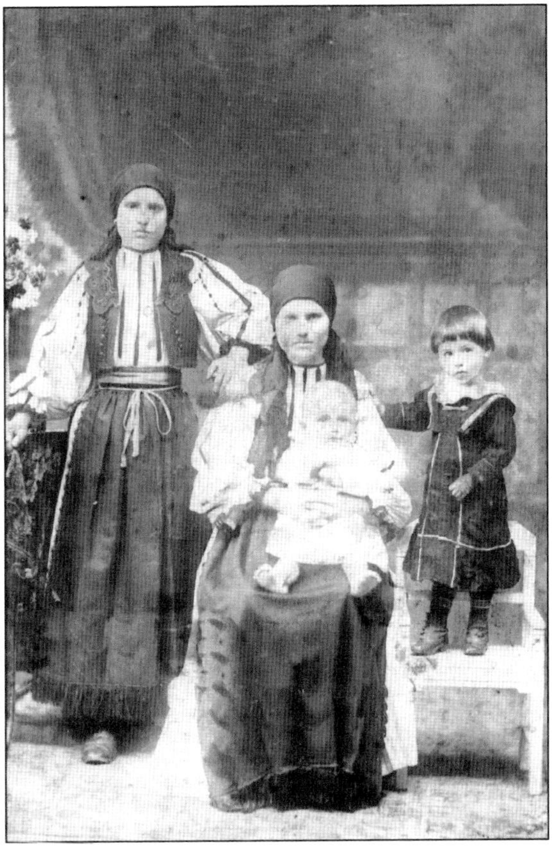

In 1919, Nick Schiau came back to the United States with his father, who stayed with him for one year to assist with his son's adjustment. In 1923, Nick Schiau married a Youngstown girl whose parents were also from Transylvania, one Romanian and one Hungarian. Schiau became a naturalized American citizen on September 26, 1927. (Courtesy of Alan Brandt.)

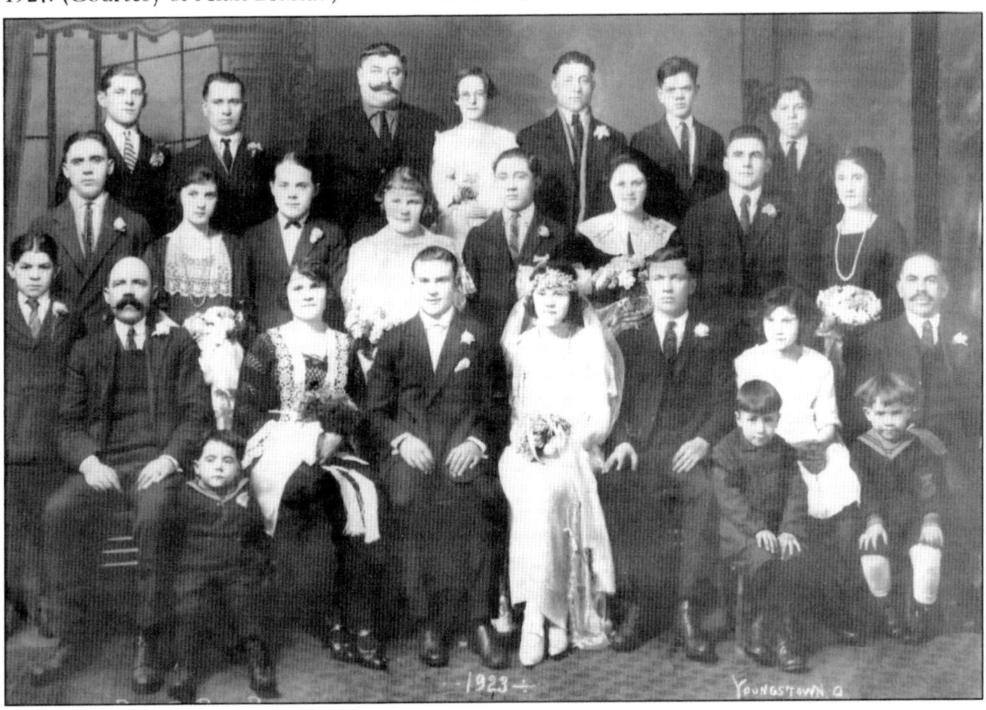

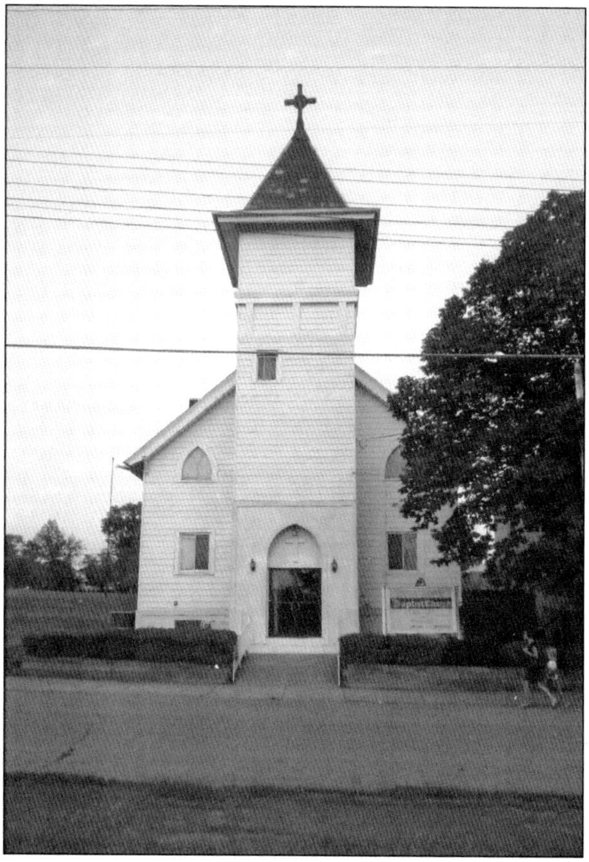

By World War II, Nick Schiau, like many members of Holy Cross Romanian Orthodox Church born in Transylvania, belonged to the United Romanian Societies, Transilvania, Bistritana, and the America Club, known as the Romanian Club, located at 918 Darr Avenue. Seen here, the former Holy Cross Romanian Orthodox Church is the current site of New Hope Baptist Church, located at 909 Lee Avenue. In 1950, Nick moved the Ideal Cash Market from Market Avenue uptown. Nick and Rose are behind the counter in the store on Roemer Boulevard. In the 1950s, he was involved in the Crusade for Freedom, a national program launched as a deterrent to the spread of communism in the United States. In 1979, he retired and sold his store to Joe Ferrence of Gibbs Flower Shop. (Left, author's collection; below, courtesy of Alan Brandt)

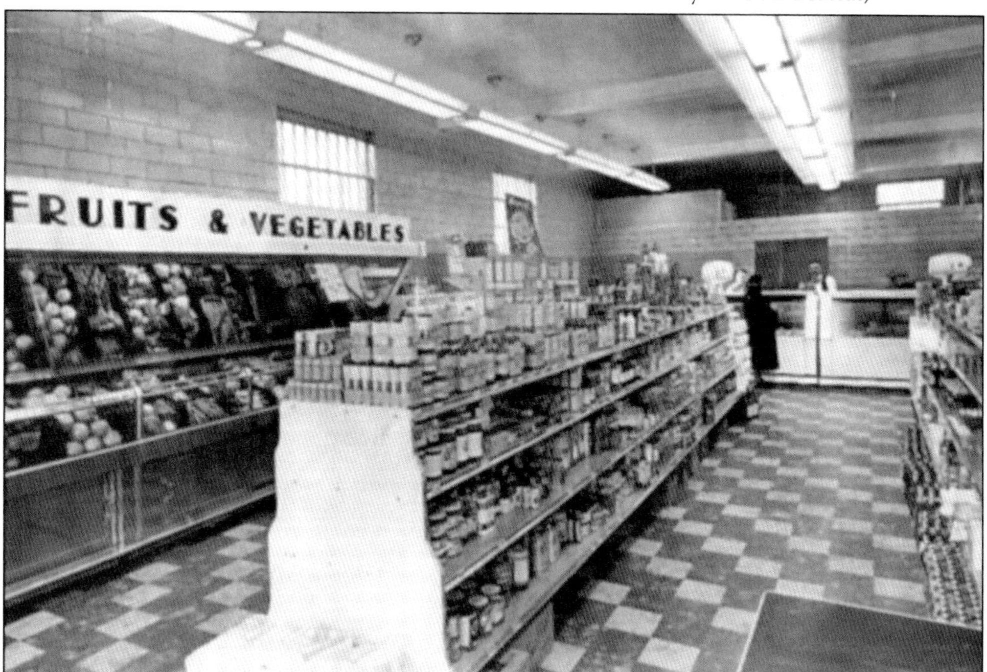

Germans who migrated from Transylvania shared common threads with many Romanian emigrants in Farrell. These Germans supported the local Transylvanian youth dance team. In Transylvania, Nick Schiau (second from left) had participated in a youth dance team. (Courtesy of Alan Brandt.)

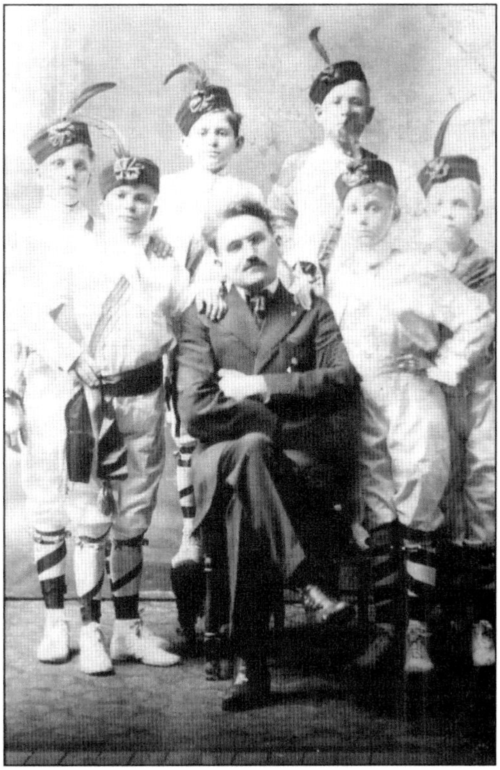

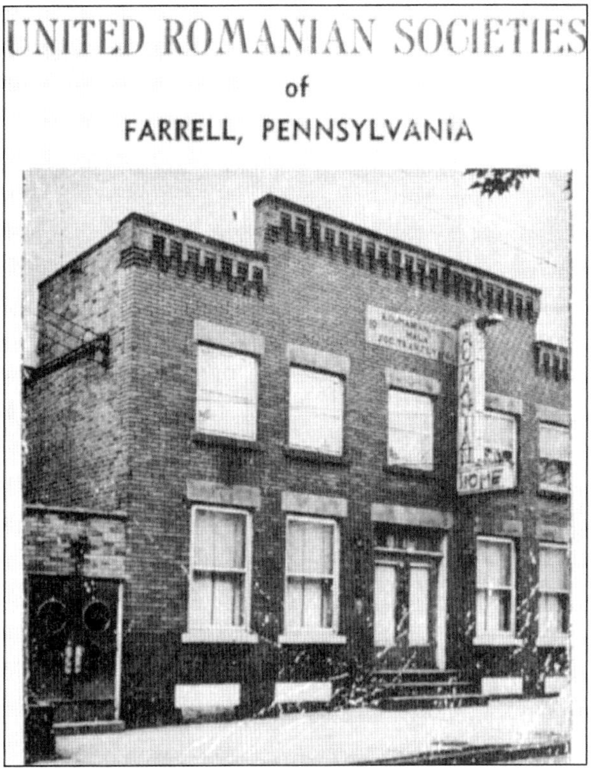

During the 1909 strike, the Romanian Society of South Sharon found itself embroiled in a heated meeting. The November 4, 1909, *Sharon Herald* recounted that 40 society members refused to pay monthly dues when the new society president became a strikebreaker. By the next meeting, plans were afoot to oust the president. (Courtesy of Alan Brandt.)

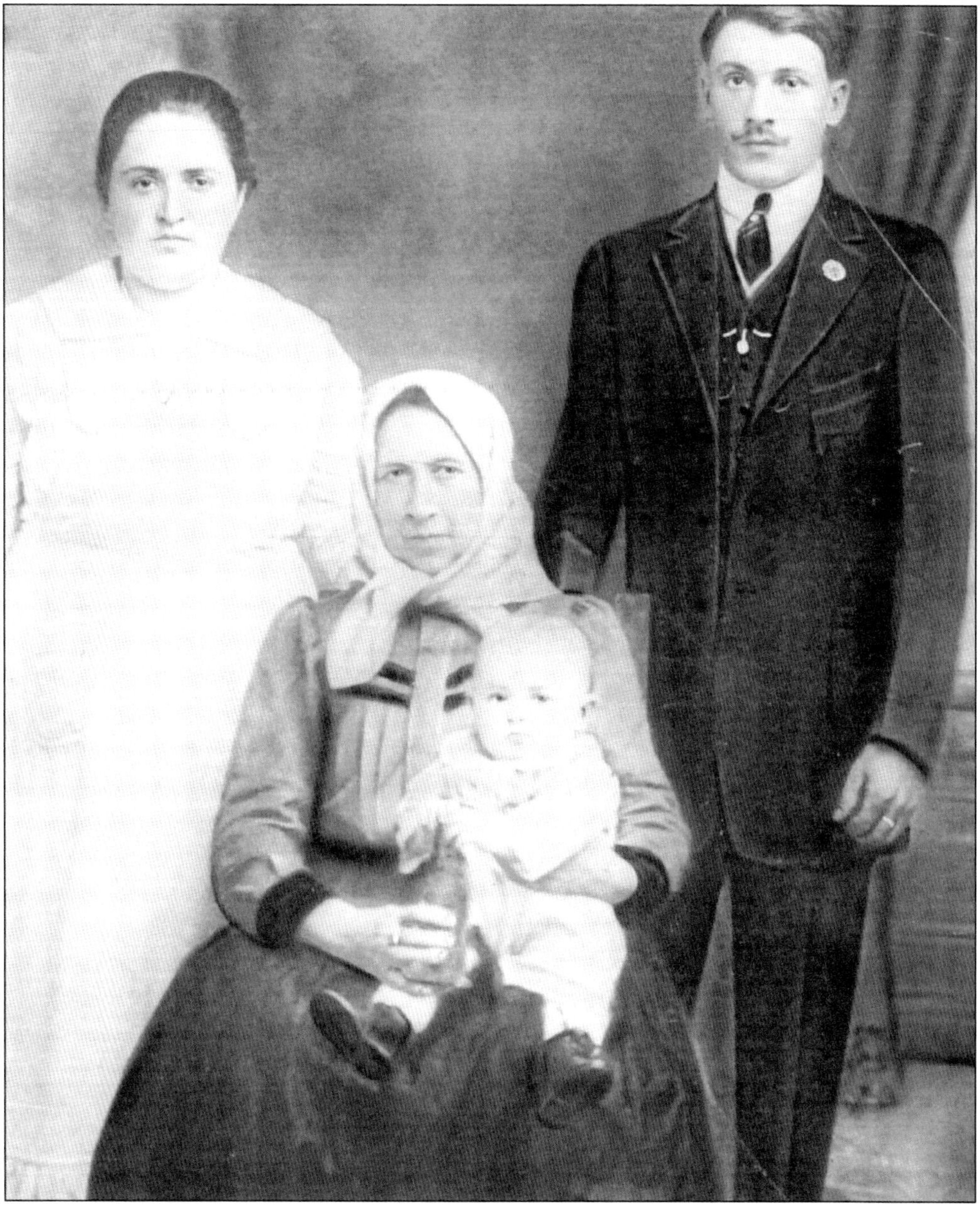

Three generations of the Aszlos family sit for a portrait of family life in America. A Hungarian immigrant, Grandma Aszlos (seated) holds her grandson Joseph Aszalos. Her son Paul Aszalos Sr. (standing, far right) was born in 1889 in Hungary. Grandma Aszlos ran a boardinghouse located in South Sharon's Little Italy until returning to Hungary. Her son paid for her travel from and back to Hungary, but he remained in America where he and his wife, Stella Toth, also a Hungarian immigrant, raised two sons, Joseph Aszalos, Paul Aszalos Jr., and five daughters, Julia Aszalos, Justine Aszalos, Margaret Aszalos Seladi, Velma Aszalos Vargo, and Rose Aszalos Chiki. Paul Aszalos Jr. later owned and operated the Thorton Hall Golden Dawn in Sharon. The woman (standing, far left) is unrelated and from the boardinghouse in Little Italy. Immigrants rented rooms at ethnic club homes and boardinghouses, where they found camaraderie, savory ethnic dishes, and others speaking a familiar language. (Courtesy of Karen Vargo Wildman.)

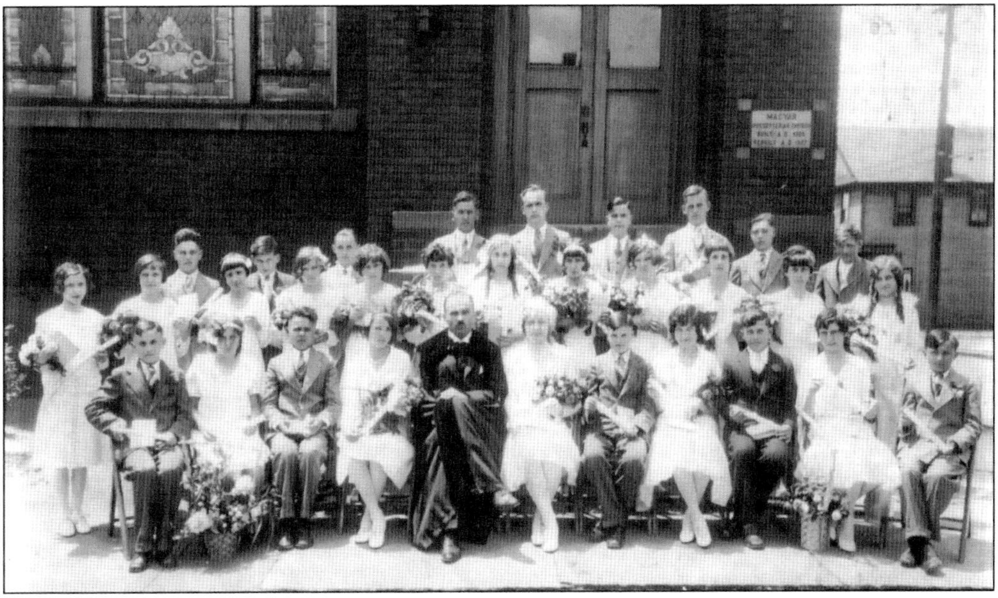

The Magyar Presbyterian Church offered Hungarian-language services. Nationalist churches supported group cohesion, ethnic identities, and community stability. Shown here is the confirmation class of Julia Aszalos (second row, fifth from left) at Darr and Staunton in the 1920s. During the Great Depression, Julia and her sister Margaret found employment as nannies in the Bronx, New York, and sent money back home to support their family. (Courtesy of Karen Vargo Wildman.)

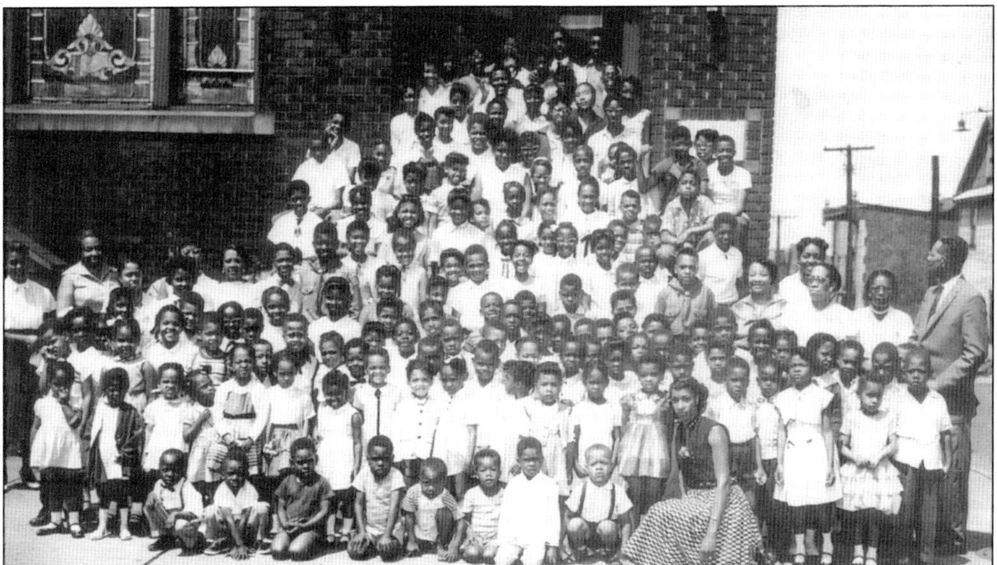

The First Baptist Church, founded in 1901, moved to its present site—the former home of the Maygar Presbyterian Church—in 1950. Rev. Ira Lavigne (first row, far right) is seen here with the first African American joint Vacation Bible School. Youths from First Baptist Church, Morris Chapel African Methodist Episcopal Church of Farrell, Community Baptist Church of Farrell, Valley Baptist Church of Wheatland, and Bethlehem Baptist Church of Sharon all participated in the 1950s. In 2011, the pastor of First Baptist Church was Rev. C. Nolan Howell. (Courtesy of Dorothy Jackson.)

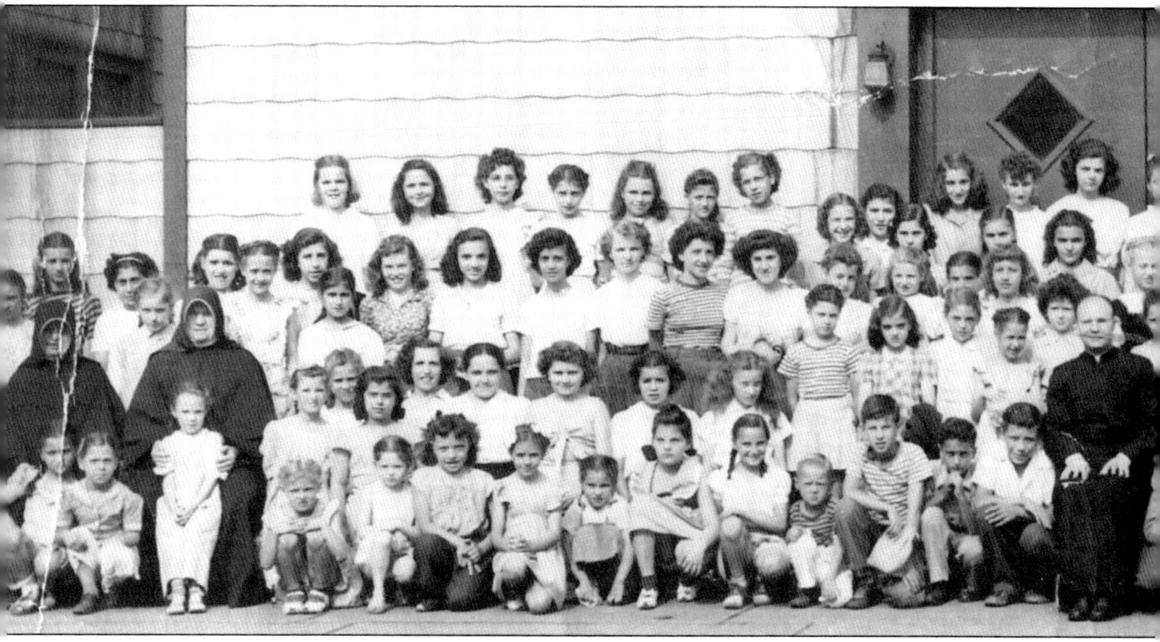

Fr. Geno Monti was the fourth and final pastor of St. Anthony de Padua Italian Catholic Church. Italian immigrants were excited when construction of the 40-foot-by-60-foot frame sanctuary on the hill was completed in 1905; Farrell was still was known as South Sharon. Little Italy was built on the floodplain and consisted of cramped boardinghouses close to the mill in South Sharon. In 1915, the adjacent parish house was built. In 1997, the Our Lady of Fatima Historical Committee and chairperson William Lombardo compiled *The Mother Church: Church Histories*

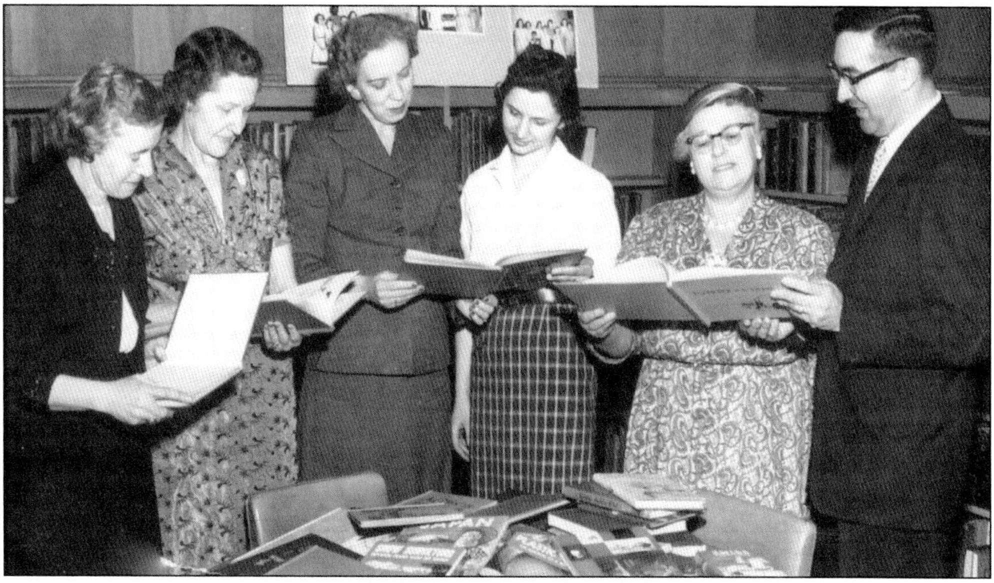

In commemoration of the Farrell Public Library's 25th anniversary, Mildred Roux, librarian (far left), received $116 worth of books from, from left to right, Ida Nugent, Nedra Ingram, Rose Husnick, Juanita Lloyd, and William Lombardo, compiler of *The Mother Church: Church Histories of: St. Elizabeth Church, St. Anthony de Padua Church, and Our Lady of Fatima Church.* (Courtesy of SNPL)

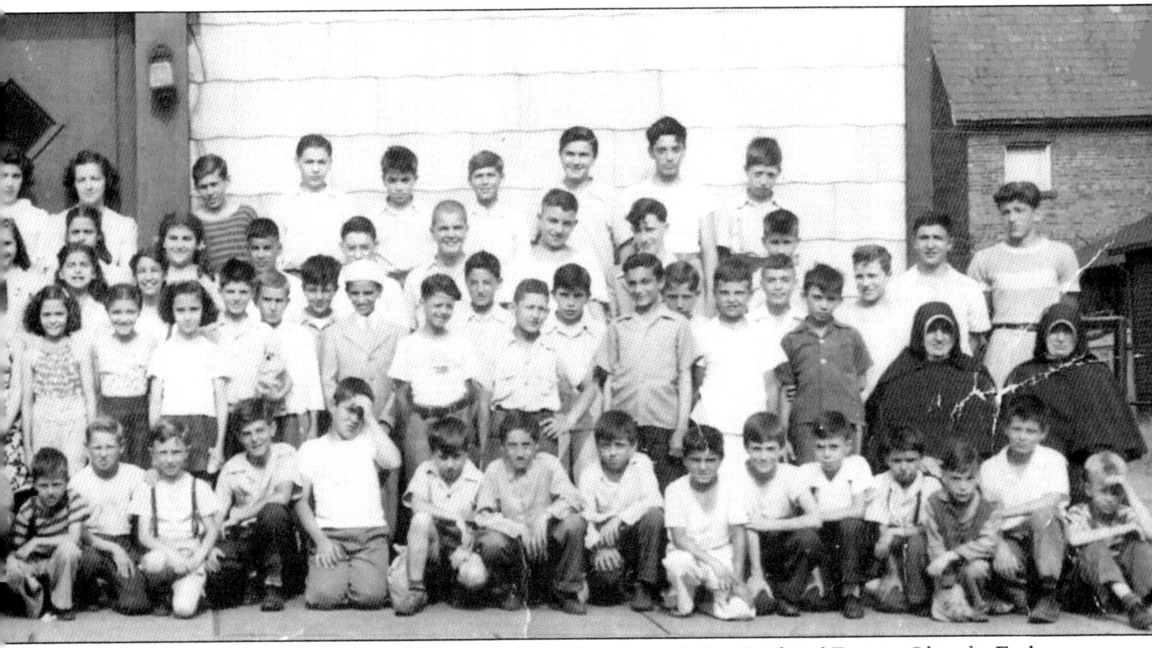

of: St. Elizabeth Church, St. Anthony de Padua Church, and Our Lady of Fatima Church. Father Monti (first row, center) gathered for this photograph with Franciscan Sisters, from left to right, Mother Matilde, Sister Leonilda, Sister Immaculate, Sister Theresa, Joanne Mastrian, and the summer religious class in front of St. Anthony's at 1947 Spearman Avenue. (Courtesy of Msgr. Geno Monti School of Our Lady of Fatima.)

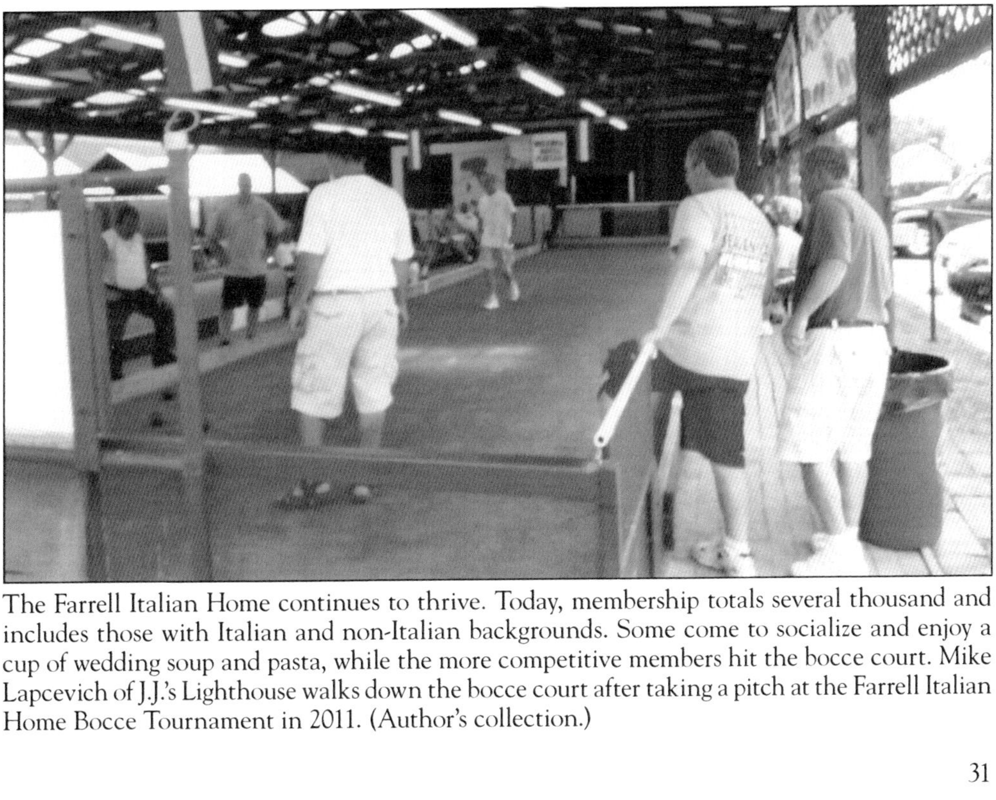

The Farrell Italian Home continues to thrive. Today, membership totals several thousand and includes those with Italian and non-Italian backgrounds. Some come to socialize and enjoy a cup of wedding soup and pasta, while the more competitive members hit the bocce court. Mike Lapcevich of J.J.'s Lighthouse walks down the bocce court after taking a pitch at the Farrell Italian Home Bocce Tournament in 2011. (Author's collection.)

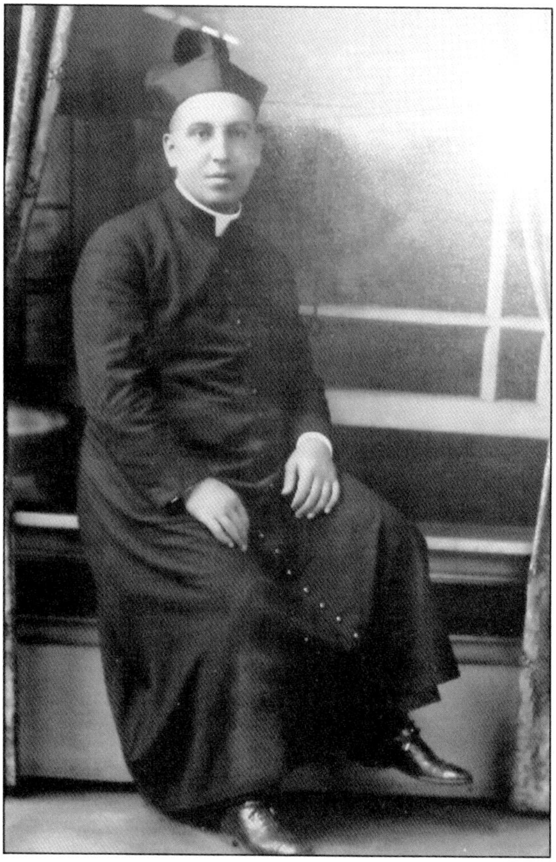

In the 1930s, the affable Rev. Joseph Vacanti (1894–1939), a native of Italy, introduced spaghetti to those not of Italian heritage. He was the second pastor of St. Anthony Italian de Padua Catholic Church and won friends with his popular spaghetti dinners. The church sponsored several Scout troops, and Father Vacanti served on the public library planning committee. (Courtesy of Msgr. Geno Monti School of Our Lady of Fatima.)

Since the 1950s, the Cavatelli Ladies of Our Lady of Fatima have prepared the special style of pasta as a fundraiser to support the parish's parochial school. Their *cavatelli* is sold at local grocery stores and has been used by the Italian Home of Farrell and restaurants. Here, the Cavatelli Ladies work in the cafeteria of the Geno Monti School. (Courtesy of Msgr. Geno Monti School of Our Lady of Fatima.)

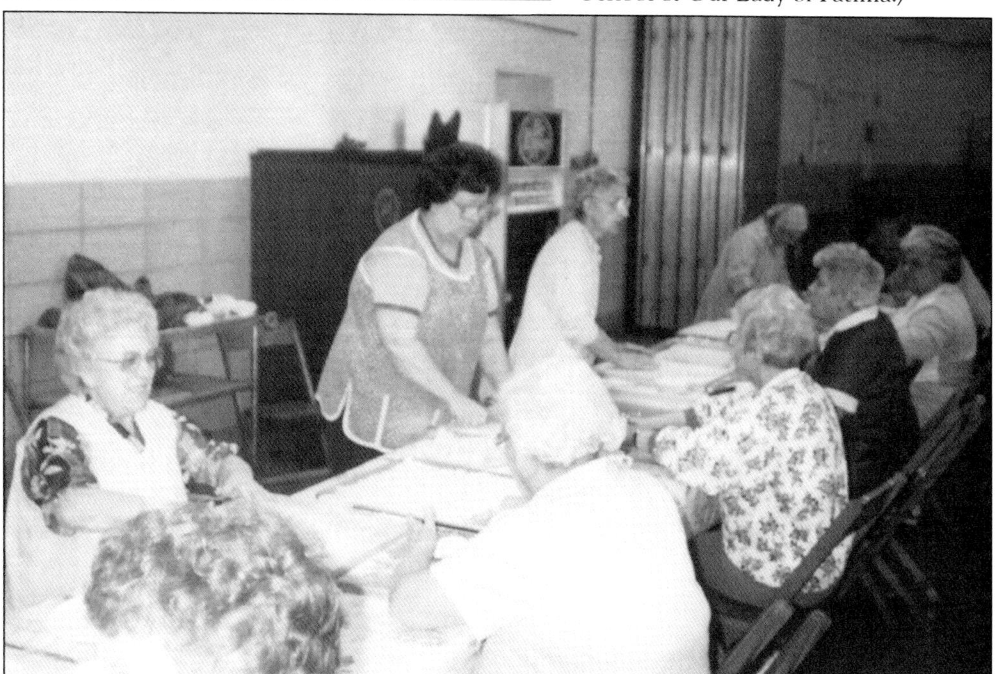

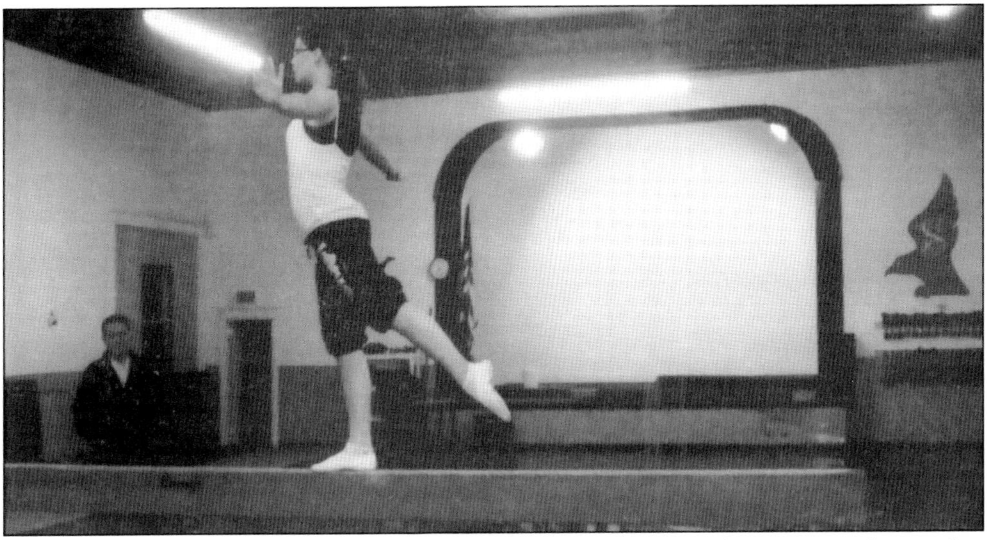

The First Slovak Workingmen's Educational Club, known as the Slovak Home, was chartered in 1912. The Slovak Home's Sokol program, which included a visible gymnastics component, had roots in their homeland's freedom struggle. Here, a youth trains on the balance beam on the third floor of the Slovak Home. Sokol members learn about teamwork and experience pride, bringing home honors in international gymnastic competitions. (Courtesy of First Slovak Workingmen's Educational Club.)

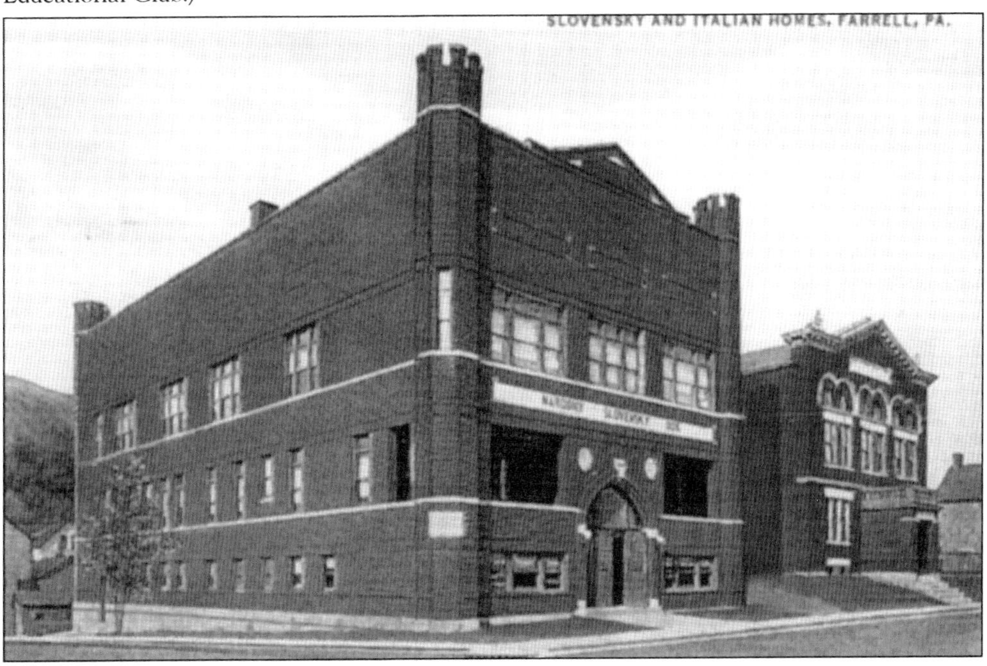

The Slovak community rallied in building what locally was known as the "National Slovak Home." Construction of the three-story building, completed in an amazing five months, was a tribute to the work ethic and dedication of the Slovak community. The cornerstone for the home was laid on October 10, 1915, and the building was ready for occupancy on February 28, 1916. The kick off for the 100th anniversary celebration of the First Slovak Workingmen's Club is scheduled for August 18, 2012. (Courtesy of First Slovak Workingmen's Educational Club.)

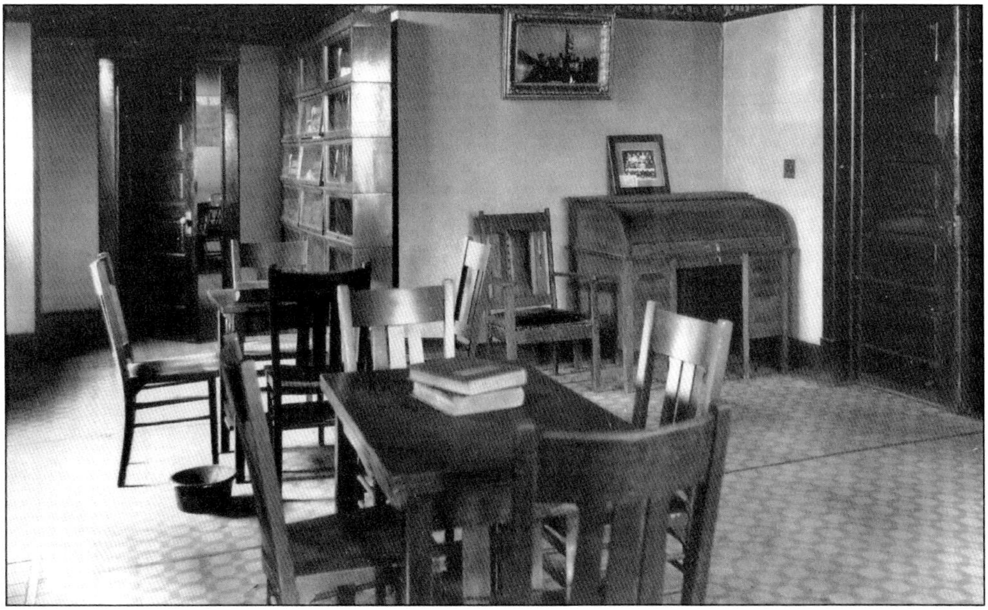

After war was declared on April 6, 1917, forty members of the Young Men's Slovak Association called a special meeting. They immediately telegraphed Pres. Woodrow Wilson that they were volunteering for military service. Shown above is the Slovak Workingmen's second-floor library, where members learned English and studied to become US citizens. The first floor initially included the caretaker's quarters, a barbershop, poolroom, bowling lanes, and cigar shop. Patriotic banquets were held on the third floor, as seen below. Steelworkers were served meals on the third floor while workingmen lived on the second floor. Today, the Sokols gymnastic team is housed on the third floor. St. Ann's Sokol Drill Team No. 6, all members of St Ann's Lodge No. 153 and the First Ladies Catholic Slovak Union, organized in 1936, won many awards. (Both, courtesy of First Slovak Workingmen's Educational Club.)

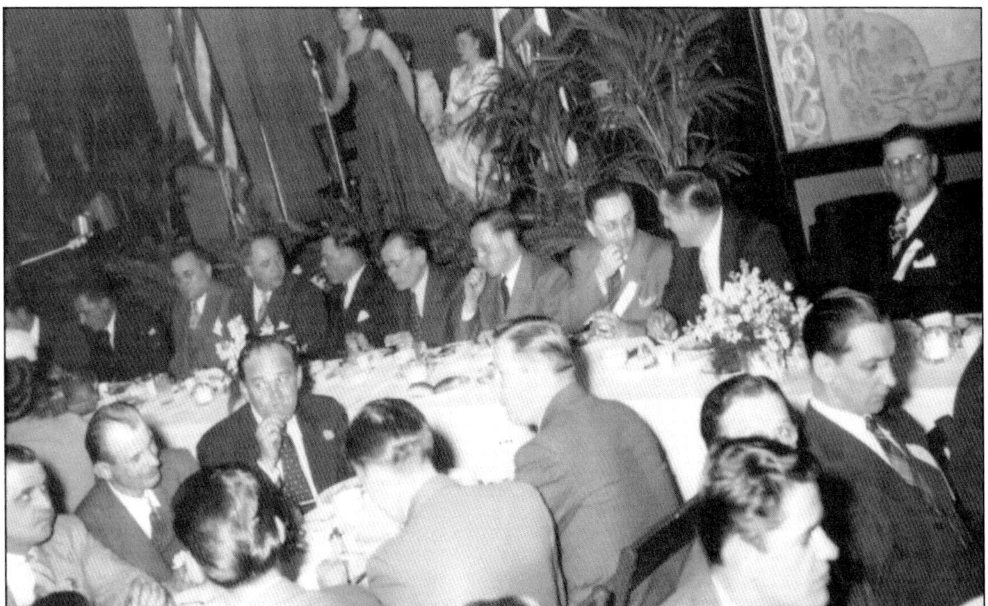

St. Ann's Church, organized in 1903, constructed a regal, commanding, brown stone building with sanctuary, parochial school, and convent. The pastor of St. Ann's Church in 1907 was Fr. Anton Bednar. Fr. George M. Duritsa (1924–2009) attended St. Ann's parochial school and was awarded a diocesan scholarship to study at the North American College in Rome. Below, graduates of the eighth grade class of St. Ann's in 1958 are, from left to right, (first row) unidentified, Kathleen ?, Annette Pugliese, Fr. John S. Cizmar (1916–1996), Barbara ?, Vicky Mack, and unidentified; (second row) Bill Grega, Denise Andrak, unidentified, Genieve Torzek, unidentified, Joyce Matsko, and Don Cheza; (third row) Ralph Russo, John Mudrinich, Joe Balluch, John Harvilla, Mike Morocco, and Emil Stone; (fourth row) Andy Torok, Bob Konnen, Ray Medvec, unidentified, Billy Horvath, and Steve Kuharik. (Right, author's collection; below, courtesy of Andrea Bohach Grega.)

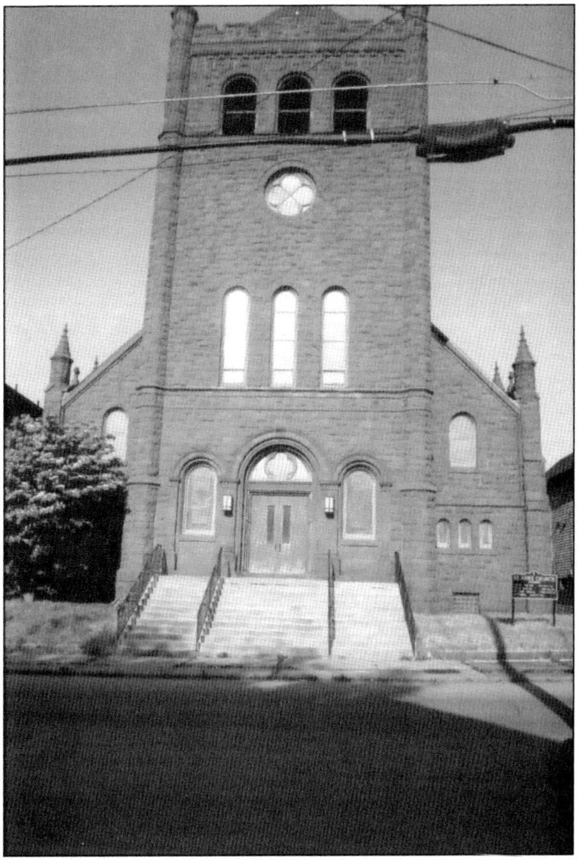

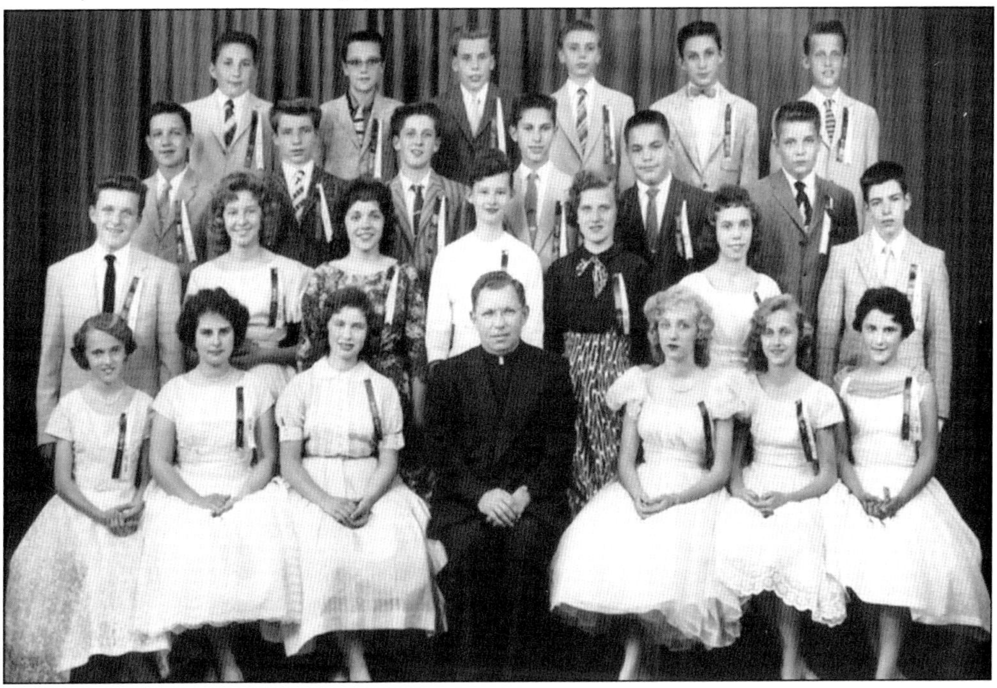

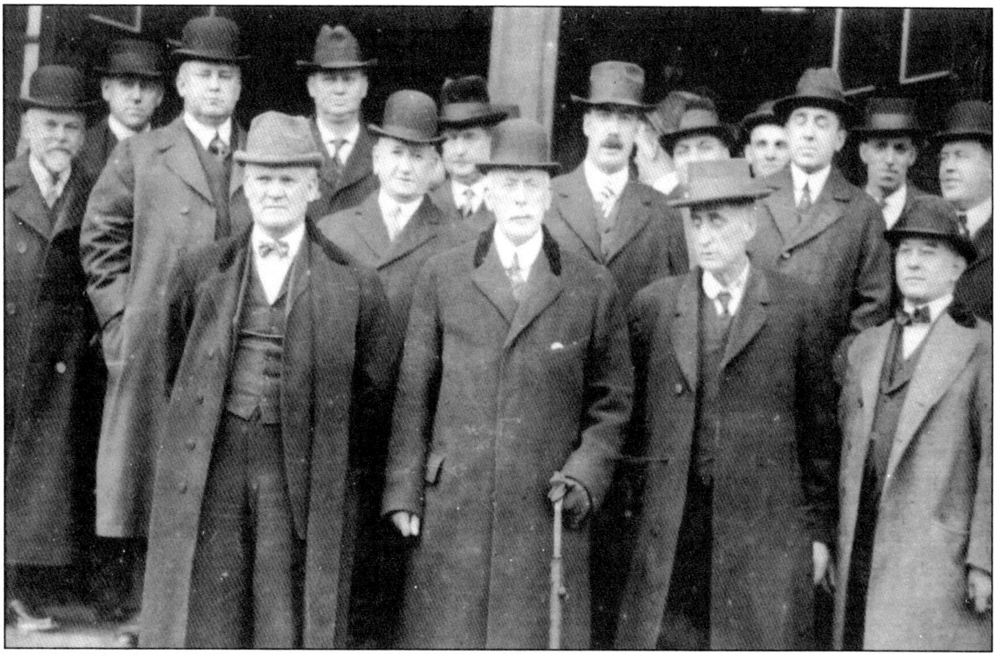

In 1912, the borough of Farrell took its name from James A. Farrell (1863–1943), the president of United States Steel at the time. Contemporaries viewed James A. Farrell, who headed US Steel from 1911 to 1931, as a Horatio Alger of the day. Farrell came to the community on two separate occasions, both in his honor. Here, Farrell (center front) attends the ceremony when the borough took his name. (Courtesy of MCHS.)

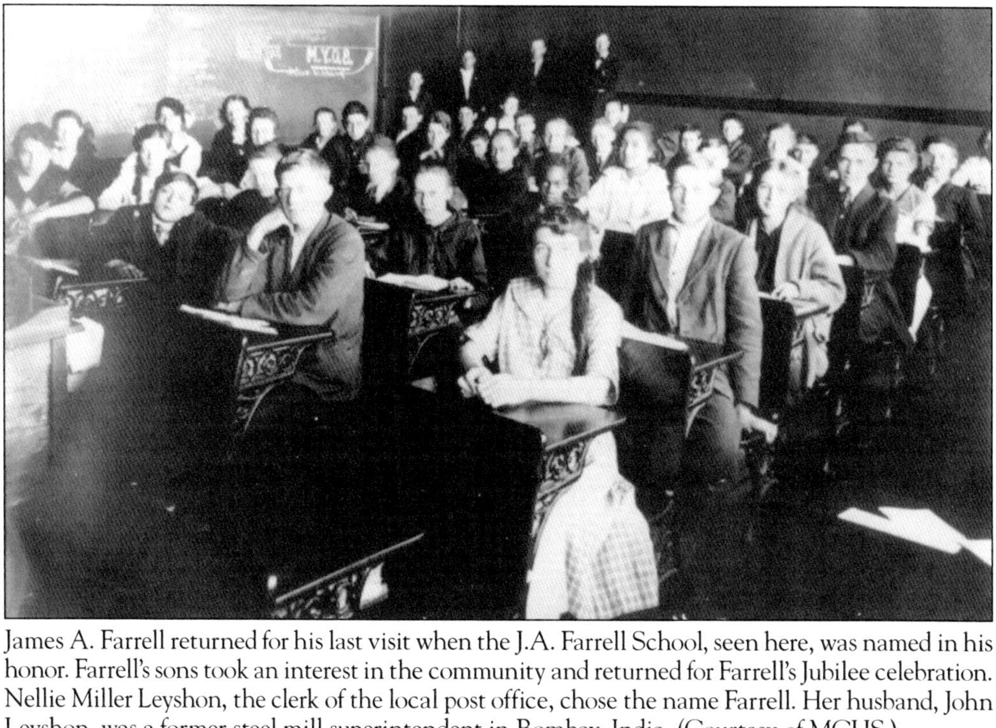

James A. Farrell returned for his last visit when the J.A. Farrell School, seen here, was named in his honor. Farrell's sons took an interest in the community and returned for Farrell's Jubilee celebration. Nellie Miller Leyshon, the clerk of the local post office, chose the name Farrell. Her husband, John Leyshon, was a former steel mill superintendent in Bombay, India. (Courtesy of MCHS.)

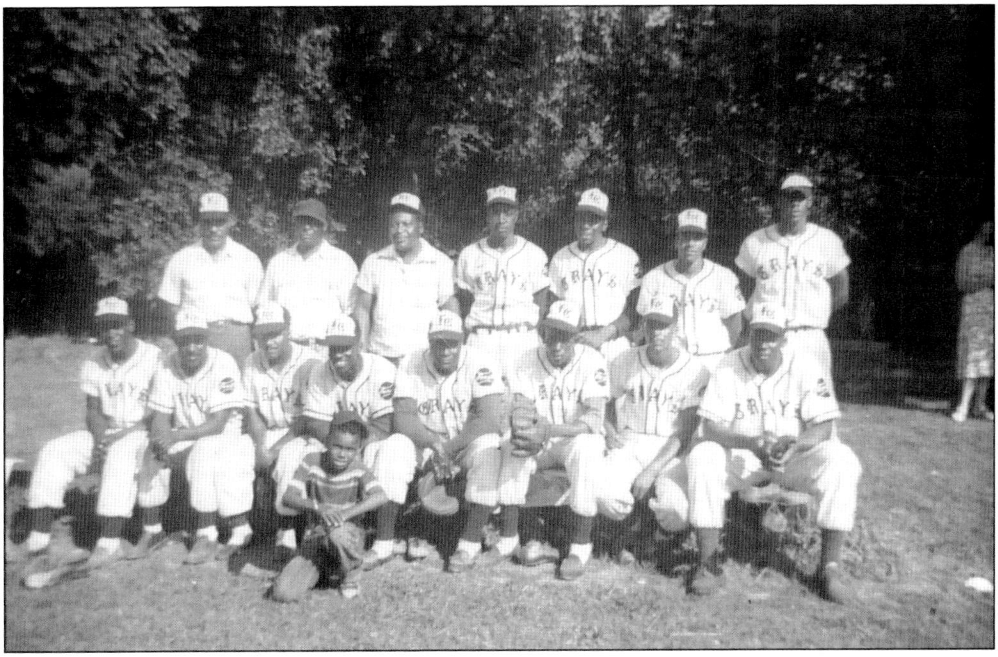

The transition from farming to manufacturing, coupled with the end of the 12-hour workday, brought a rise in recreational, leisure-time activities. The Farrell Grays lineup included James A. Mitchell (first row, third from left), Leroy Smith (first row, fifth from left), Harry Cannon (first row, seventh from left), and Alphonso James (second row, second from right) in the 1950s. (Author's collection.)

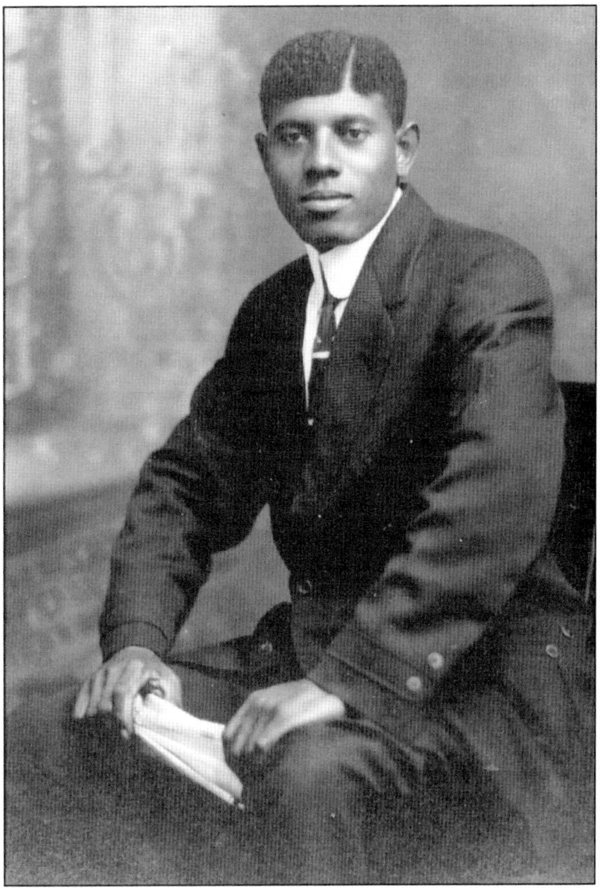

James E. Matthews was offered a position in the National Colored Baseball League, but the pay was not sufficient to support a family; blacks were not permitted to play in the major leagues when Matthews played in the early 1900s. Matthews threw both right-handed and left-handed against the Cuban Giants, the first black professional baseball club. (Courtesy of Shirley Matthew Williams.)

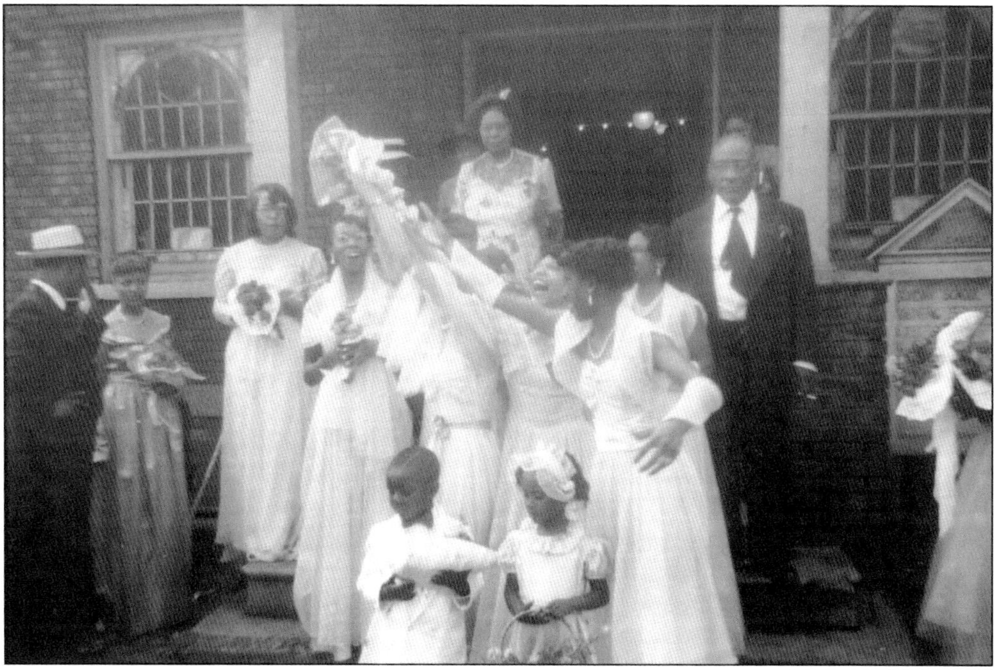

The wedding party of Henry K. Sanders and Martha Jane Wiley stands in front of Second Baptist Church, located at 1116 Market Street, on June 31, 1951. The party includes James Wiley (far right), father of the bride, and Alice Scott (top center). In 1956, a tornado damaged the former church building. (Courtesy of Selma Sanders-West.)

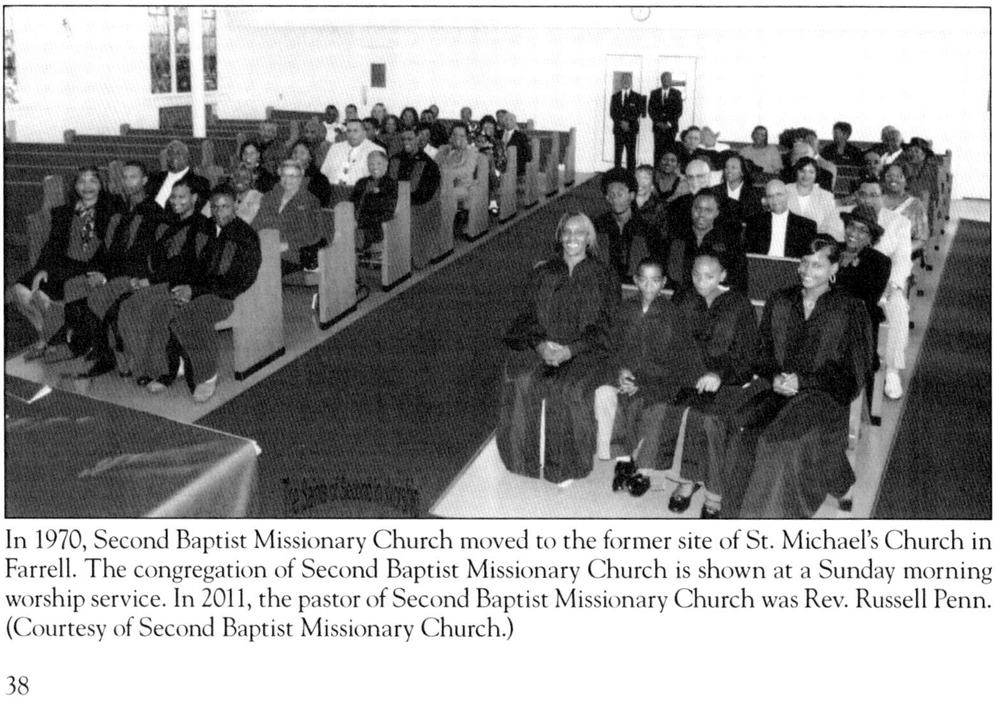

In 1970, Second Baptist Missionary Church moved to the former site of St. Michael's Church in Farrell. The congregation of Second Baptist Missionary Church is shown at a Sunday morning worship service. In 2011, the pastor of Second Baptist Missionary Church was Rev. Russell Penn. (Courtesy of Second Baptist Missionary Church.)

Three

Children of Strangers

From Many We Are One

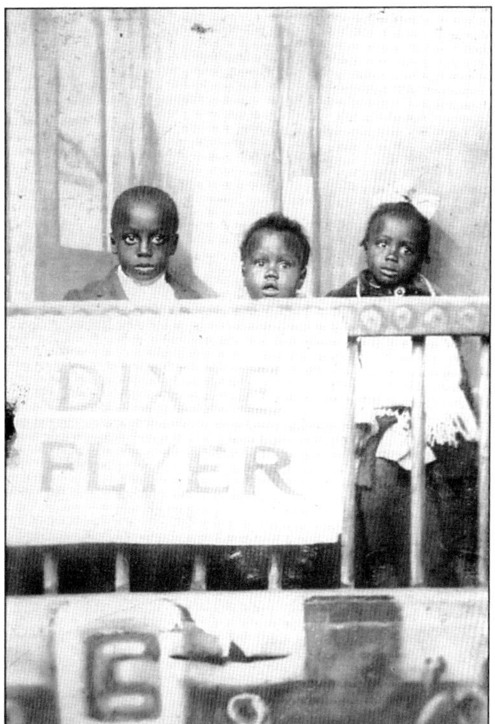

In Georgia, prior to leaving for Farrell, Luther Will Stevenson (1913–1933, left) and Dorothy Stevenson (1915–1996, right) take a photograph with their cousin Earnest Fielder Jr., who remains in the American South. The poem "Dixie Flyer" by this book's author highlights the quasi-freedom of blacks in the South: "At another time the hummmmmm of the Dixie Flyer carried coffee people, shoebox lunches, chickens, both alive and fried, packed in Jim Crow cars unable to relieve themselves; bushes blot their shame." (Author's collection.)

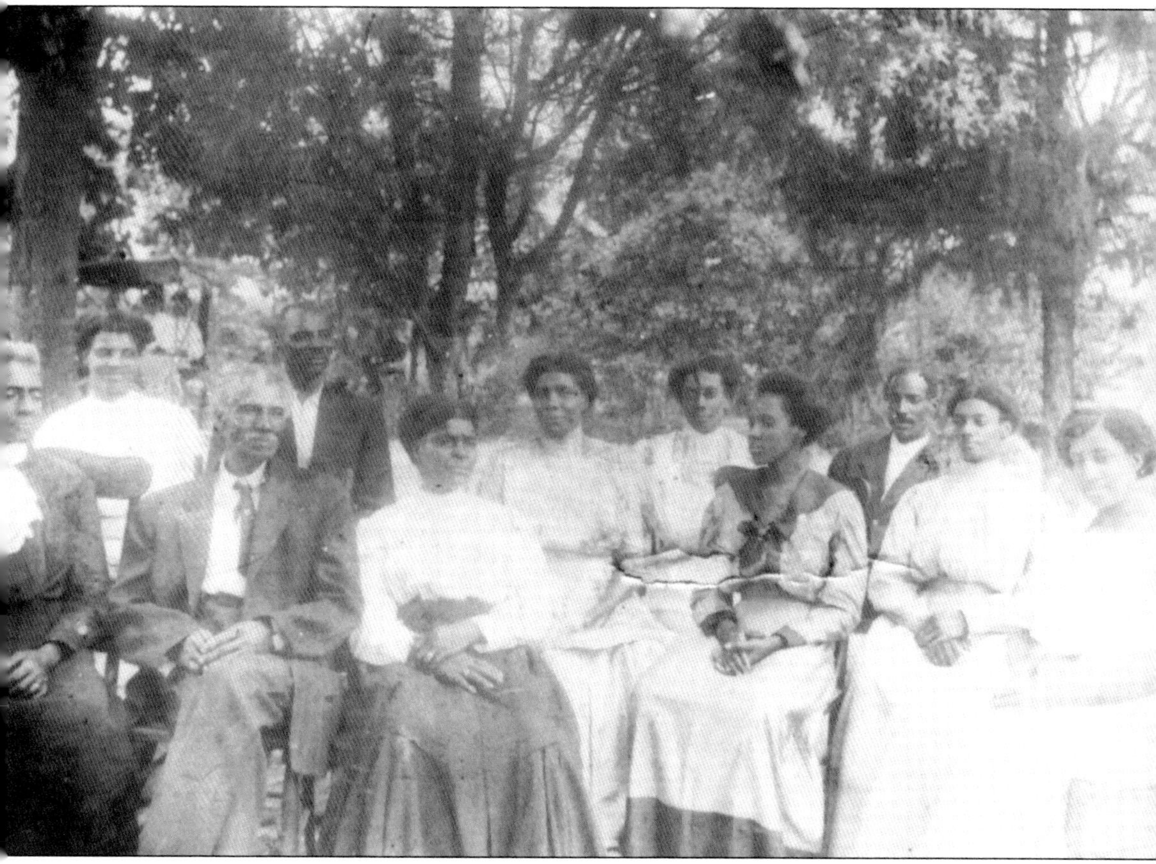

From 1916 to 1930, over one million African Americans fled the Southern states for economic opportunities in the North. During that period, known as the Great Migration, the *Birmingham Age-Herald* reported: "It is not the riffraff of the race, the worthless Negroes, who are leaving in such large numbers. There are, to be sure, many poor Negroes among them who have little more than clothes on their backs, but others have property and good positions which they are sacrificing in order to get away at the first opportunity." The values of the fleeing African Americans remained deeply rooted in their southern past, but northern circumstances provided opportunity. In the 1870s, Wilson Steverson worked as a farm laborer, logger, and peddler to purchase his 80-acre farm. After World War I, Steverson, daughter Mary Steverson McClendon, and son-in-law Joseph S. McClendon moved from Ensley, Alabama, to Erie, Pennsylvania, where both men found employment as laborers at a paper mill. They later moved to Farrell. In this photograph, Wilson Steverson (first row, second from left) relaxes at a family reunion on his farm in Georgia. (Author's collection.)

Southern migrants typically chose a community after a series of careful choices. Wilson Steverson sent money for his son's family to come up north, and by 1921, Etania Steverson; his wife, Mamie; and their five children joined others in Farrell. Joseph McClendon, Wilson's son-in-law, helped his brother-in-law find a position as a laborer at the Farrell Works of Carnegie Steel. Pictured are Anna and Clyde Steverson in "pretty clothing" supplied by an aunt in Detroit, Michigan. (Author's collection.)

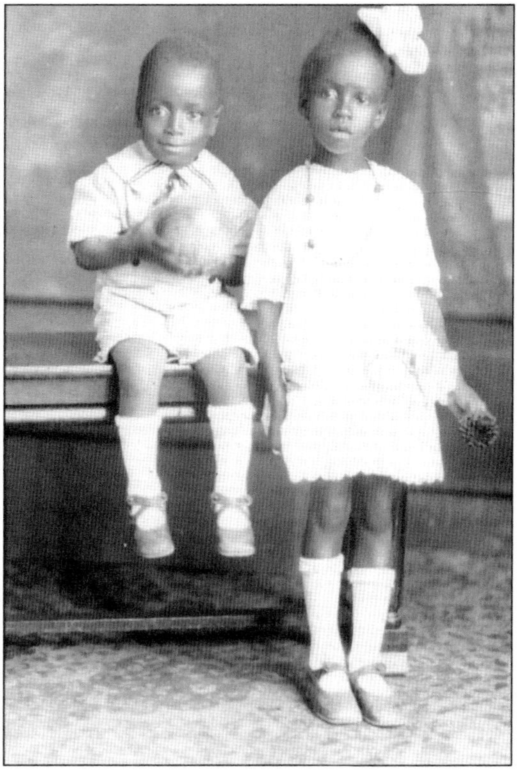

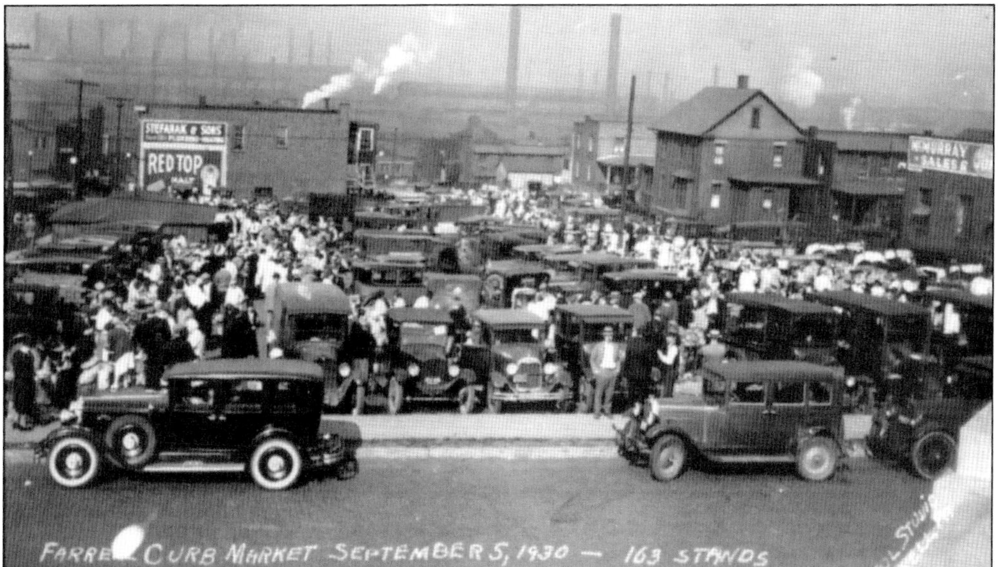

The majority of immigrants came from farmland either in Europe or in the American South. Some worked as peasants, goat herders, peddlers, or cotton pickers and were considered greenhorns. Joseph and Mary McClendon operated a stand at the Farrell Curb Market, where they sold butter, fruit, and pork. McClendon would hang fresh chickens on the rafters in the basement of the house his family rented from Carnegie Steel, so that varmints could not reach them. The post office now occupies the former site of the Farrell Curb Market. (Courtesy of SNPL.)

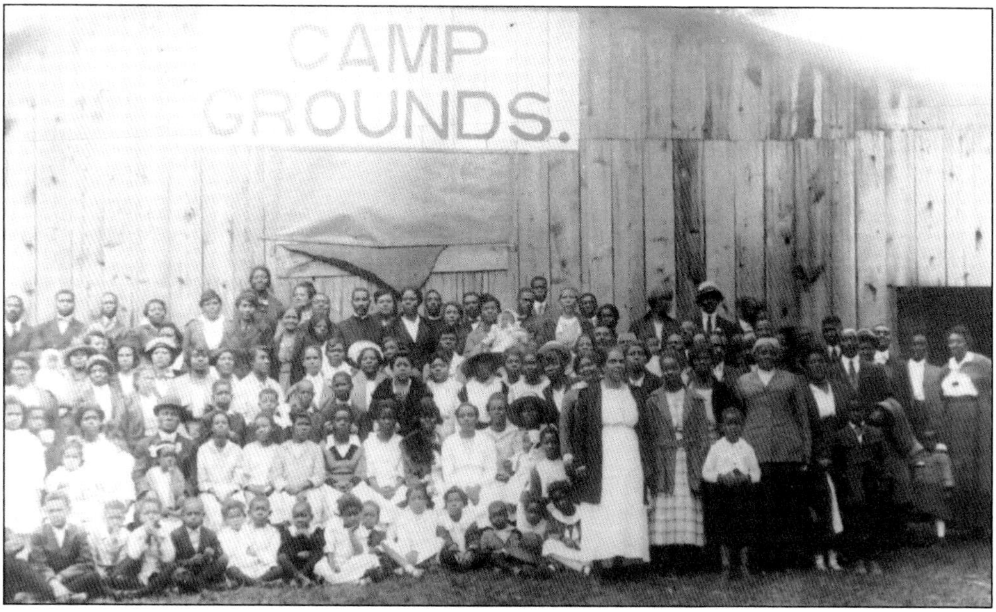

The campgrounds provided southern migrants a chance to maintain their rural traditions. Campground builders mortgaged and sometimes sold their homes. James Crosswhite, former campground manager, recalled that Farrell "produced the Christmans, Phillips, Mitchells, McClendons, Redferns, Smoots, Moores, Waynes and many others who played a great part in its development and maintenance with very little compensation, if any." Below, James E. Matthews and family visited the campgrounds around 1936. The family included, from left to right, (first row) Roy and Carl Matthews; (second row) Kenneth, Elmer, and Frank Matthews; (third row) Sadie (holding baby Shirley), James, Gertrude, Harold, and Shelton Matthews. The tin-roofed cabins of the camp, which were situated along what was known as Tin Row and became quite warm in the summer, are visible in the background. (Above, courtesy of the National Association of the Church of God; below, courtesy of Shirley Matthews Williams.)

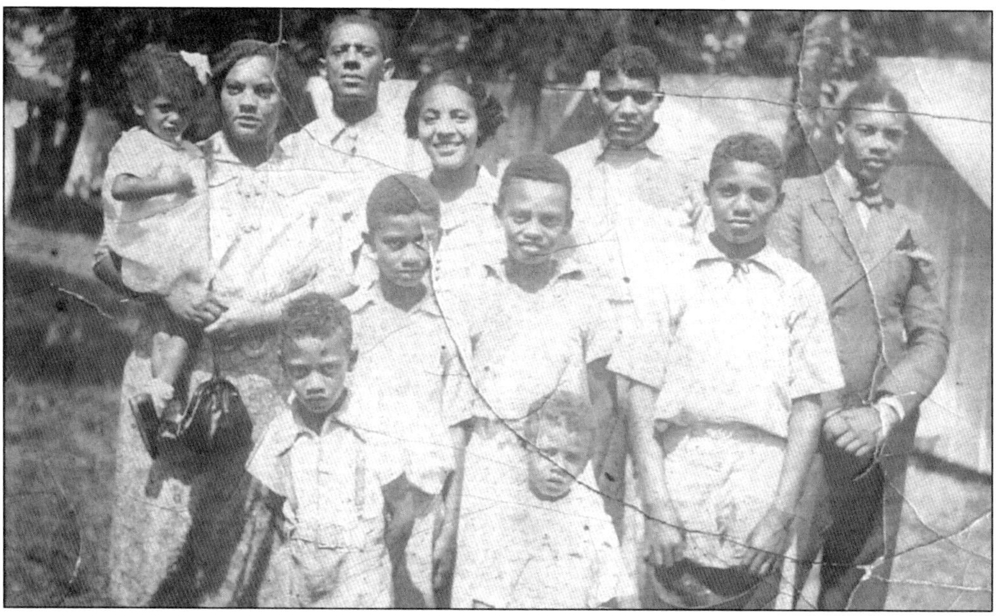

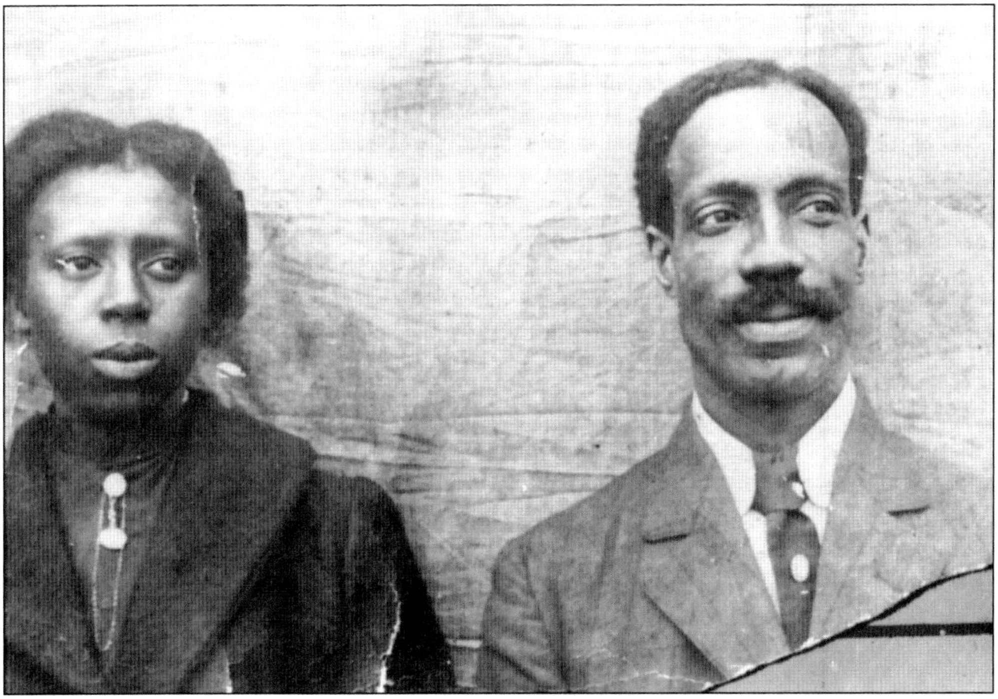

Etania and Mamie Steverson are seen here on their wedding day in 1912, before their migration to Farrell. Three generations lived together in a three-bedroom company house on Hamilton Avenue for almost a year. Wilson Steverson lived with his son Etania, his daughter-in-law Mamie, his daughter Mary, his son-in-law Joseph, and six grandchildren. The children, accustomed to eating coarse foods like cornbread and greens, found corn flakes to be a special treat. (Author's collection.)

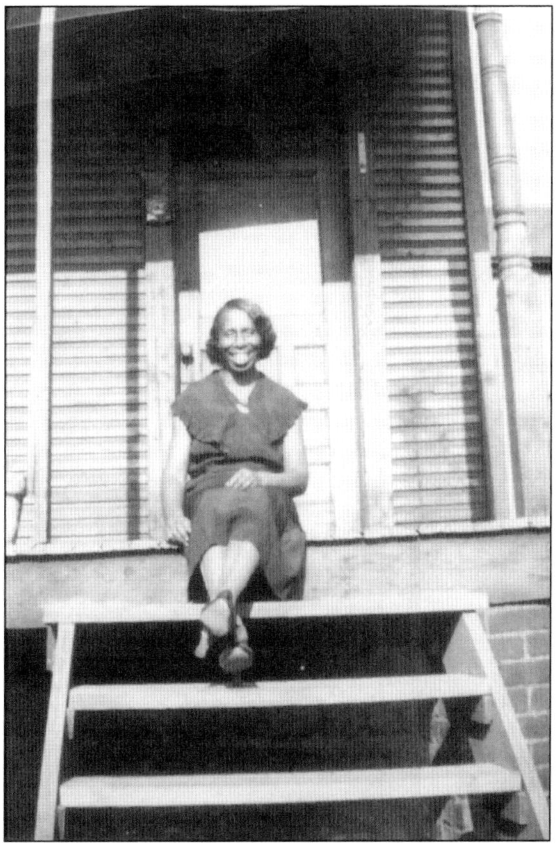

Seen here on the back porch at 1012 Lee Avenue in the 1930s, Mamie Steverson enjoyed life in Farrell. Before their migration, Etania and Mamie were cotton pickers and sharecroppers. But in the North, circumstances were different, and Etania even raised chickens and rabbits in the backyard, with Mamie using an upstairs incubator to hatch peeps. During the Great Depression, she fed hoboes who came to their back door, saying they might be "angels unaware." (Author's collection.)

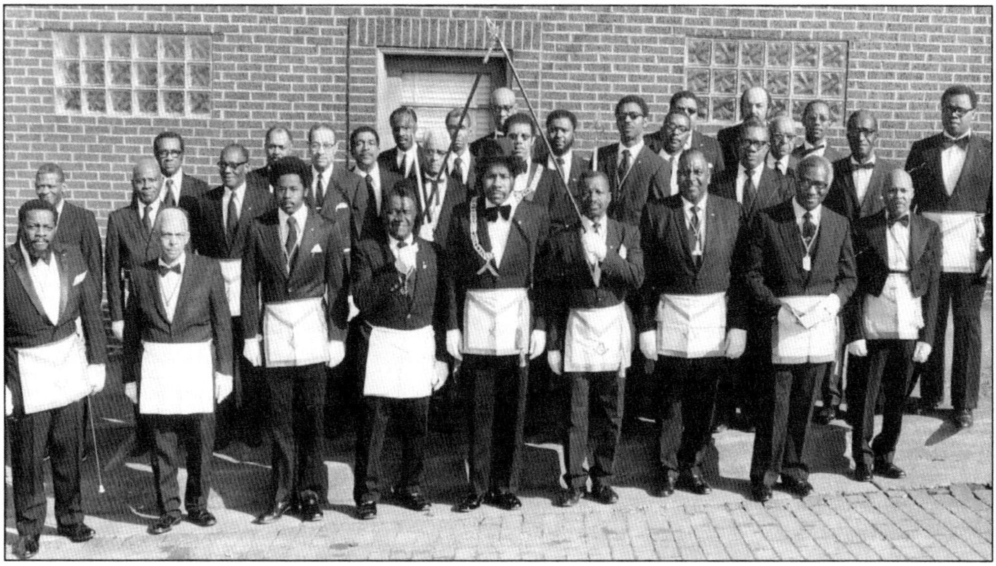

Prince Hall Masons became a stronghold of the African American community leaders; in 1920, its 41 members reflected the middle class. The hierarchy included four chiefs, three clergymen, two barbers, two proprietors, two chauffeurs, two teamsters, a postal employee, a policeman, a mechanic, and a messenger. Posing for a group photograph here are, from left to right, (first row) ? Johnson, Henry Wells, William Samuels, Nelson Miller, John Singleton, Isaac Clarke, John Askerneese, Alphonso Ford, and William Jones; (second row) Melvin Wilson, Sylvester Ward, Jesse Dobie, Morris Bagsby, Clarence Austin, Maurice Carey, ? Seltzer, unidentified, Henry McDonald, unidentified, Shade Speight, and Robert Dunlap; (third row) Toby Jackson, Harold Wiley, William Hobbs, David Myers, Fred Chambers, Henry K. Sanders, two unidentified people, and George B. Thomas. (Author's collection.)

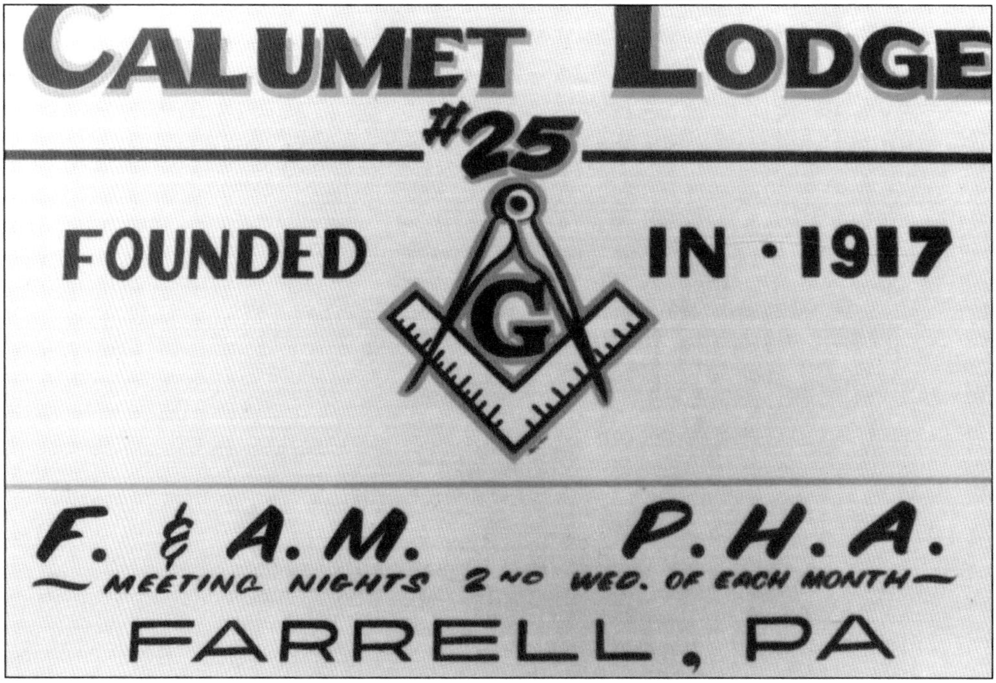

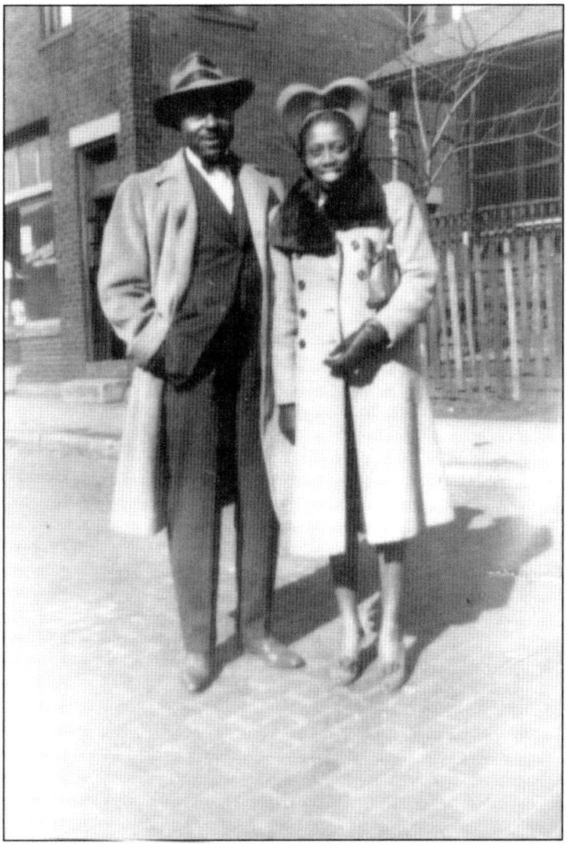

Samuel Malloy and his wife, Dorothy Steverson Crosby Malloy, pose in stylish clothes on the street. Malloy, who lived on the 900 block of Market Street, was worshipful master of Calumet Lodge 25, Free and Accepted Masons, Prince Hall Affiliation in the 1940s. He was also a member of the Knights of Pythias and the Elks. Dorothy Malloy belonged to the female auxiliaries. (Author's collection.)

In 1916, Charles S. Butler (first row, fourth from right) moved from Canonsburg to Farrell and found employment at the American Sheet and Tin Plate Company. One year later, he and a few other migrants, many of them former members of Payne Chapel in Canonsburg, organized Morris Chapel African Methodist Episcopal Church in Farrell, which Samuel and Dorothy Steverson Malloy helped in building. (Courtesy of Debbie Matthews Walters.)

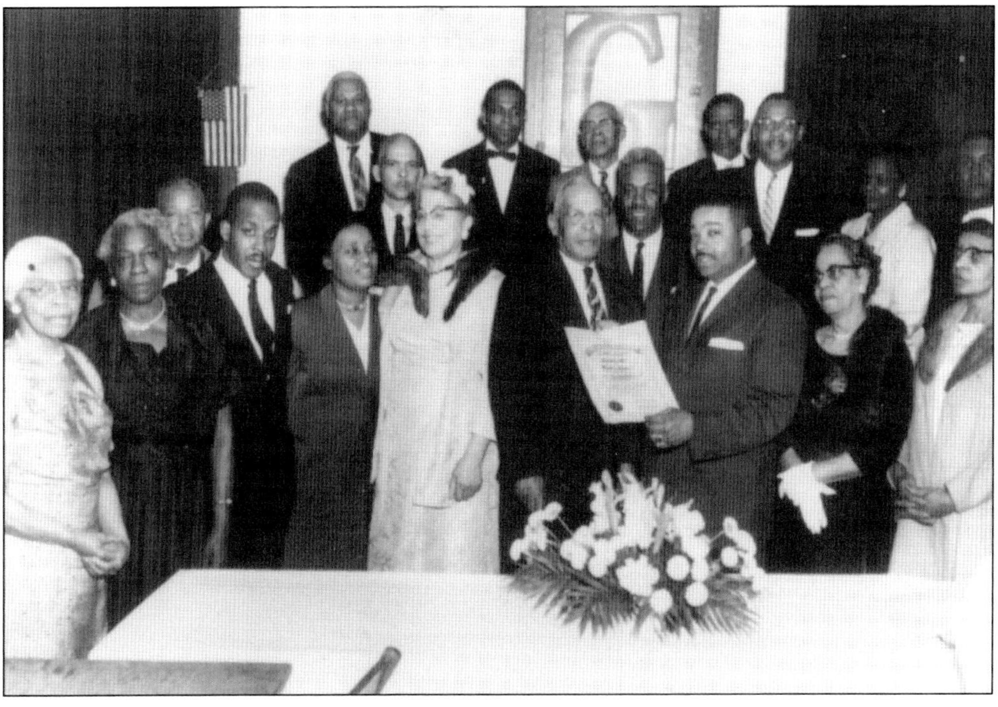

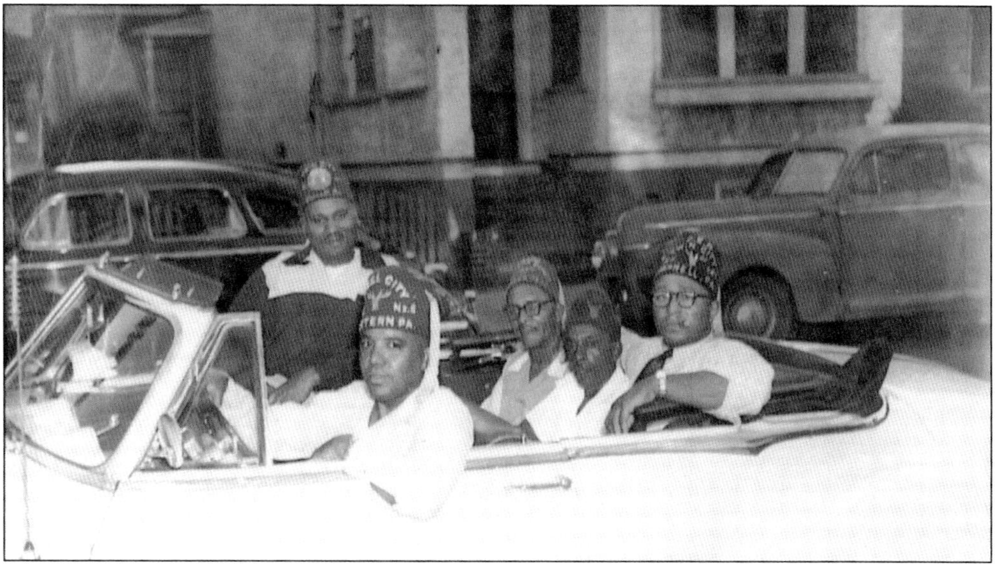

A national lodge dignitary, the dynamic J. Finley Wilson traveled across the country telling people, "If you want to see somebody with money, go to Farrell, Pa." The Twin City Elks officers seen here in the late 1940s are Lewis Greene (1907–1990) driving, Odell B. Matthews Jr. (b. 1914) in the front passenger seat, and Charles Vactor Sr. in the back seat, center. Between 1938 and 1951, Charles Vactor Sr. was the spokesman for Twin City Elks, Farrell's largest community-based African American organization. (Author's collection.)

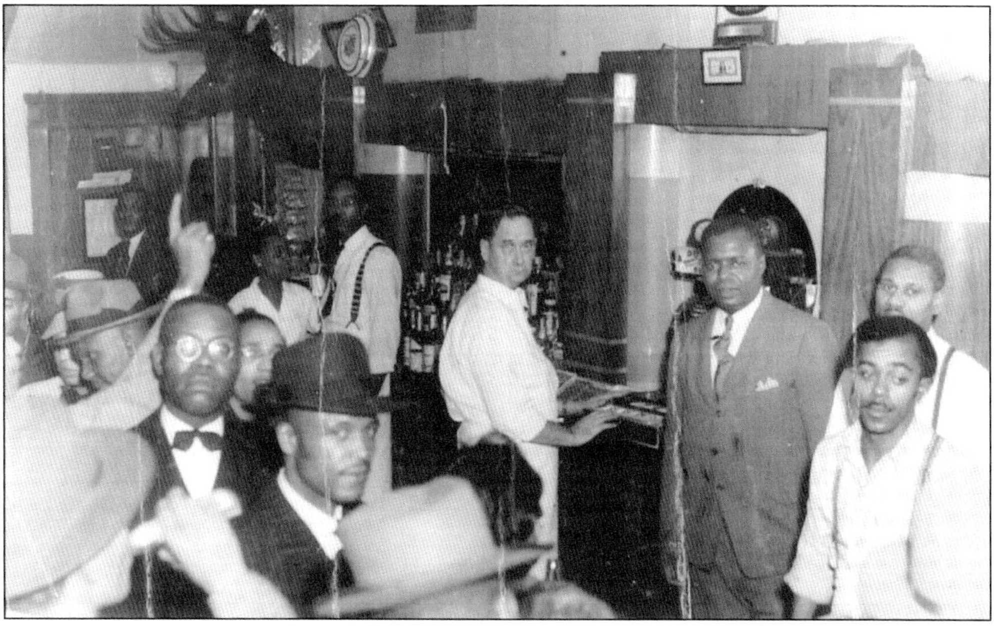

Twin City was an extraordinary organization indeed, with community-based programs and activities of wide appeal. Bands and private orchestras often performed at Twin City–sponsored events. The bar at Twin City Elks Rest is crowded with people from out of town on the weekend, as server Roy Parker (fourth from the left in back, head turned towards camera) heads out the door to the kitchen. Odell Matthews Jr. (far right, behind man in suspenders) assists. (Courtesy of Debbie Matthews Walters.)

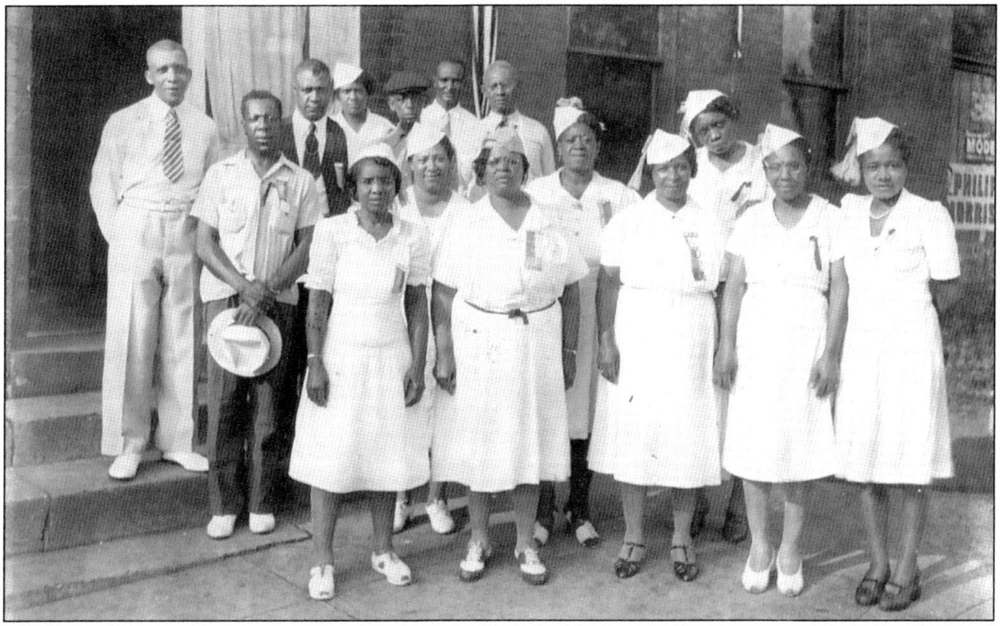

The Elks was a happening place in the 1940s and 1950s, with African Americans traveling over 60 miles to socialize there. Organized in 1914, it remained intact in an era marked by social upheaval and gave African American steelworkers an opportunity to participate in community building. Pictured are members of the Twin City Elks. Regulars came from Erie, Warren, Pittsburgh, and Youngstown and Cleveland, Ohio. (Courtesy of Debbie Matthews Walters.)

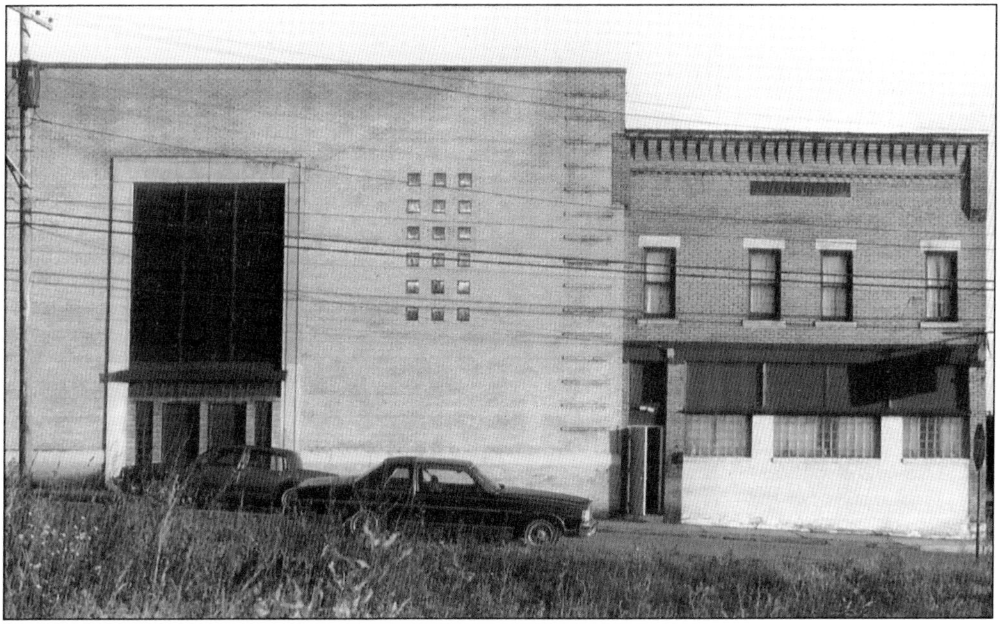

This is the prosperous intersection of Lee Avenue and Staunton Street, which housed the Twin City Elks, Miss Jessie's Café, and Pete's. Known as "The Corner" in the African American community, it was a place of high traffic. The lodge snagged popular national entertainers as they traveled between Chicago and New York, including the Temptations, the Four Tops, Duke Ellington, Ray Charles, Peg Leg Bates, and Jesse Owens. (Author's collection.)

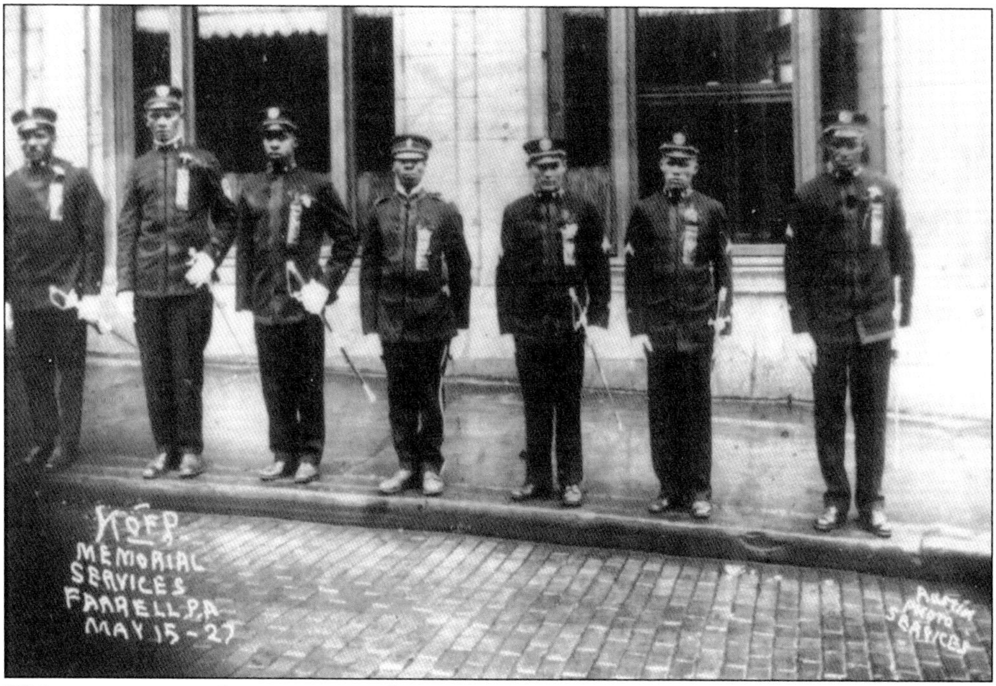

With more money and more property than many of its competitors, the African American Knights of Pythias Lodge was recognized as an exclusive organization in the nation. Due to its exorbitant fees and exclusionary practices, membership in Farrell never exceeded 40. (Author's collection.)

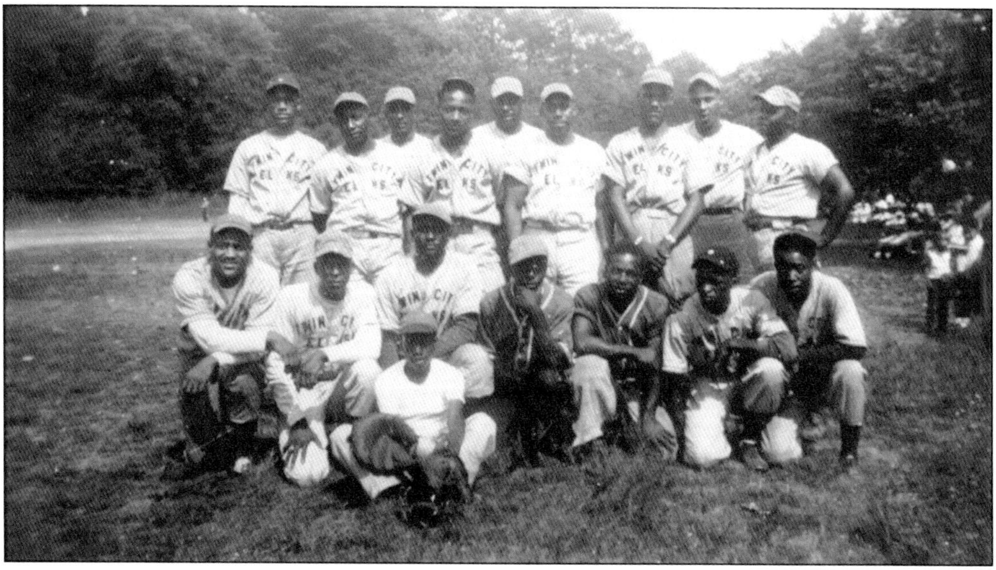

During segregation, Twin City Elks sports programs provided a constructive outlet to relieve pent-up frustrations. The softball team held home games at the Mill Street Field in Sharon's Flats, regularly having 1,000 people in attendance. Samuel Malloy (second row, center) and his teammates, including Clindo Truesdale, T. Johnson, ? Kellum, Wee Henderson, and William "Kitty" Hyatt (second row, far right), pose for a team picture at the Pine Hollow Field in Sharon around 1955. (Author's collection.)

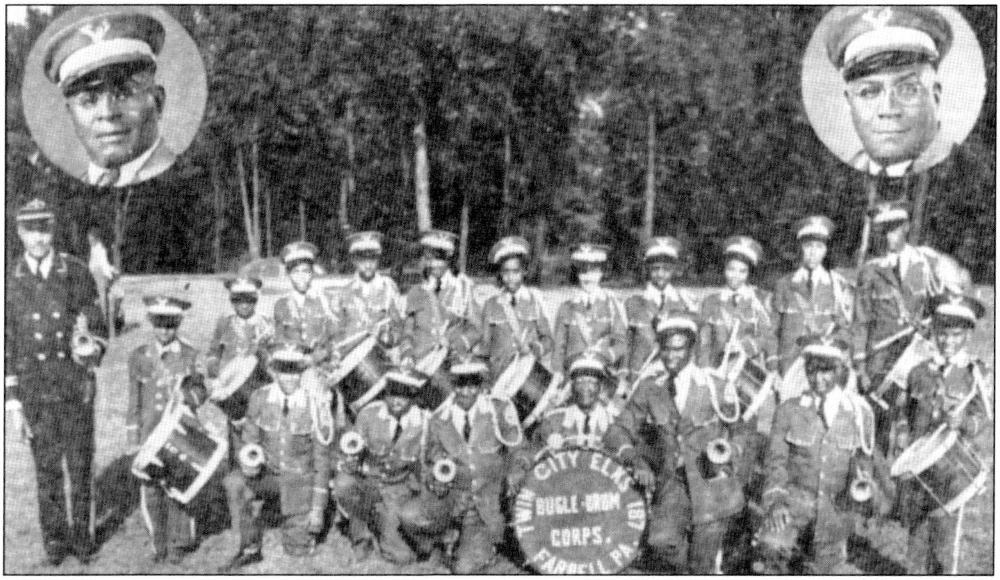

The Elks hired a music instructor to lead the adults in the award-winning Twin City Elks Band. In 1950, the completion of a $75,000 gymnasium, where the music department and sports groups practiced, was considered a great advancement. The Twin City Drum and Bugle Corps was a youth band under the leadership of a Mr. Hyatt (upper left) and Edward Smith (upper right) in the 1950s. (Author's collection.)

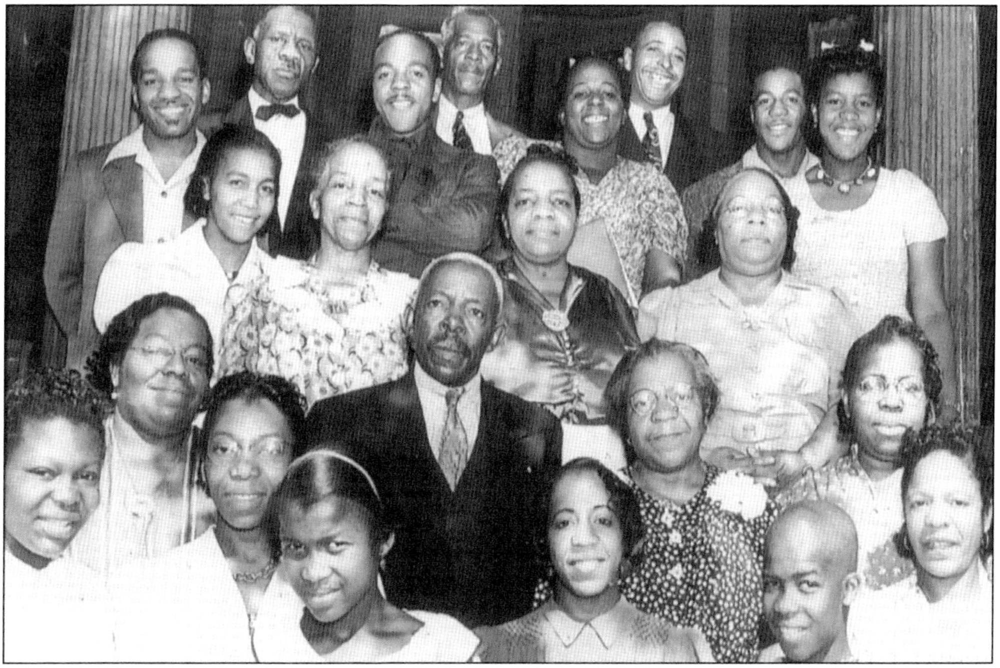

In 1912, Edward Robinson, a native of Virginia, moved from Donora to Farrell, working at the Farrell works of Carnegie Steel. He became a member of First Baptist Church and Twin City Elks. In 1953, Edward Robinson (back row, second from right) and Sarah B. Inge Robinson celebrated their 50th wedding anniversary with family at their residence, 903 ½ Market Street. (Courtesy of Iris Robinson.)

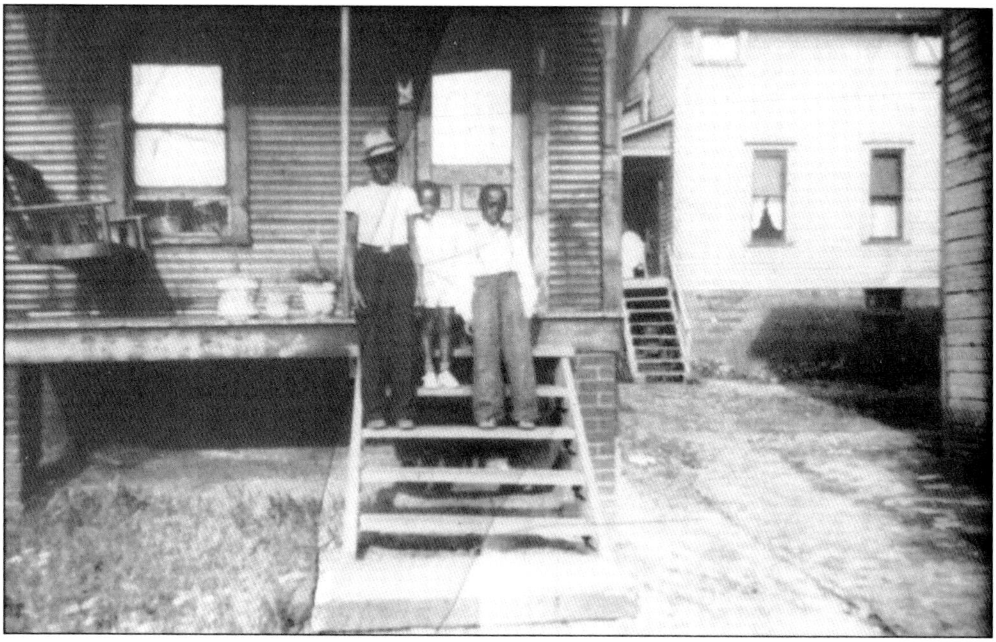

Ronald Crosby (1933–1994), of the 1952 championship team, played for the Virginia State Trojans and Ettrick Lakers, an independent team that won the Virginia All-State Tournament championship, where he received Most Valuable Player. Crosby (center) with his uncles Raymond Steverson (left) and Virgil Steverson (right) are on the back porch at 1012 Lee Avenue. (Author's collection)

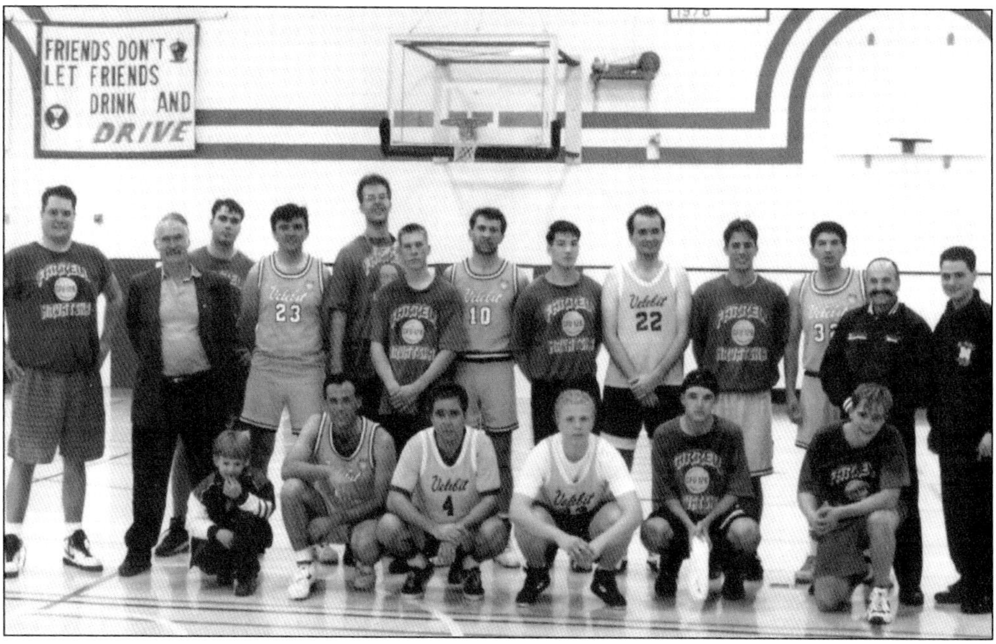

The community's competitive sports programs, supported by ethnic homes, fostered a culture of winning basketball. Farrell's Croatian Fraternal Union Lodge 126 has had a distinguished basketball program. In 1942, the local boys' youth team won a national championship in Cleveland, Ohio. Basketball team members included K. Frankovich, E. Bietatta, ? Gaus, T. Koskos, M. Schimp, S. Kennedy, K. Boldish, and J. Jacobson in the 1980s. (Courtesy of Ann Yazvac.)

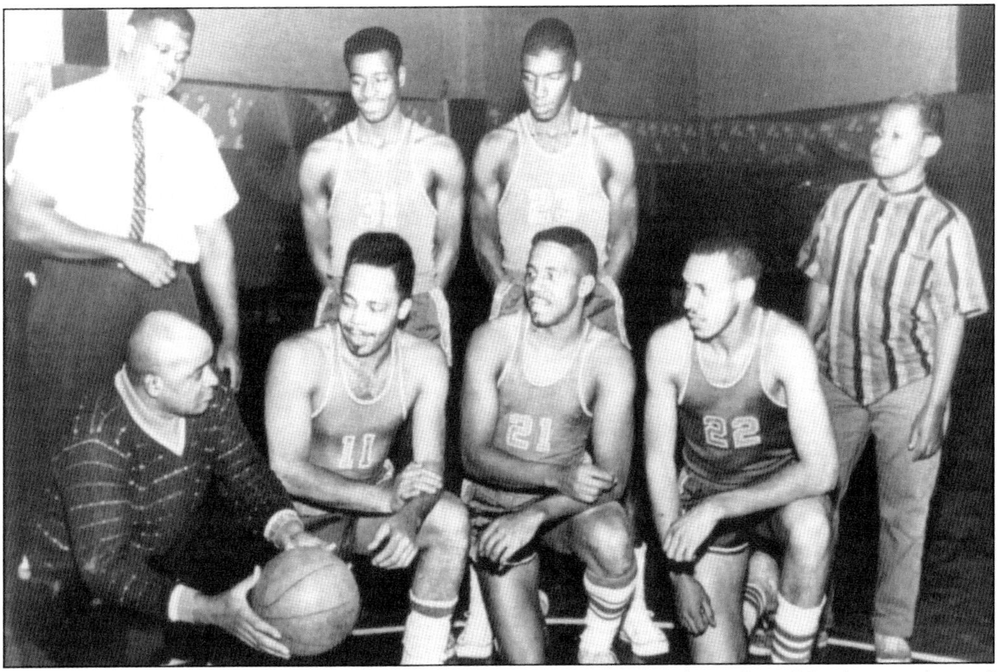

Helping to meet the aspirations of African American migrants—those from Northern industrial communities as well as those from the rural South—Farrell's Twin City Lodge touched many lives. The last Twin City Elks basketball team, in 1962, included, from left to right, (kneeling) coach Bobby Rapper, Hugo Washington, Charles Mitchell, and Leon Ponder; (standing) assistant coach and financial officer Samuel Satterwhite, ? Ferguson, ? Thompson, and unidentified. (Author's collection.)

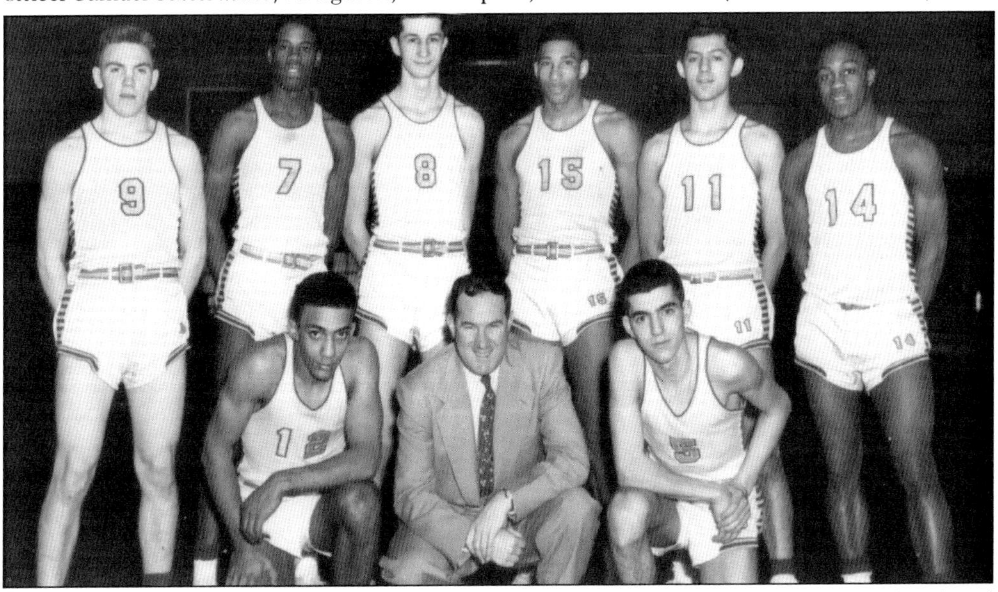

Here, the 1952 state championship team is, from left to right, (first row) Sy Alli, coach Edward "Eddie" McCluskey, and Anthony DeCello; (second row) Robert Hoffman, Ronald Crosby, James Yazvac, Julius McCoy, Nicholas Dan, and Paul Flint. In 1956, Ronald Crosby played ball for South Jersey's Super Subs where his skills led to being featured on the cover of the May 1956 *Tide* as "Mr. Basketball of Atlantic City." (Courtesy of William Jarrett.)

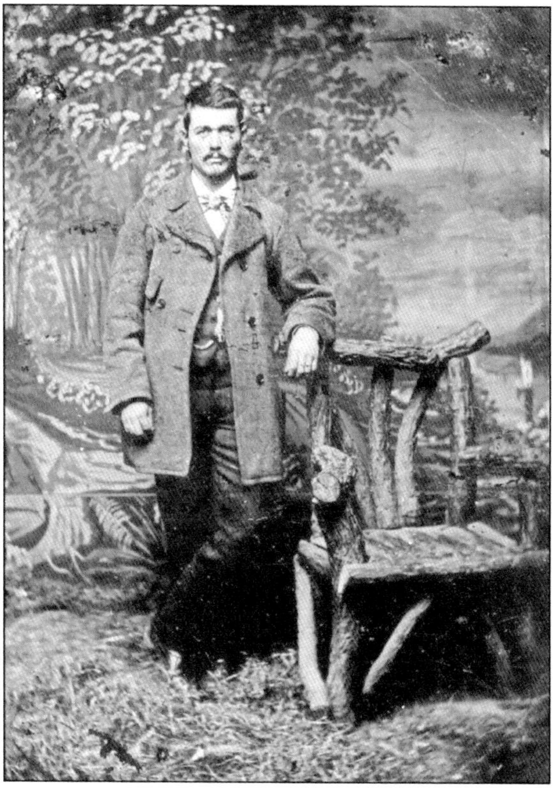

The bulk of the earliest Jewish settlers arrived from eastern Europe. Shown here is Jacob Gross, born in 1860 in Hungary before he immigrated to the United States in 1877. Many Jewish migrants typically chose a community after a series of careful choices. Below, Jacob Gross operates a general store in Commerce, Texas, in late 1880s. Gross, later attracted by the opportunities in the new industrial center, relocated to South Sharon around 1900, where he and his family had a business and maintained a vibrant Jewish life. In 1902, the framed wood synagogue on Greenfield Avenue, today known as Market Avenue, rooted the Jewish presence in the community. First trustees included Frank Gross, Leipold Klein, Morris Neiman, Joseph Goldberger, and Joseph M. Goldberg. In 1918, the landmark brick B'Nai Zion Synagogue at Spearman Avenue and Union Street was built. (Both, courtesy of SJHPRHC.)

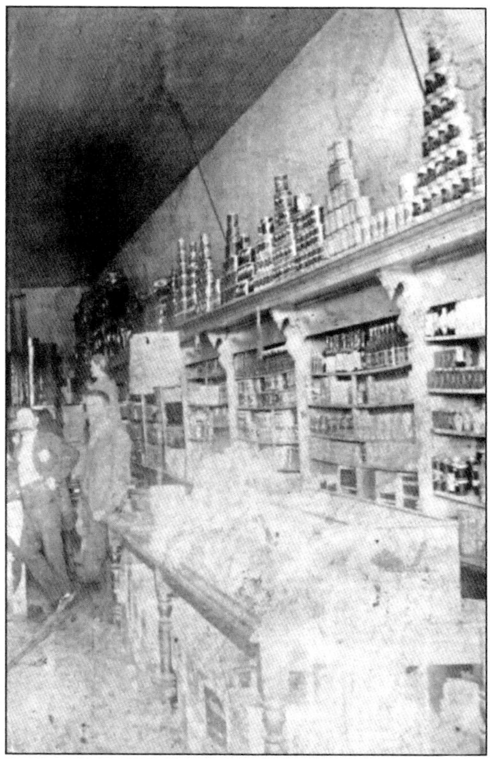

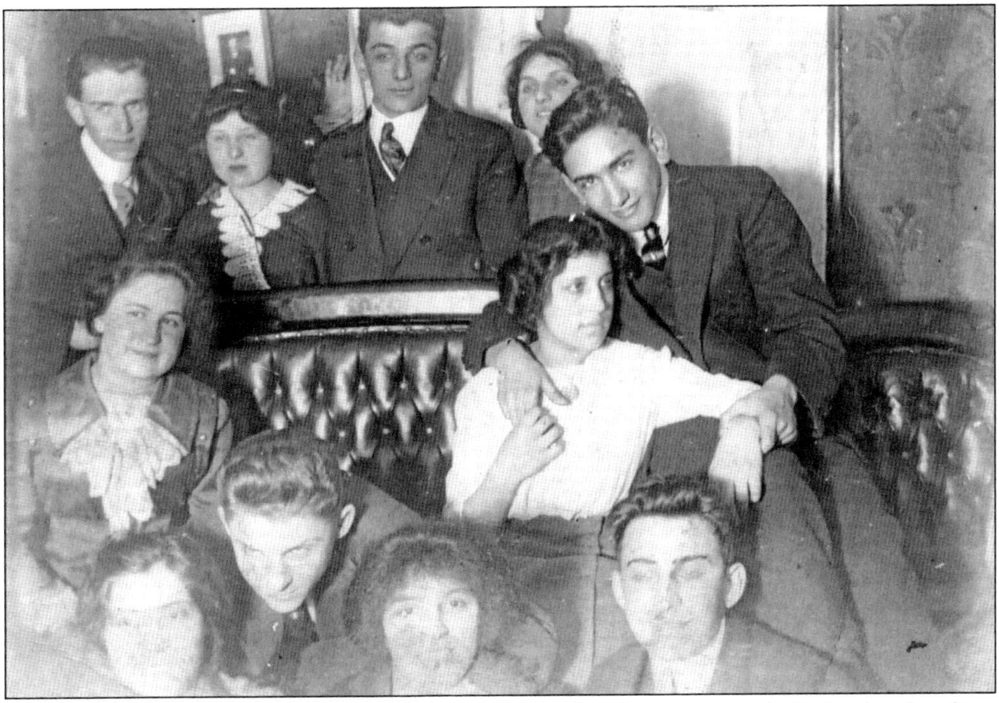

The Jewish community maintained its traditions. A Mr. Fleischman operated a kosher butcher shop. The Hebrew Independent Social Club, located at Idaho and Wallis, was a communal meeting spot. Shown here are Jewish members from Farrell and Sharon at a social gathering. From left to right are (first row) ? Garfunkel, Benjamin H. Markovitz (Marks), Ruth Greenstone, and Morris Bennett; (second row) Lena Weiner Greenstone, Ruth Bennett, and Morris Gluck; (third row) Max Gross, Sarah Markovitz (Marks), Rube Slavonsky, and Grace Rosenberg. (Courtesy of SJHPRHC.)

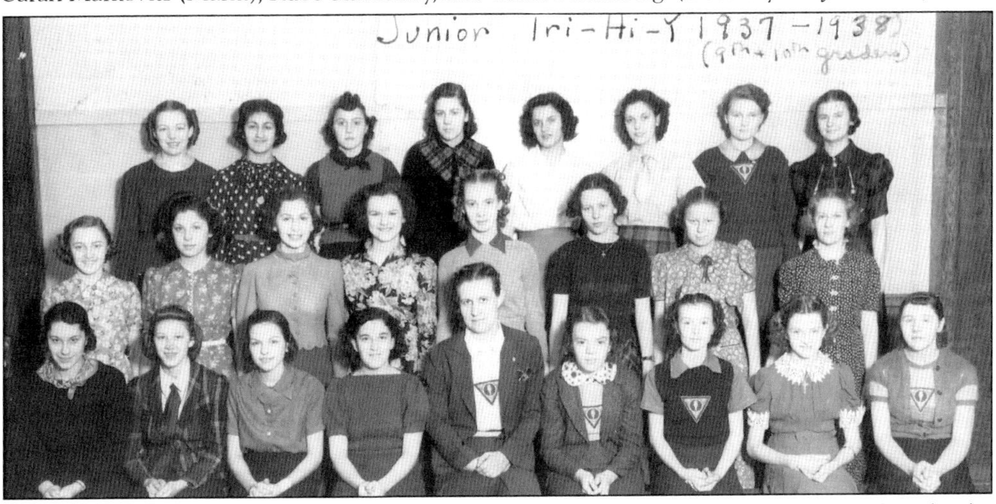

Before 1950, prominent Jewish members actively participated at Farrell High School (FHS). The ranks included school board members Dr. R.L. Landay, also treasurer, and Sophia Polangin; Dr. Irvin E Rosenberg (1920 FHS graduate), school physician; and Dr. Louis Applebaum (1923 FHS graduate), school dentist. Lena Weiner Greenstone (1910 FHS graduate) and son-in-law Dr. Charles Brier taught in the school system. In 1937, Kolma Greenstone Brier (second row, third from left) belonged to the Junior Tri-Hi-Y. (Courtesy of SNPL.)

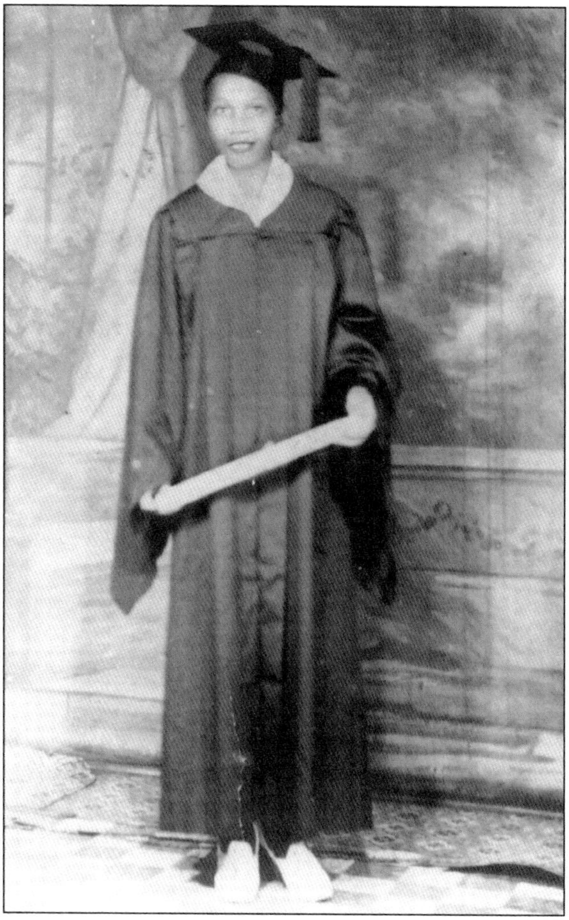

A quality education became the passport to future success. Anna Steverson holds her Farrell High School diploma in 1937. A professional seamstress, Steverson began her quilting with remnants of what might have been deemed ready for discard; they yielded an enormity of textures, contours, colors, sizes, and patterns. The poem "Crazy Quilt" by this book's author draws parallels to how diverse nationalities, languages, and creeds contributed to the social mosaic that was Farrell. Below, basketball coach Raymond Giardina and his wife, Joanne Mastrian Giardina, the Msgr. Geno Monti School librarian, pose for a picture with Drew Barksdale Hall, grandson of Anna Steverson, outside the Marian Room after a parochial school sports banquet. Hall attended Duquesne University. (Both, author's collection.)

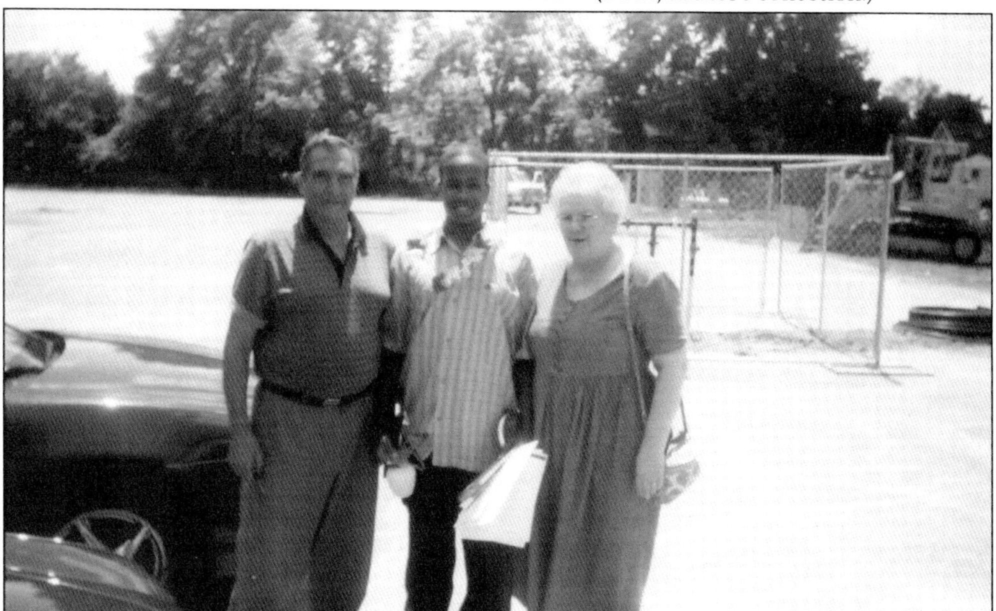

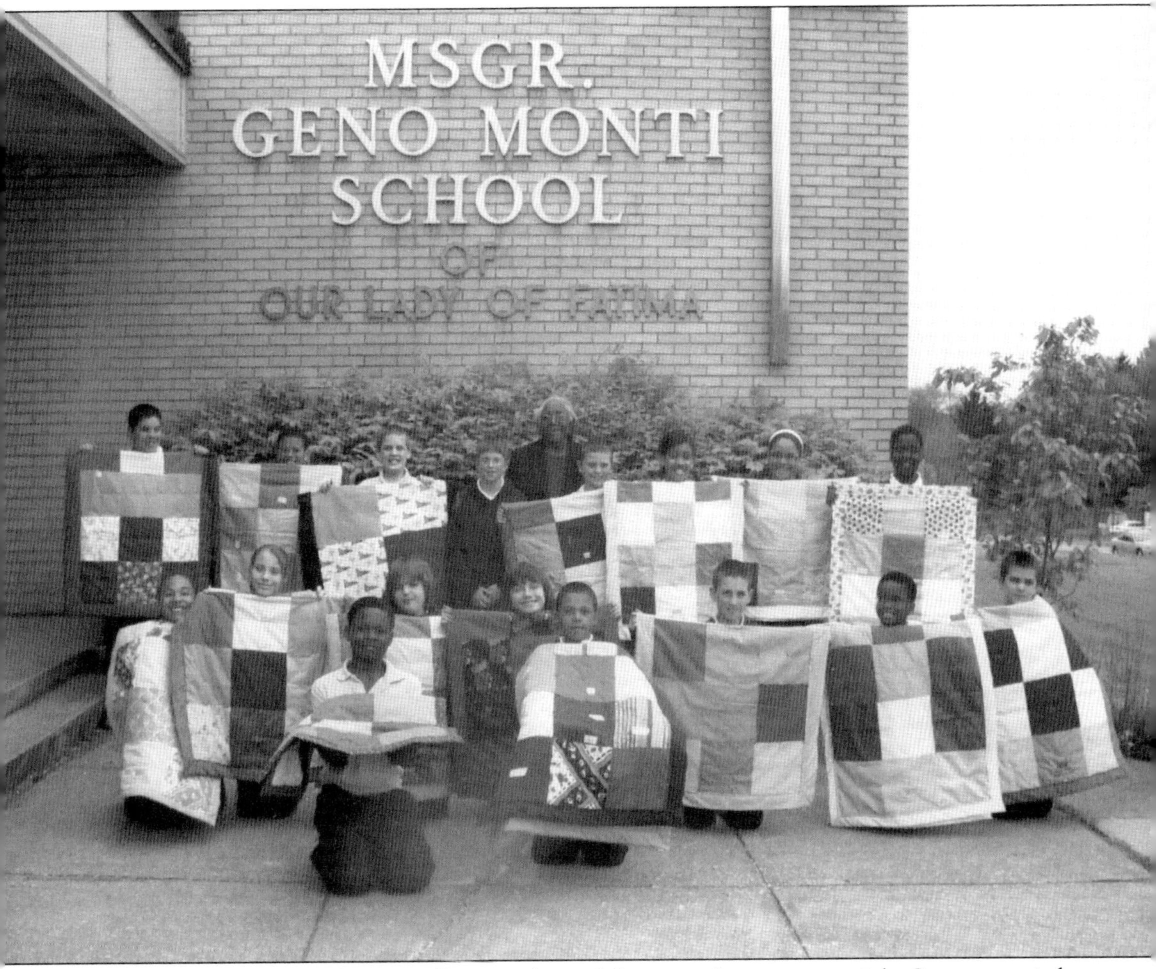

Authentic patchwork quilts typically were derived from gently worn materials. Sources varied "from purples of sister's frock to papa's green flannel, removed from work shirt must," as the poem "Crazy Quilt" says. Quilts were stuffed with old rugs to add warmth during the blustery winters. The next generation of quilters proudly displayed their original handcrafted designs. These young quilters were exposed to the celebrated African American quilting tradition by third grade teacher Rev. Willie E. Peagler (back center). The students are, from right to left, (first row) Elijah Ruff and Andre Campbell; (second row) Ariana Brezner, Sabrina Yassem, Matthew Sposito, Ashley Zanolli, Mario Cannone, Imanuel Hall, and Merle Woodring; (third row) Hunter Grande, Jason Reed, Cole George, Zachary Baker, Geno Burdick, Oriana Smith, Skylar Harris, and Jazmine Pegues. (Courtesy of Msgr. Geno Monti School of Our Lady of Fatima.)

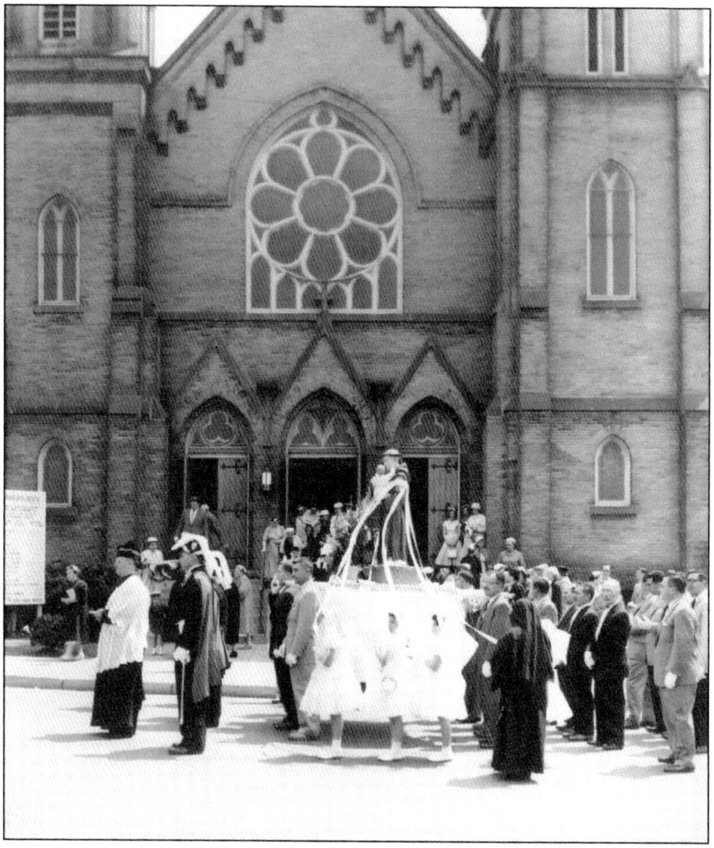

In 1952, the unification of St. Elizabeth Church and St. Anthony de Padua Italian Catholic Church by Papal decree resulted in Our Lady of Fatima Church. Here, Msgr. Geno Monti leads a feast day parade in front of Our Lady of Fatima, at the corner of Roemer Boulevard and Wallis Avenue. Below, inside the church, Fr. Donald Berdis leads a processional for the eighth grade graduation ceremony. Domenico Lombardi is the altar boy. (Left, courtesy of Msgr. Geno Monti School of Our Lady of Fatima.; below, author's collection.)

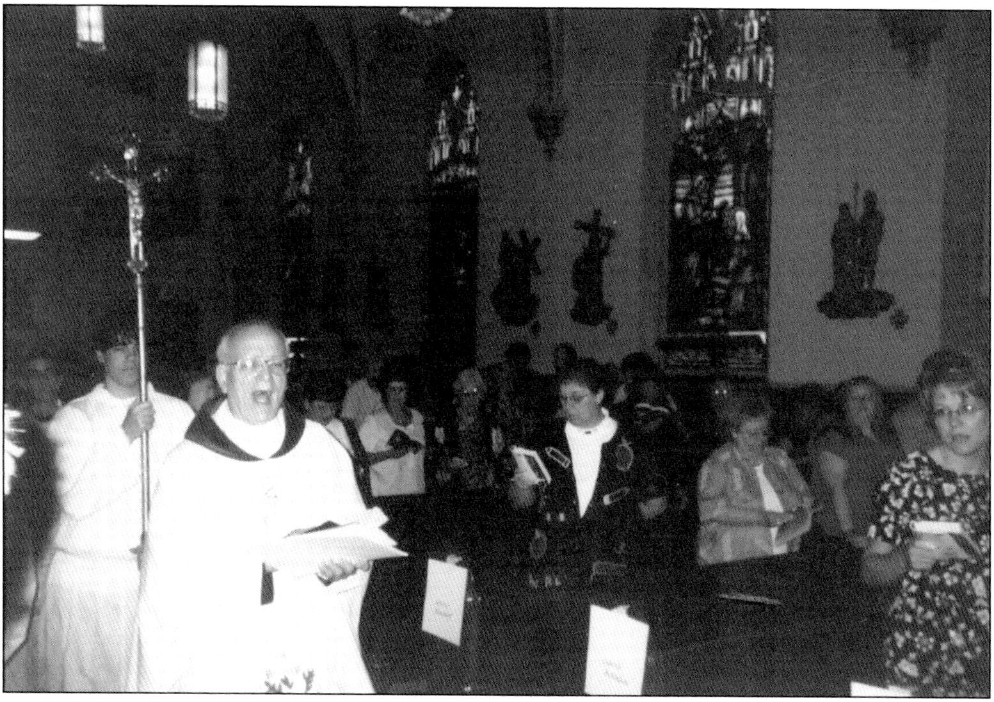

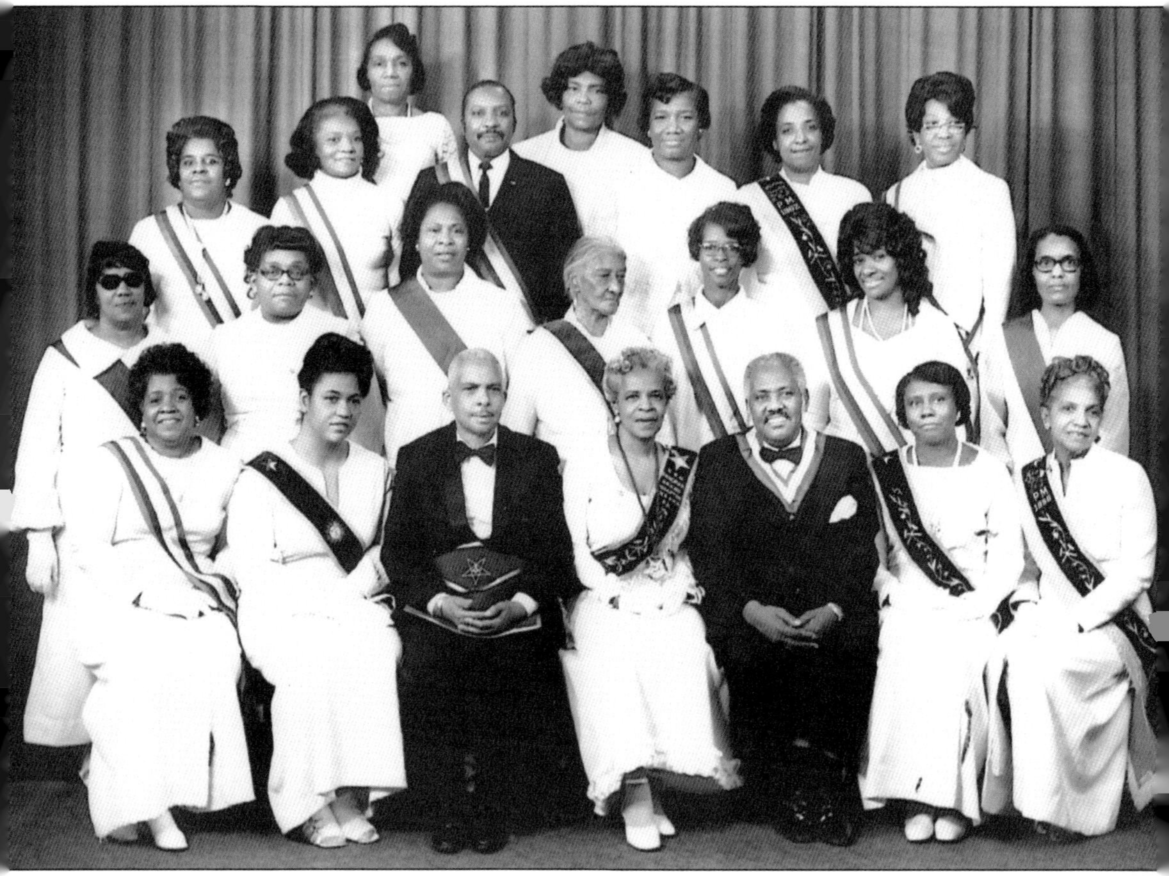

Many prominent African American women belonged to the Order of the Eastern Star. When Sara Dillard Austin (first row, center) served as statewide grand worthy matron, Order of the Eastern Star, members of Miriam Chapter included, from left to right, (first row) Rosetta Ragster, Carolyn Miller Roberts, Henry Wells, Austin, W.D. Mason, Jessie M. Alford Winston Bugg, and Helen Green; (second row) Estelle Campbell, Isabelle Hailey, unidentified, Belle Wright, Marquetta Flint, and two unidentified; (third row) unidentified, Anne McMillan, William McMillan, and three unidentified; (fourth row) two unidentified. During the Great Depression, Jessie M. Alford Winston Bugg's mother, Elizabeth Alford, a southern migrant, moved to Farrell and operated Mrs. Alford's Restaurant, where a cheeseburger, fries, and soda cost 50¢ in the 1950s. In 1958, Jessie, a 1939 Farrell High School graduate, inherited the restaurant on her mother's passing, becoming the second generation of an African American female-owned business. She changed the name to Jessie's Café and operated the restaurant, on the busy corner of Staunton Street and Lee Avenue, until 1977. The Temptations, Bo Didley, and the Four Tops, in town for shows across the street at the Twin City Elks, all tasted her fried fish. (Courtesy of Frances Flemon Ward.)

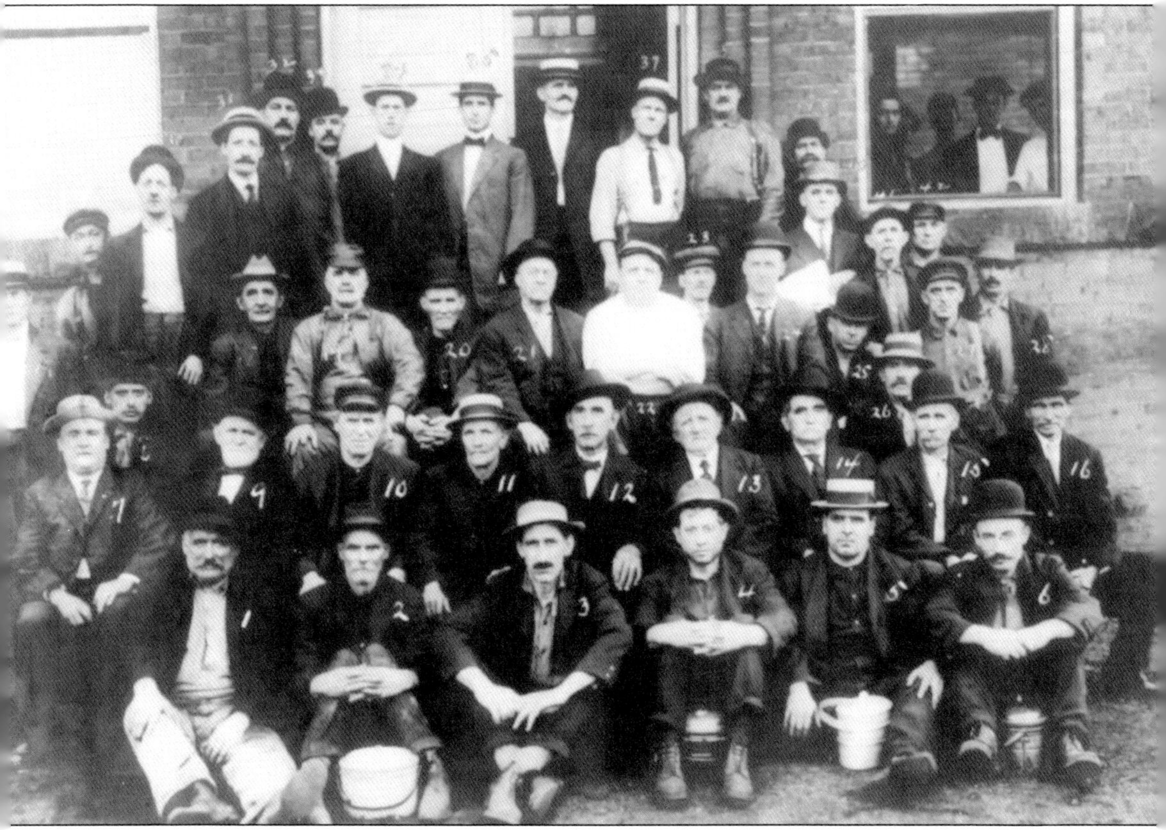

Veterans of Carnegie-Illinois Farrell Works with 20-plus years of service are pictured in the 1920s. From left to right are (first row) Charles Thomas, heater; H.E. Bell, millwright helper; David I. Davis, heater; William F. Warren, roller; John Watkins, roller; and Patrick Morrison, heater; (second row) John G. Lewis, foreman boiler house; William H. Donner, shape worker; Evan D. Thomas, foreman and weigher; Patrick Carney, engineer; Nick Pitz, laborer; Henry I. Davis, police; John W. Jones, oiler; Nicholas Wiesen, carpenter; John Hynd, foreman; and George Richards, stamper; (third row) William Pearce, finisher; John W. Davis, engineer; Griffith Saunders, engineer; William Magee, laborer; Edward Randolph, warehouseman; D.W. Christie, superintendent; William Peat, superintendent; J.V. Rigby, master mechanic; Daniel Letcher, pitman; Thomas Johns, ladle liner; Fred Bees, millwright; and Michael Letishon, stripper; (fourth row) Casper Miller, ladler; Charles F. Moore, machinist; W.H. Moore, assistant; James Phillips, foreman; Edward R. Hoagland, machinist; James Benbow, auditor; N.B. Price, clerk; F.L. Mathay, roll turner; Matt Carnes, bricklayer; Martin Letcher, foreman; Frank Letcher, foreman; W.T. May, chief shipper; Thomas Henrahan, pit man; and Henry Smith, ladle man. (Courtesy of MCHS.)

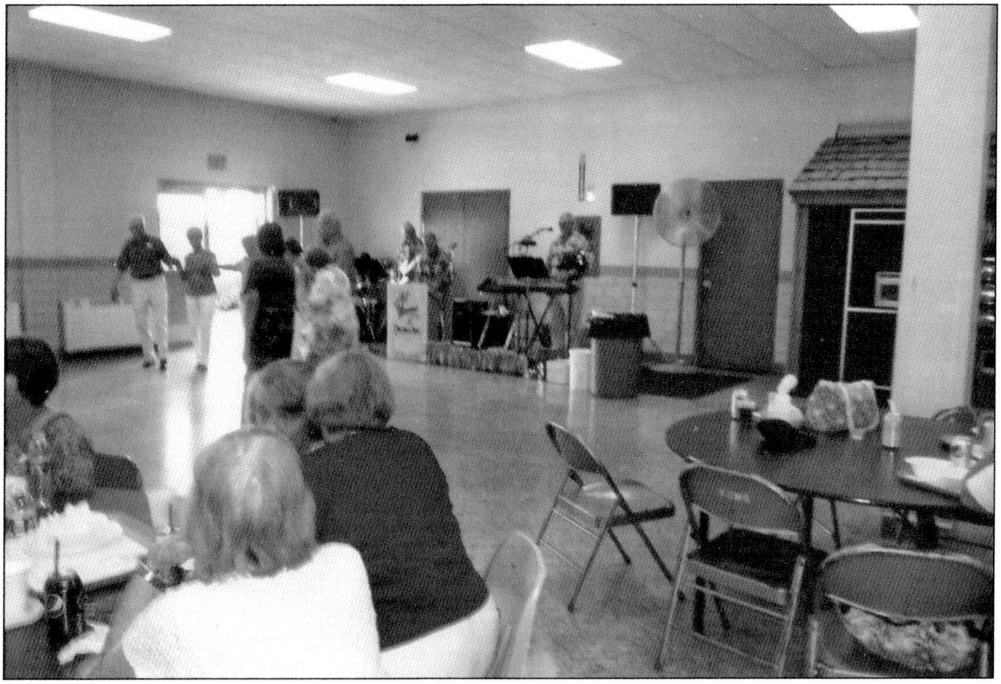

Polish life and culture continue to be celebrated in Farrell. St. Adalbert Polish Catholic Church holds its annual festival in June, with prized colorful babushkas, line dancing, and food, such as tasty cabbage and rice, pierogies, and piping hot sausage smothered with tomatoes, peppers, and onions on a bun. In 2005, Ludima Gus Burton, a Polish-theme-oriented romance writer, joined the first Farrell High School Alumni Hall of Fame class. (Author's collection.)

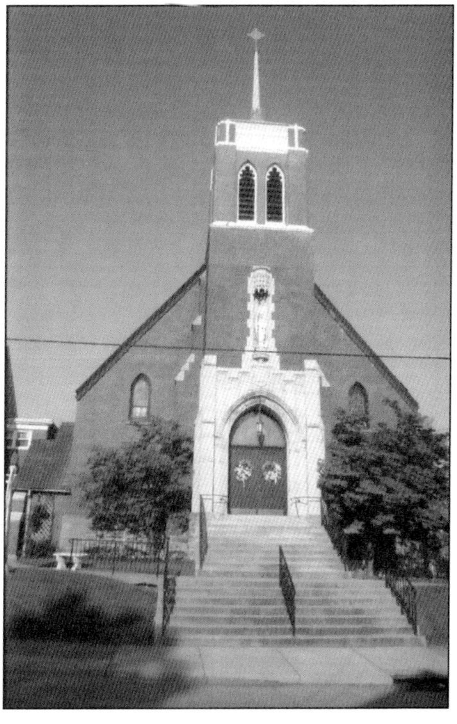

Fruit Avenue was known by residents as "Church Row" for its many nationalist churches. Immigrants found a foreign language service, familiar worship style, and cultural life helpful in making the transition to life in America. Leo J. Yankevich, a prominent poet and 1980 alumnus of Farrell High School, attended St. Adalbert's Roman Catholic Church, pictured here at 1035 Fruit Avenue. Today, Yankevich lives in Gilwice, Poland. (Author's collection.)

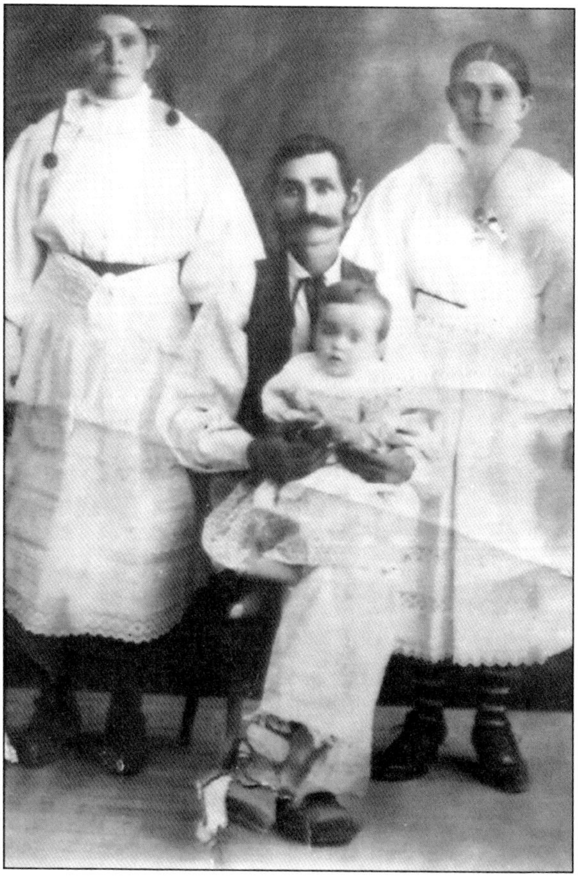

Steve Yazvac (1882–1965) first came to America from Dragnic, Croatia, in 1905, returned to Croatia in 1917, and married Barbara Bene in 1919. In Croatia, Barbara Bene Yazvac (right) takes a picture with Katich Bene (left) and Ivan Bene, holding his grandson John Yazvac, before coming to America. In 1920, Steve Yazvac, wife Barbara, and son John immigrated to the United States, where they had a cow, chickens, and a truck garden. (Courtesy of Ann Yazvac.)

First generation Croatian immigrants sometimes faced social exclusion. They and their children found one of the Croatian lodges (there were three in the area) a safe haven and home away from home. Banquets and other social events were well attended from the 1930s through 1950s. (Courtesy of Ann Yazvac.)

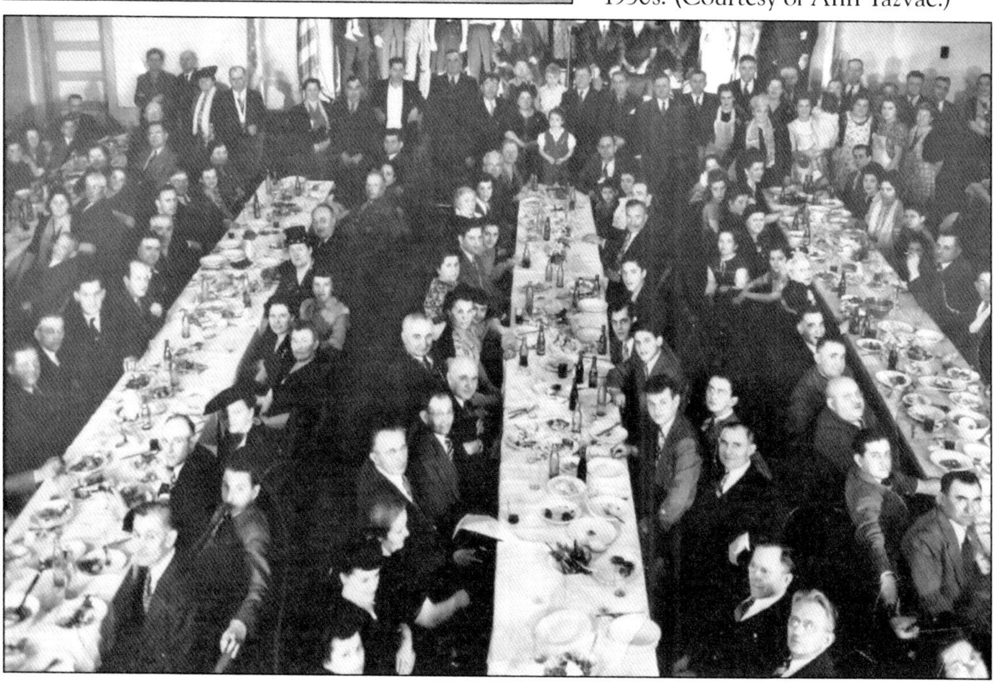

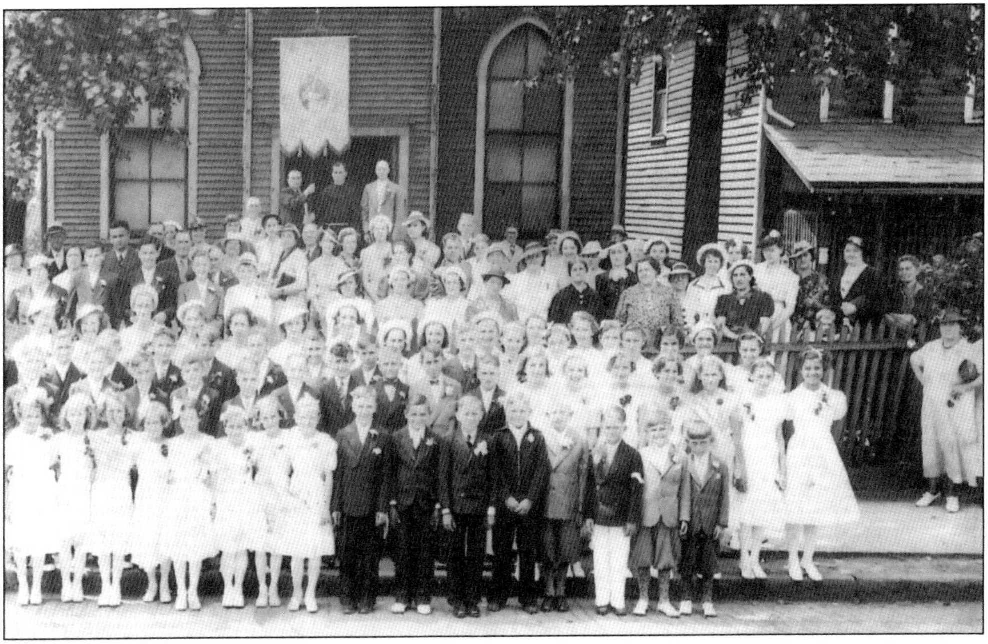

In 1937, Fr. Anzelmo Sliskovic was pastor for the confirmation class at St. Anthony American Croatian Roman Catholic Church on Market Avenue. Shown here are, among others, Barbara Yazvac (first row, far left), Anne Yazvac (second row, far right), Mary Yazvac (third row, far right), Steve Yazvac (third row, seventh from left), John Yazvac (back row, in front of window), and Barbara Yazvac (behind fence, seventh from right in a print dress). (Courtesy of Ann Yazvac.)

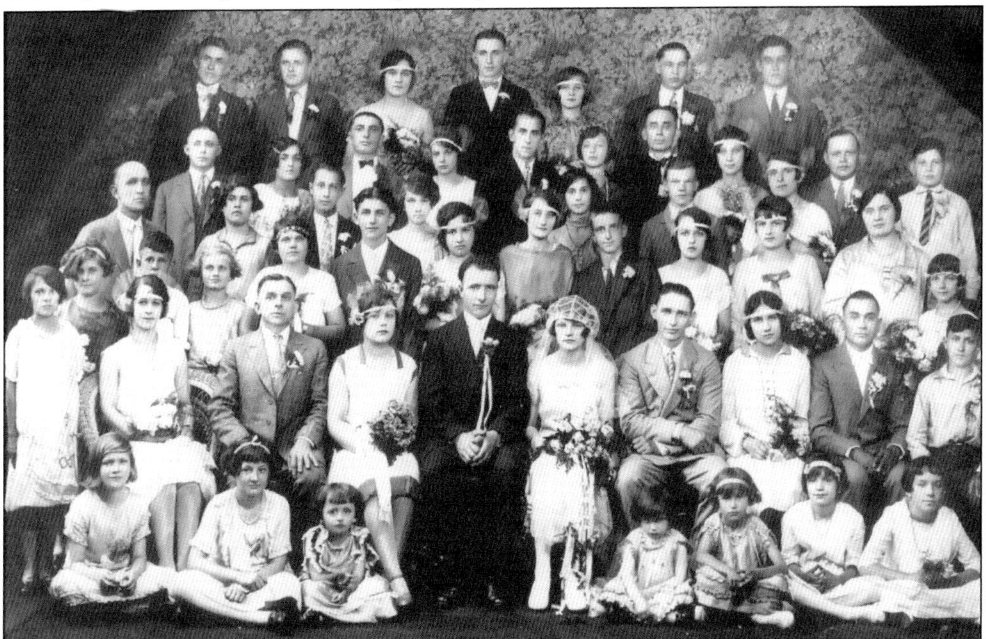

On June 26, 1926, Fred Husnick and Katherine Egercic were married. Katherine Egercic was 15 years old. Husnick was 28 and employed at American Steel and Wire. Members of the wedding party were all Croatian. (Courtesy of Ann Yazvac.)

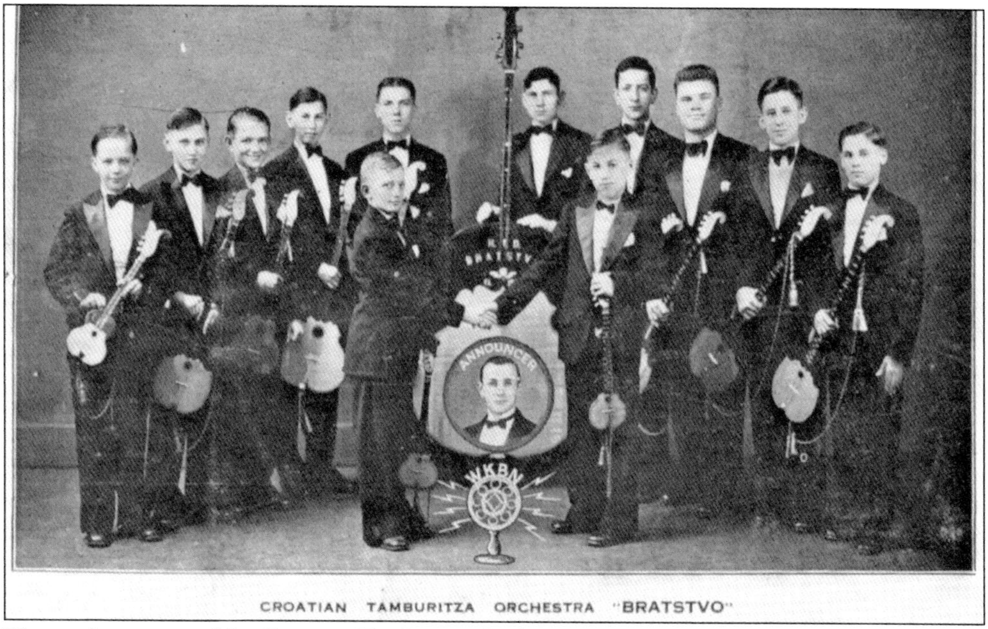

The performances of the Croatian Tamburitza Orchestra Bratstvo were broadcasted over WKBN in Youngstown, Ohio. This iteration of the orchestra included, from left to right, (first row) Joe Bobich and Mile Bakmus; (second row) Mike Golub, Andy Bakmus, Joe Brachich, Emil Bossick, Nick Yurcich, Frank Egercic, Bill Vatavuck, Frank Spicko, Tom Egercic, and Tony Bralich. (Courtesy of Ann Yazvac.)

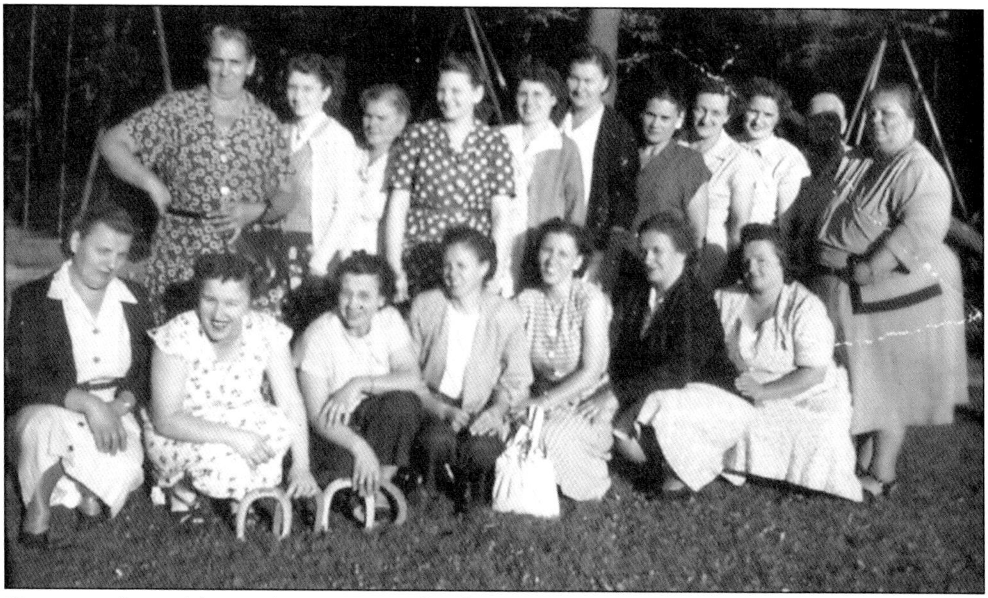

Croatians, Jews, African Americans, and Italians all figured prominently within their precinct. In 1928, elements in the Croatian community encouraged John Edmunds, an African American, to run for office, fully supporting his candidacy. Candidate endorsements were decided at joint political meetings. In the late 1940s, the Ladies Auxiliary of the Croatian American Civic Club included Anna Pilipovich (first row, far left) and Katherine Husnick (second row, fourth from left). (Courtesy of Ann Yazvac.)

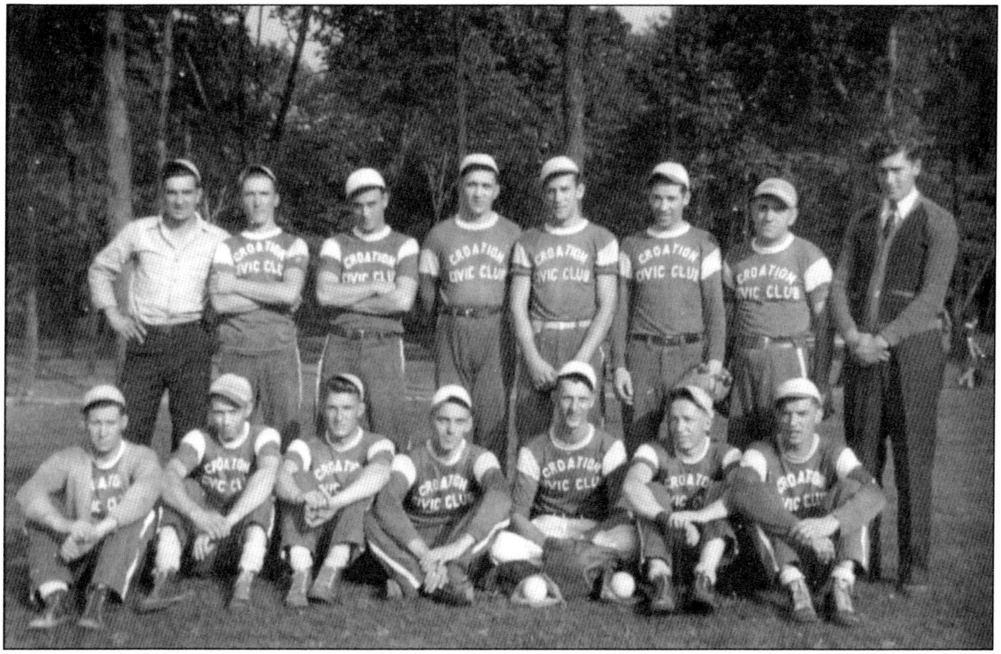

Farrell was an athletic community, as evidenced by the vibrant sports programs developed by ethnic homes. Like the Twin City Elks, the Croatian American Civic Club sponsored a baseball team. Both clubs had national championship basketball teams in the 1940s. (Courtesy of Ann Yazvac.)

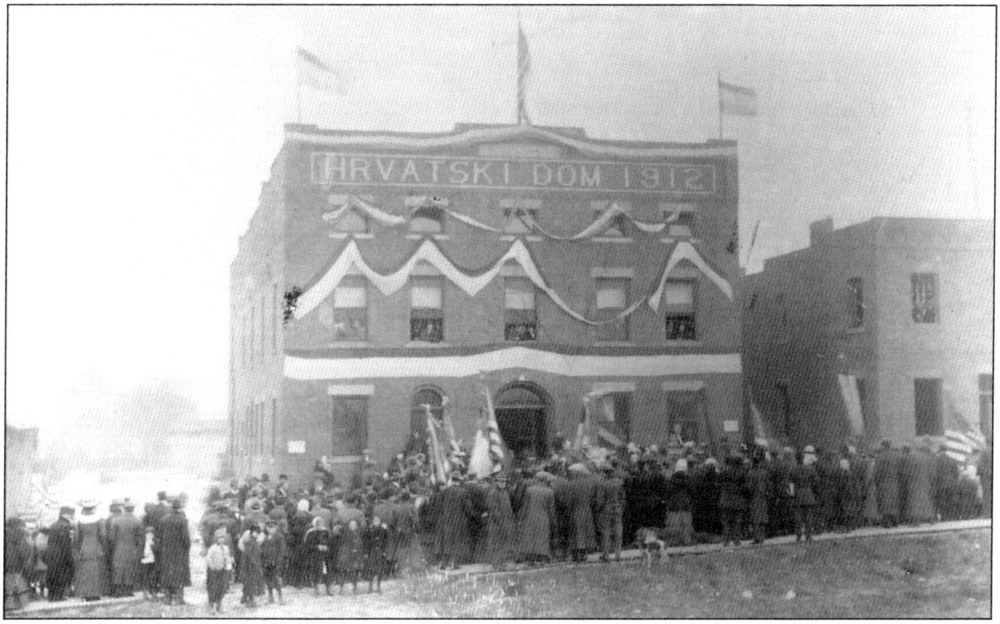

On Thanksgiving Day, November 28, 1912, the dedication for the Croatian Home drew a large crowd. According to the August 23, 1946, *Farrell Press*, the Croatian American Civic Club developed from the old Croatian Political Club. The Civic Club, originally headquartered at the Croatian Home, moved to the Pintar Building before returning to purchase the Croatian Home around 1946, when John "Bucky" Pandza was the president. The 100th anniversary celebration of the dedication of the Croatian Home will be held October 14, 2012. (Courtesy of Ann Yazvac.)

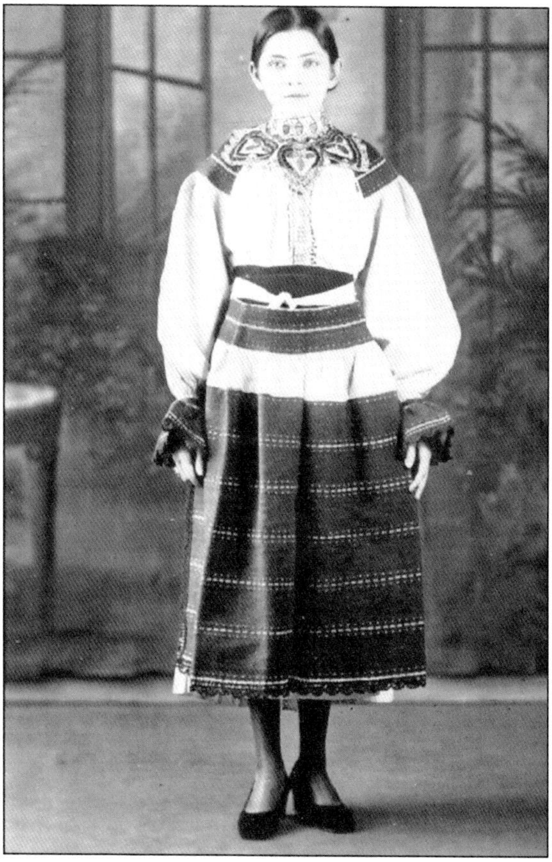

The Croatian Home, at 412 Staunton Street, was in the heart of a mixed neighborhood comprised largely of Jews, Italians, African Americans, and Croatians. As early as 1915, joint political meetings were held in Farrell, where Croatians actively participated in the American political process. Here, Mildred Egercic wears a traditional Draganic dress from Croatia at the Elite Studio in Farrell. Descendants of the natives of Draganic and a neighboring Croatian village populated Farrell. (Courtesy of Ann Yazvac.)

The Croatian community was socially conservative and widely known for its excellent Tamburitza orchestras. Partially due to developments in their homeland and because of a few agitators, the Croatian American Civic League was falsely branded a Communist organization and many wrongly suffered for the mistakes of a few. (Courtesy of Ann Yazvac.)

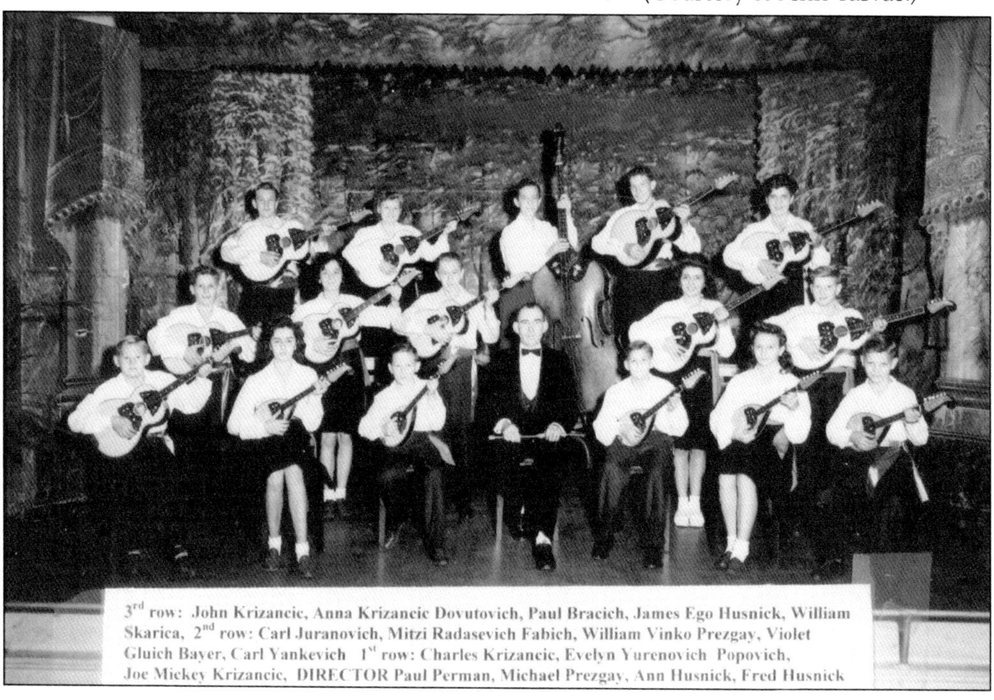

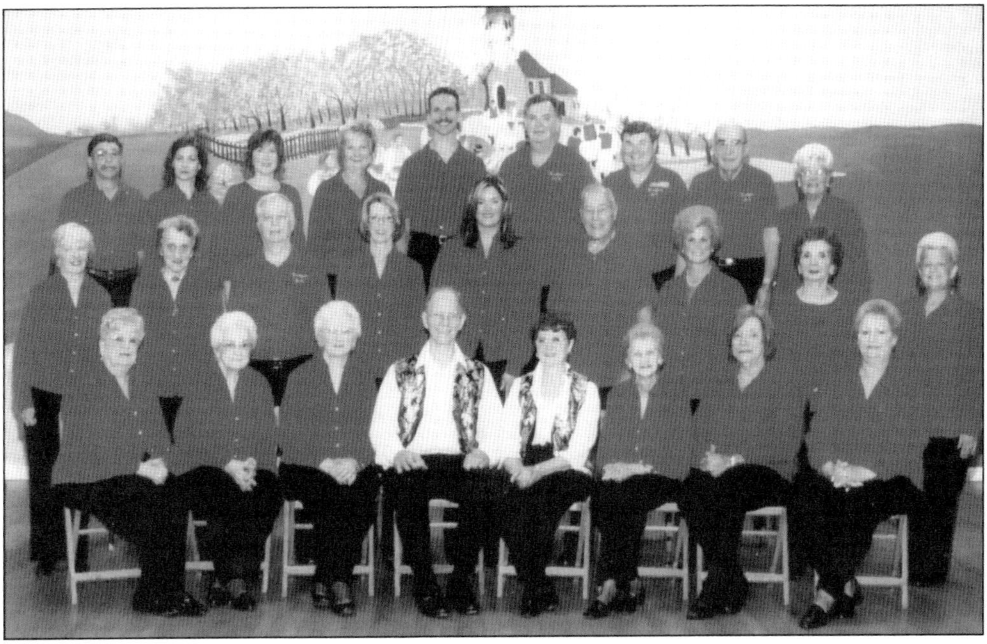

The famous Vesli Tamburitzans, formed by Fred Husnick, has numerous recordings and has been on tour to Yugoslavia. In 1989, Fred Husnick was inducted at Las Vegas into the Tamburitza Association of America Hall of Fame. Husnick's instrumental accompaniment and wife Rose's voice have made the recordings a huge success. Here, Fred and Rose Husnick (front row, center) sit with the current Farrell Croatian Home's Tamburitza orchestra on the stage. (Courtesy of Ann Yazvac.)

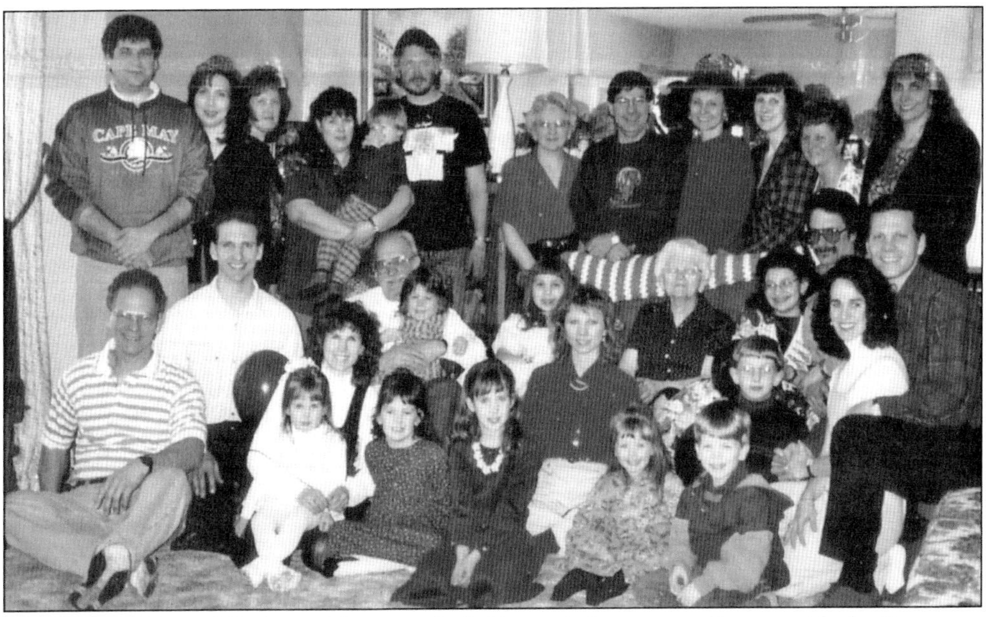

In 1952, Fred Husnick Jr. (seated first row, far left) traveled on tour to Europe with the Duquesne University Tamburitzans, where he met his grandmother Husnick for the first time. His children Mark and Diana, like their dad, were members of the Junior Sloga Tamburitzans and the Duquesne University Tamburitzans. Family members gather for 80th birthday celebration of Katherine Egercic Husnick (seated on sofa, center). (Courtesy of Ann Yazvac.)

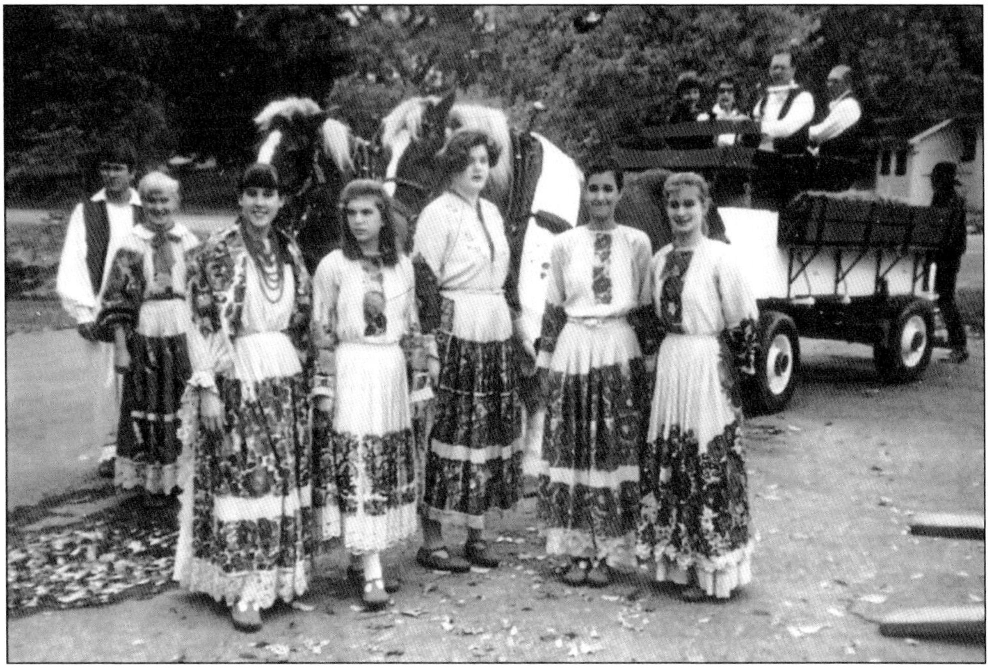

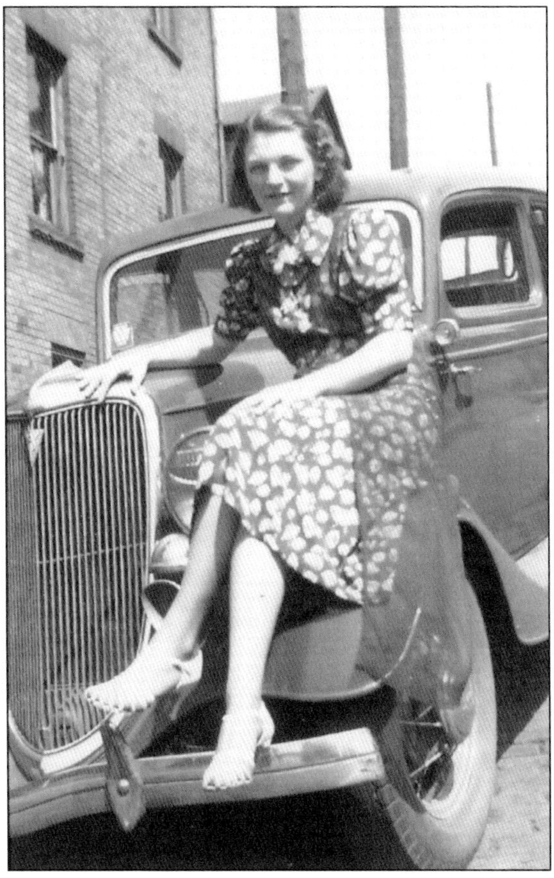

In October 1996, Priscilla Fister and Davis Earhart wanted to reconnect with their roots and hold a traditional Croatian wedding. The bridal party included Adam Allhouse, Valerie Taylor, Stacey Pipic, Allison Minoff, Catherine Bralich, Tanya Matijevic, and Sarah Minoff. Behind the bridal party in the dowry wagon was the orchestra—Rose Husnick, Libby Fill, Fred Husnick, and Mike Jurich—in Farrell's outlying countryside near West Middlesex. (Courtesy of Ann Yazvac.)

Ethnic homes once provided a sense of belonging for first generation immigrants with language barriers. There they could have a drink, play cards, participate in sports, and maintain aspects of their cultural traditions. Kathryn Husnick models her family's first car on Staunton Street in the 1930s. With the development of the automobile and language proficiency, people no longer were forced to live close to where they worked. They even packed in and traveled to distant places on occasion. (Courtesy of Ann Yazvac.)

Four

American Enterprise

Building a Healthy Community

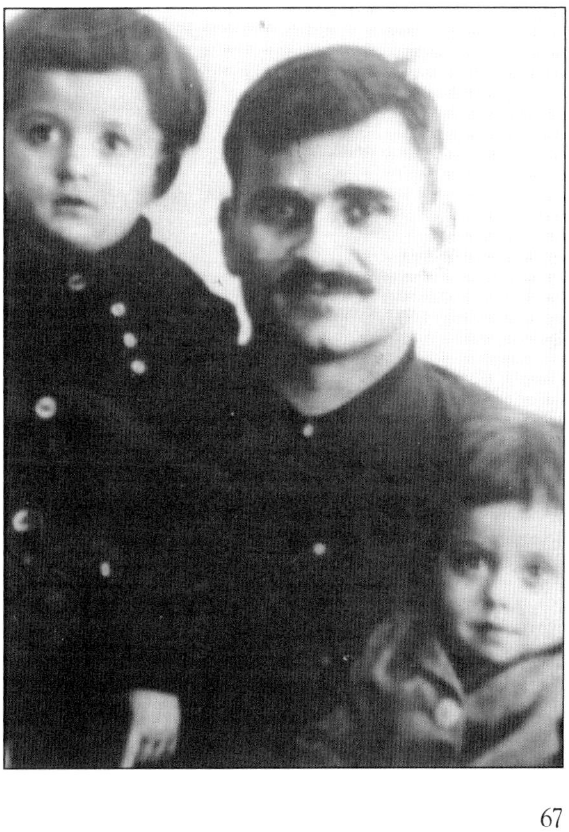

The flu epidemic following World War I killed more people than the war did. Greek native George Havas's 27-year-old wife, Mercina Cacalis, was a casualty of the epidemic. Hayas is shown here with his daughters, Angeliki and Rodopi, in 1920. (Courtesy of Marcy Pedas Sigler.)

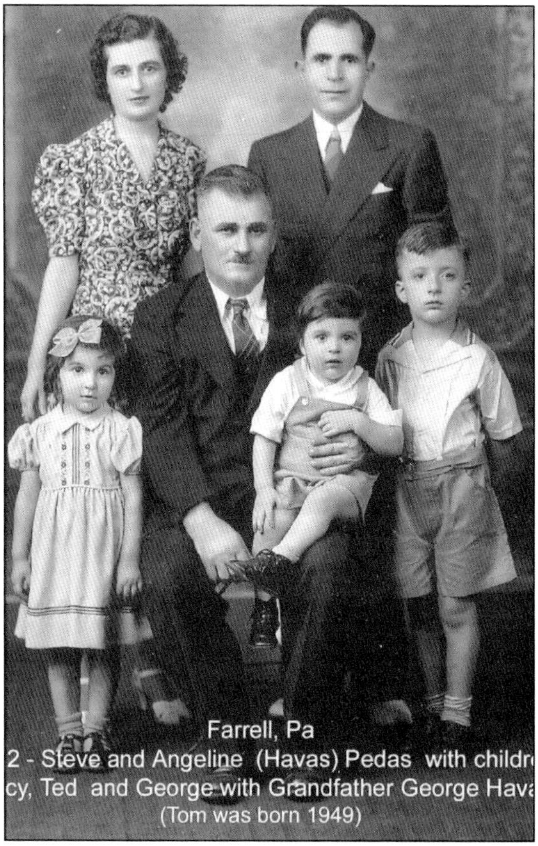

During the Great Depression, Gust Talaganis, owner of New Castle's Star Market, noticed George Havas's daughter Angeliki shopping and assisted with an introduction and arranged marriage to his friend Steve Pedas (Efstathios Tsimpedas), a Farrell businessman. Both Pedas and Talaganis were natives of Doriza, Greece. During his free time, George Havas assisted his son-in-law at the Broadway Cash Market at 745 Broadway Avenue. (Courtesy of Marcy Pedas Sigler.)

In 1938, the wedding party of Steve Pedas and Angeliki Havas Pedas included, from left to right, (first row) unidentified flower girls; (second row) bride Angeliki Havas Tsimpedas, Aglaia Zaimes, Angeliki Zentoviloni, two unidentified people, and Katina Mavropidis; (third row) groom Steve Pedas (Efstathios Tsimpedas), unidentified, ? Mouganis, unidentified, Georgios Talaganis, and Nick Mavropidis. (Courtesy of Marcy Pedas Sigler.)

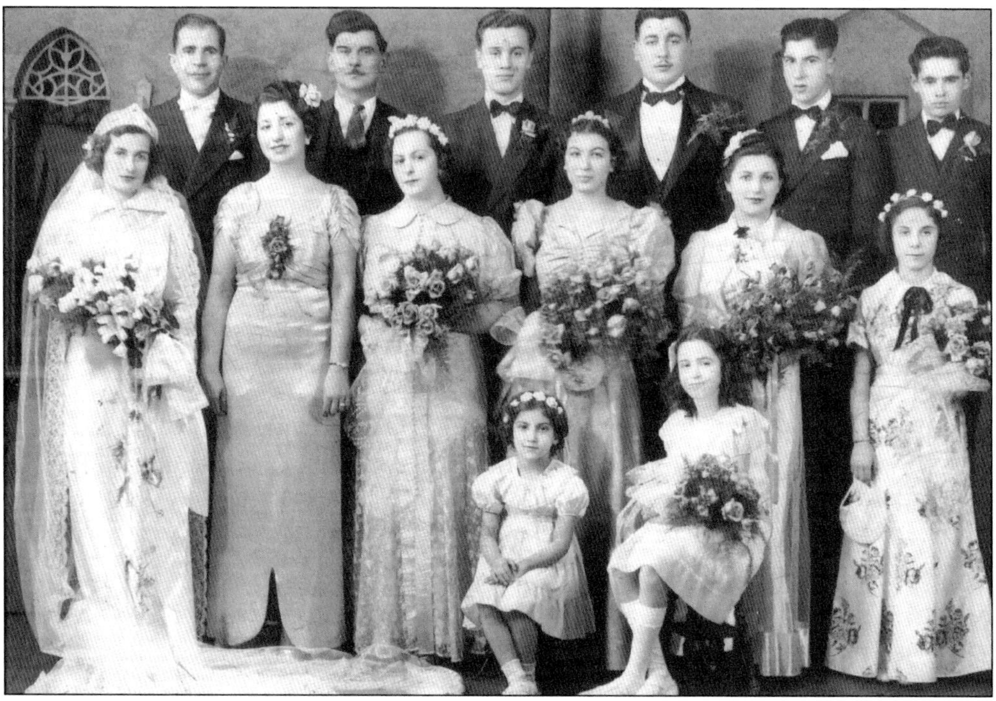

The Greek American Progressive Association was established in 1925 to promote a better understanding of the fundamentals of good American citizenship. The Greek Home was located on Roemer Boulevard. The association also built the Annunciation Greek Orthodox Church (seen here) at the corner of Washington Street and Beechwood Avenue, which was dedicated on November 15, 1942, in addition to purchasing a parsonage and maintaining a Greek language school. (Courtesy of Marcy Pedas Sigler.)

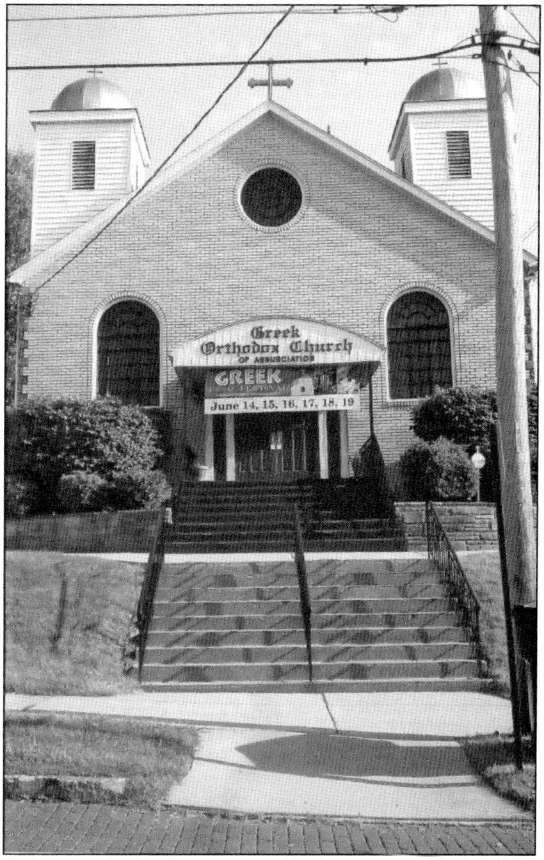

Chris L. Lampros was the first president of the Annunciation Greek Orthodox Church. In the 1950s, Lampros, along with Msgr. Geno Monti, was involved in the Crusade for Freedom, a national program developed as a deterrent to the spread of Communism. The orthodox churches annually came together for a musical celebration. Kathryn Polyzou directed the church choir, seen below, when Fr. George Stephanopolous was pastor. (Courtesy of Marcy Pedas Sigler.)

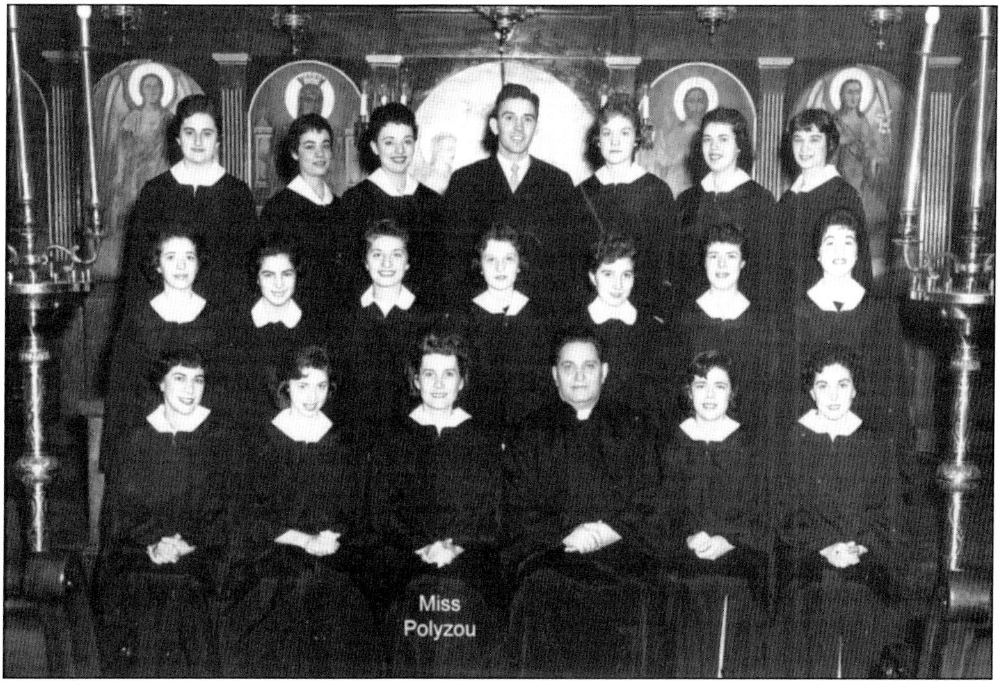

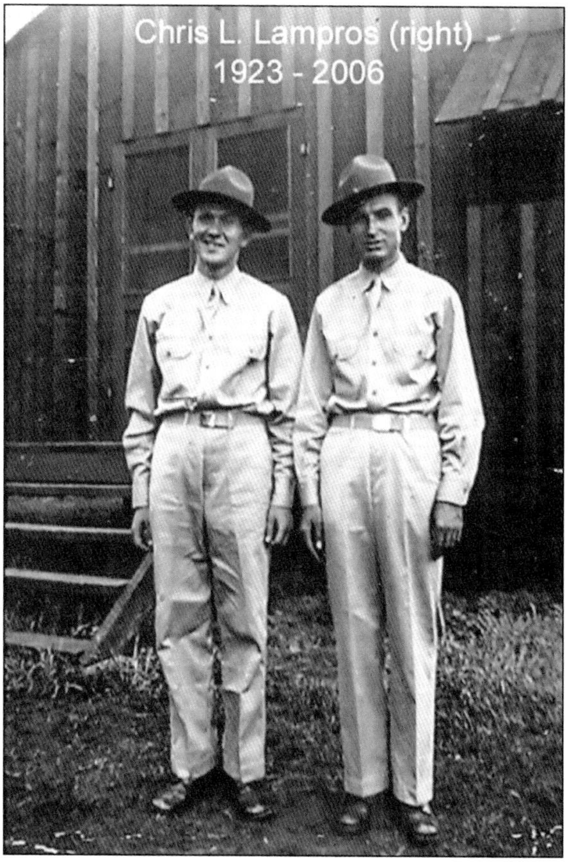

Chris L. Lampros had a rags-to-riches life story. In 1923, at age 13, Lampros left Greece and came to Farrell, where he lived with an uncle, Louis Brown, on Negley Street. He attended Eckles School and worked shining shoes in the evening for a year. In 1926, he was hired as a janitor and usher in the Strand Theater. Three years later, he purchased the bankrupt Farrell Theaters. Principal stockholders in the Lampros Brothers Theaters included his brothers John and Louis and his brother-in-law Peter Zahariou. Lampros owned the Capitol and Colonial Theaters, local landmarks on Idaho Street, where Jim Pedas and his brother Ted Pedas worked as ushers. As adults, these enterprising Pedas brothers became film producers, launching the Coen brothers career with films such as *Raising Arizona*. (Left, courtesy of Marcy Pedas Sigler; below, courtesy of Ann Yazvac.)

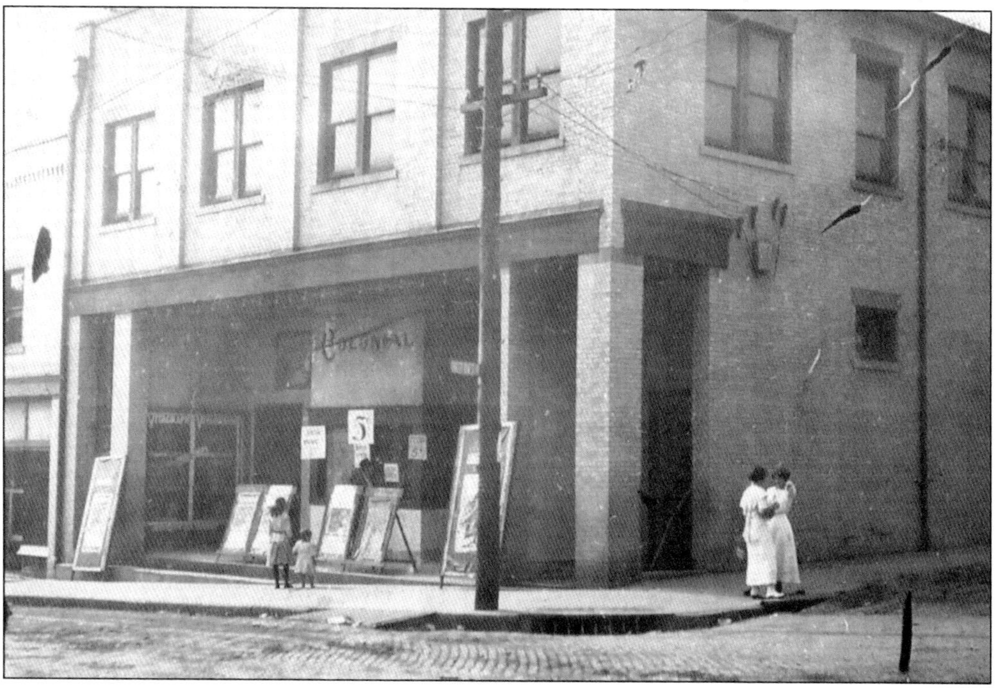

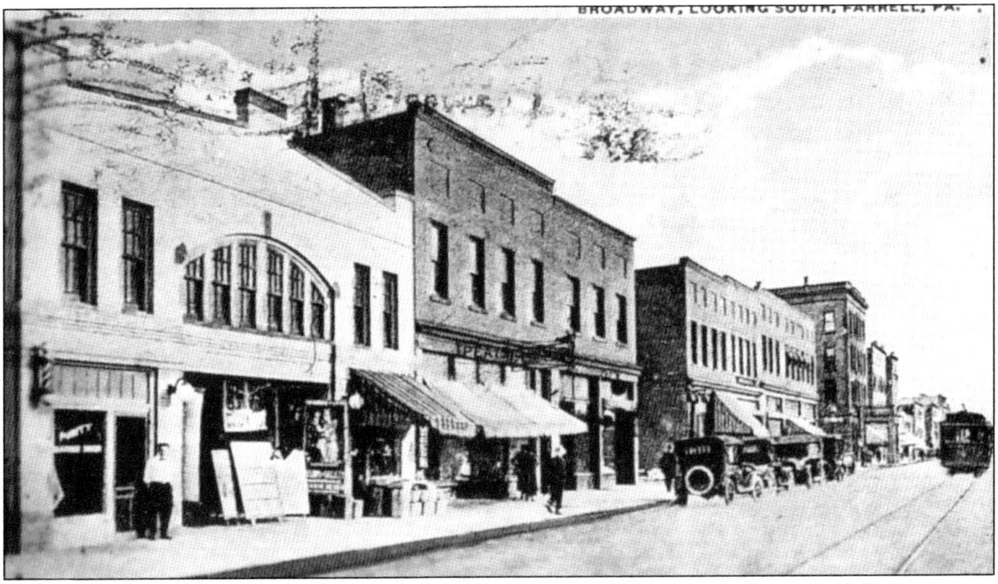

Elaine Lobl Konigsburg, a Newbery Award winner, recalled living on the second floor above a tavern her father, a Farrell businessman, operated on Broadway Avenue before her Jewish family moved to a house on Spearman Avenue. The S.J. Gully Bank, a landmark, operated on Broadway Avenue from April 1929 until 1961, when the bank was sold to First National Bank of Mercer County. Farrell banker Sol J. Gully (1878–1967), born in Catanzaro, Marina, Italy, came to the Unites States in 1900. Broadway Avenue (pictured above) with its streetcar line was a vibrant multiethnic business corridor. Below, First National Bank employees in front of the branch in Farrell are, from left to right, (first row) Debbie Turjan, Denise Jarrett, Amy Kovalchik, and Carrie Fisher; (second row) Carolyn Simoni, Amy Summers, and Christine Cieslak. (Above, courtesy of Marcy Pedas Sigler; below, photograph by Maria Stewart; courtesy of First National Bank.)

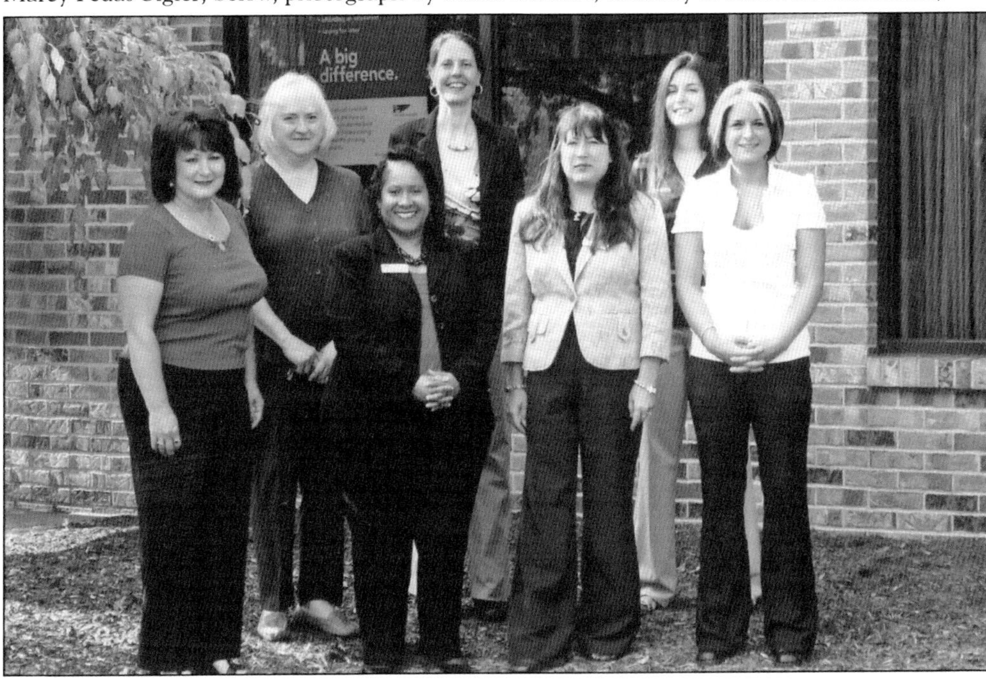

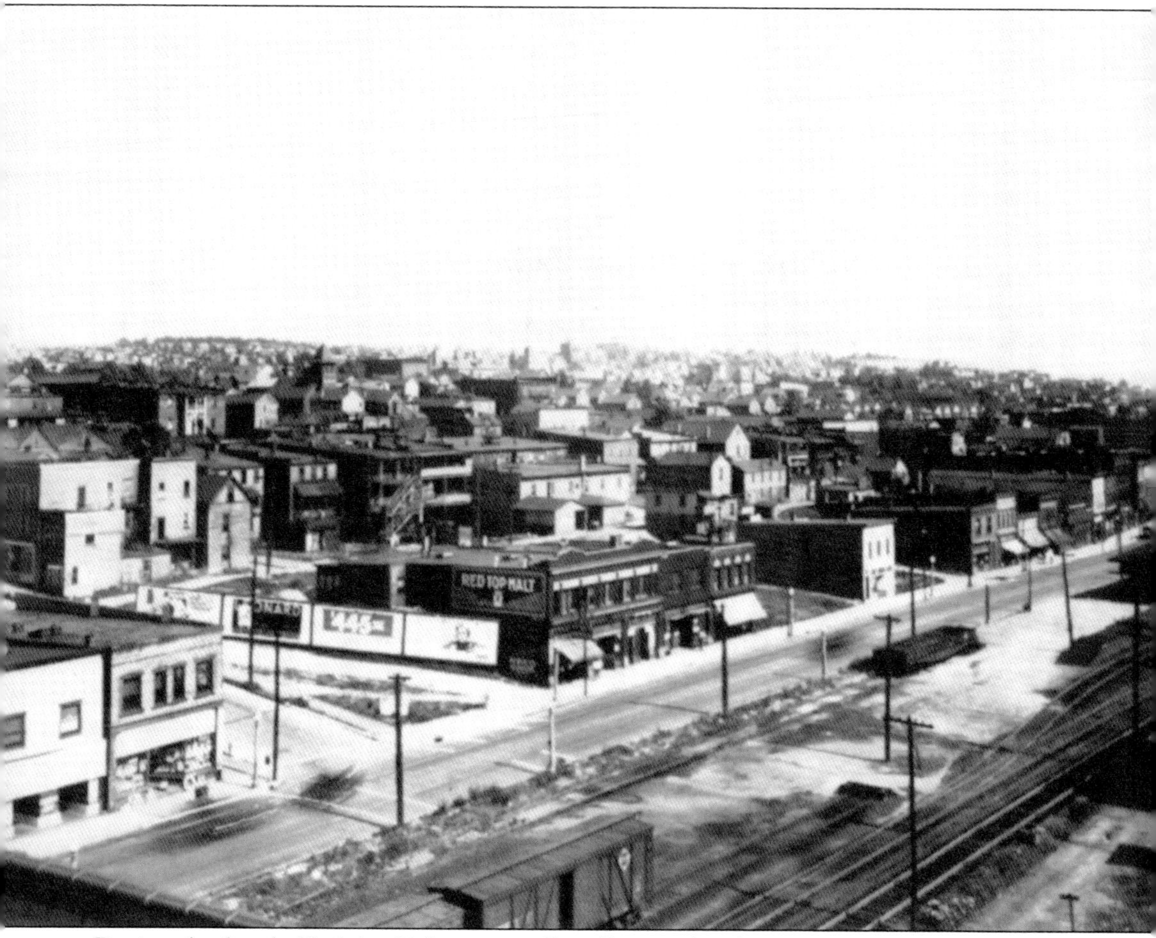

During the first half of the 20th century, Farrell was a bustling multiethnic business sector, which attracted shoppers from outlying communities. In 1914, two local newspapers—*Farrell Daily News* and *Farrell Sentinel*—competed for advertising and news. Two Chinese American laundries, one located at 322 Idaho Street and the other at 308 Negley Street, were operated by Sing Wah and Sam Yee respectively. The rise of independent grocery stores best reflected a high level of participation by eastern and southern European immigrants in America's system of free enterprise. In 1914, the Farrell City Directory listed more than 65 independent grocery stores, 18 meat markets, 6 dry goods stores, 10 clothing stores, 9 poolrooms, 6 hotels, and 3 banks. The town's recreation needs were met with three bowling alleys, two theaters, and a music store. The American dream of starting a successful small business became attainable for many from first and second generation immigrants. (Courtesy of SNPL.)

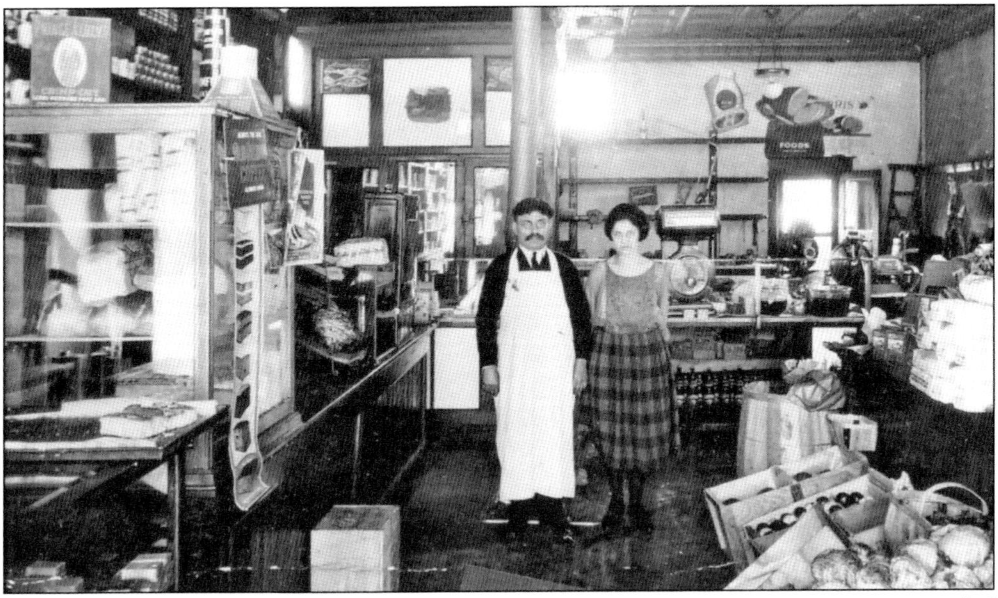

Booming steel industries meant prosperity for the community. Anglo-Saxon managers resided farthest up the hill, and the Italians who occupied neighborhoods on the lower hill gradually moved up the hill, replaced by Croatians and African Americans. The American Steel and Wire plant expanded to the former site of Little Italy. Here, M.A. Grande and his daughter pose inside his meat market on Fruit Avenue in 1911. (Courtesy of Ann Yazvac.)

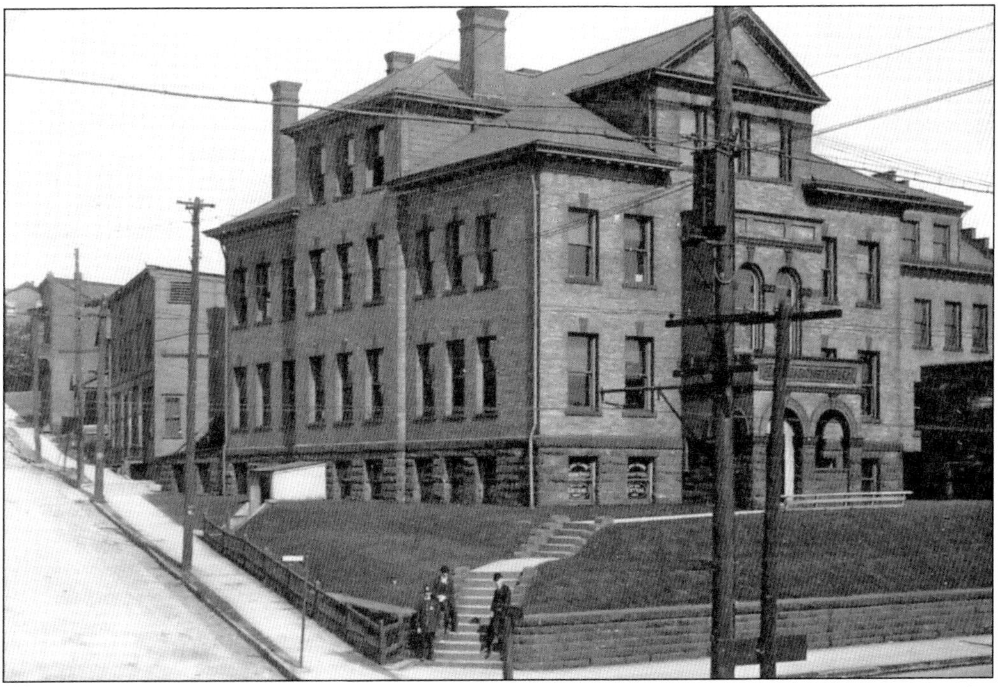

Steve Pedas had a brief stint in the steel mills. When unable to afford the cost of gloves, he returned home from his first day of work with his hands bloody and dirty. Pictured in 1910, the former Carnegie Steel main office, located at the corner of Broadway Avenue and Negley Street, is the current site of the Farrell American Legion, Post No. 160. (Courtesy of Ann Yazvac.)

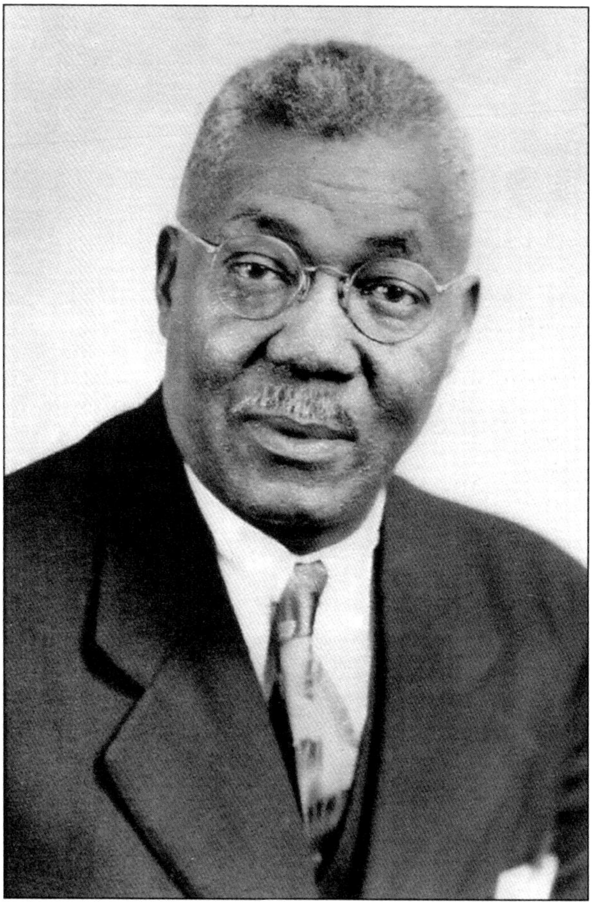

Strong families maintained business pursuits in the community. Gerald L. Mitchell, owner of Mitch's Laundromat Minimart located at 201 Idaho Street, recalled the Christman family as "multifaceted" in their pursuits. In 1914, James Abraham Christman, Sr. (1879–1966), left, established the Christman Transfer Company, located in the 900 block of Darr Avenue. He owned and operated the major concern for 33 years and served as a member of the board of directors of the Interstate Commerce Commission. In 1958, his son James Abraham Christman Jr. (1908–1984) received a patent for a brake safety device. He also developed a cold welding process for cracked engines, which attracted interest by major car manufacturers. Brothers Harry Benjamin Christman (1922–1972) and James Abraham Christman Jr. owned and operated Christman's Garage at 928 Market Avenue in the African American business corridor. (Both, courtesy of Darlynna Thompson.)

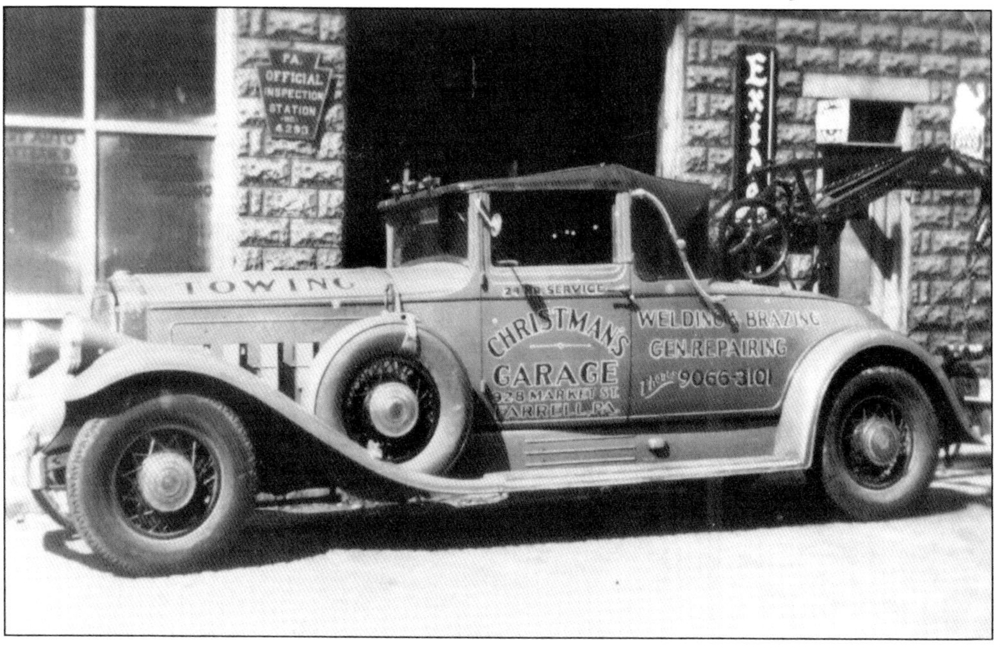

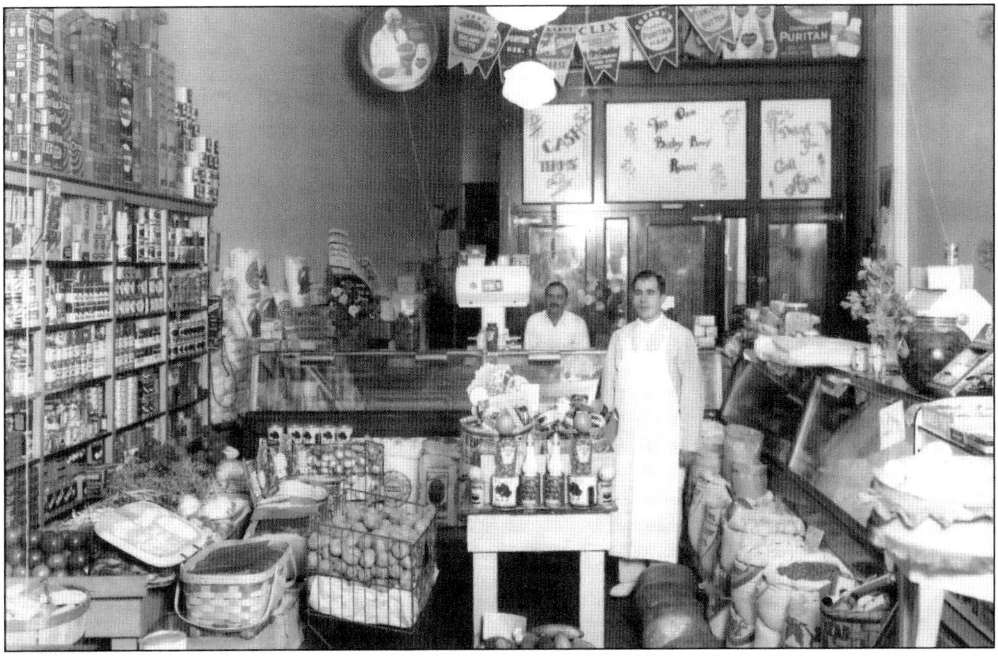

Steve Pedas (Efstathios Tsimpidis) secured a loan from the Gully Bank and opened the Broadway Cash Market, located at Broadway Avenue and Federal Street. Steve Pedas stands in front of the counter in a store loaded with stock. Behind the counter is a Greek immigrant working his way to Chicago; Pedas hired him as a temporary butcher. In 1930, Steve Pedas became a US citizen. He operated the store until 1972, when it closed. (Courtesy of Marcy Pedas Sigler.)

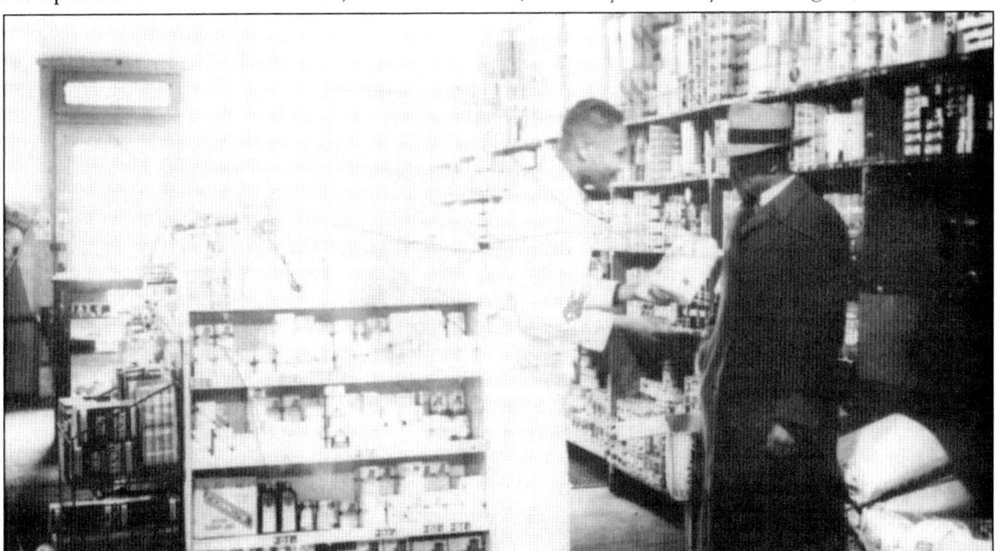

Rev. Samuel Delane, a native of Darlington, South Carolina, owned a grocery store in the 900 block of Greenfield Avenue, later known as Market Avenue, where a thriving African American business district emerged. Reverend Delane peddled fried pies made by Esther Robinson Delane from a Red Flyer wagon, which provided seed money to buy and sell canned goods from Mabel Bruce's yard before purchasing the grocery store for several hundred dollars. Leroy Green, seen here at left, was one of three butchers in Delane's Store. (Courtesy of Althea Jennings.)

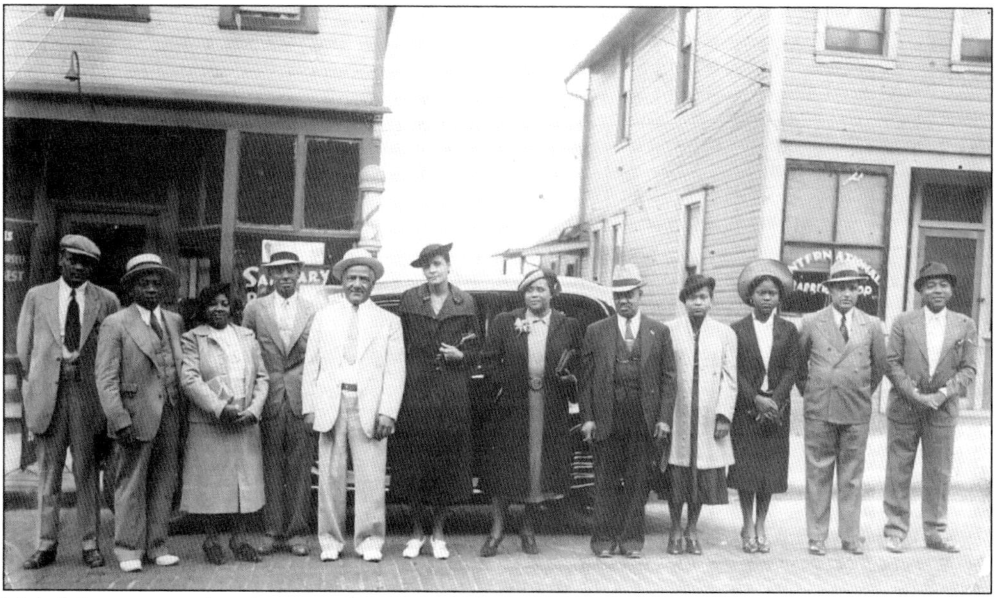

Mabel Bruce owned and operated a women's lingerie shop on Idaho Street in Farrell at a time when most African American women were relegated to staying home. Pictured from left to right are Robert Bruce, Rev. Oscar Singletary, unidentified, James Elmer Matthews, two unidentified people, Mabel Bruce, Lincoln Watson, Violet Bruce Crowder, Margaret Bruce Campbell, Thomas Dillard, and ? Counts on the Market Avenue African American business corridor in the 1940s. (Courtesy of Ethel McClain.)

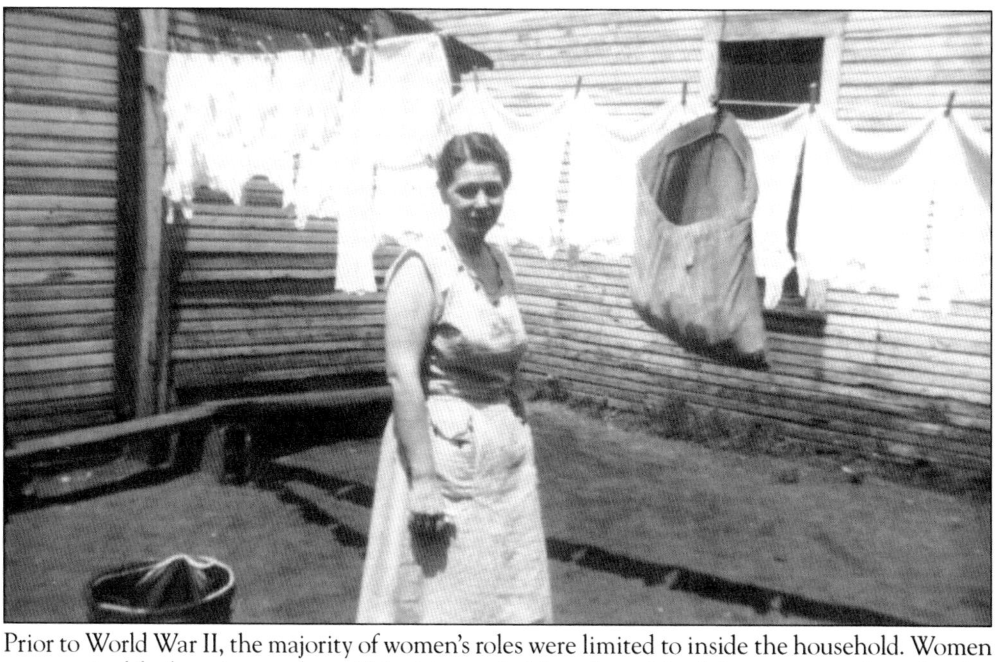

Prior to World War II, the majority of women's roles were limited to inside the household. Women were praised for hanging out beautiful white wash. Here, Joyce Harsh hangs out wash in the dirt courtyard of the multiunit framed tenement owned by Sol Rosenbloom. In the neighboring yard, where the Rosenbloom family lived, he would hang chickens outside so the blood could drain, in keeping with kosher tradition. (Courtesy of Shirley Matthews.)

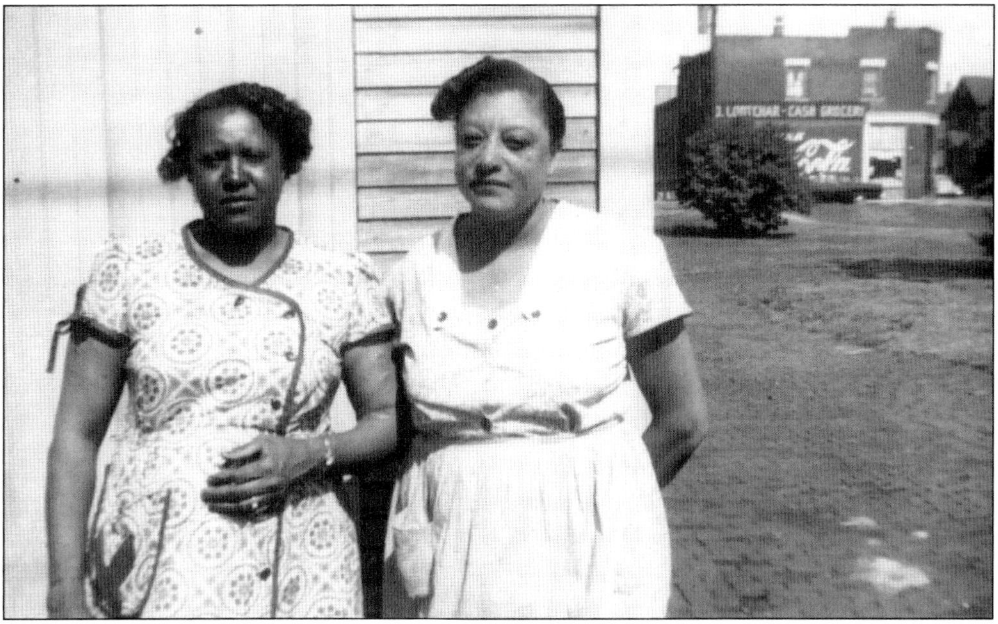

The business district around Idaho Street bustled with activity, from the Romanian Home's accordion music to aromas of roasted lamb from the pit at the Serbian Home. From the 900 block of Darr Avenue, the big brick of B'Nai Zion Synagogue was visible at the corner of Union Street and Spearman Avenue. Johnnie May Matthews (right), who lived in a tenement, maintained an account at the Serbian-owned Lontchar Cash Market in the background. (Courtesy of Shirley Matthews.)

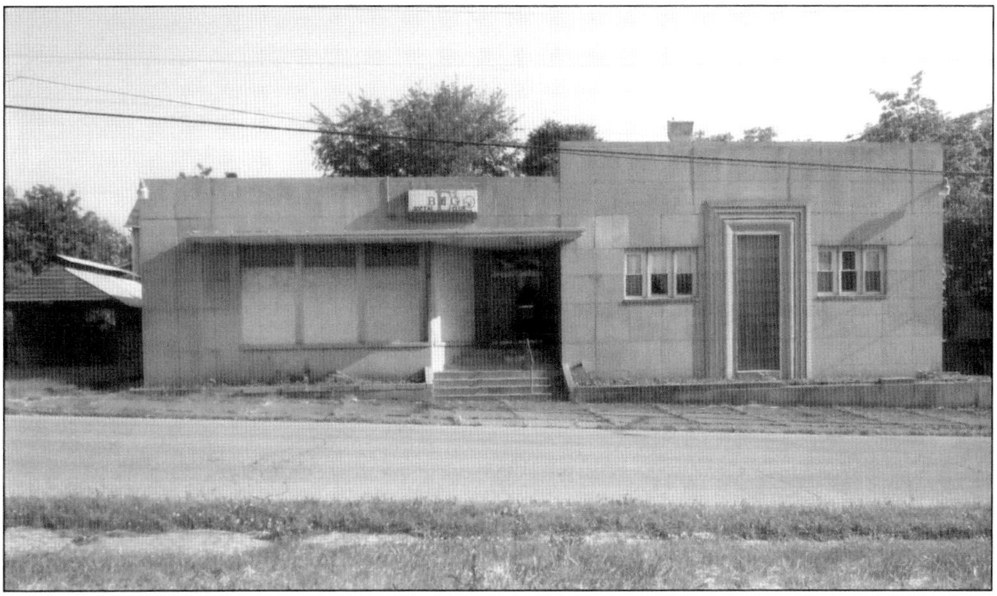

In 1939, the American Serbian Progressive and Citizens Club built the Serbian Home at 313 Union Street. Seen is the building with roasting pit to left, once rumored to have a bomb shelter. In 1924, Farrell Serbs secured permanency in building St. George Serbian Orthodox Church. In 1939, the club officers were Spiro Androich, president; Paul Kobac, vice president; Dushn Lontchar, treasurer; and Steve Sremcich, Joe Beader, and William Yankovich, trustees. In 2009, Big E Place was located at the former site of the Serbian Home. (Author's collection.)

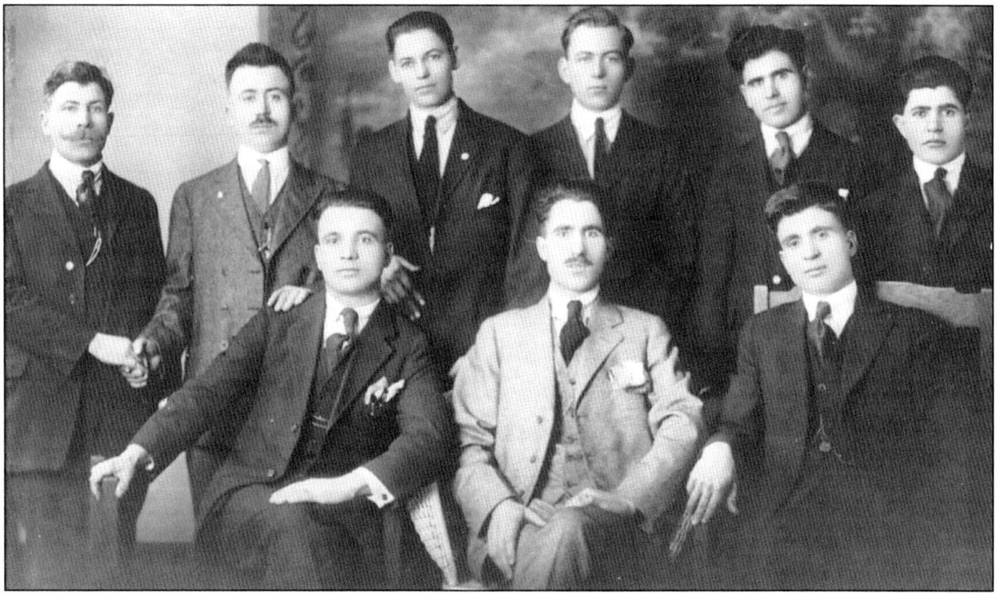

Immigrants from Doriza, Arcadia, on the Peloponesus in Greece visited one another's homes, loaned money to one another, and maintained loyal friends. Former Greek shepherds established businesses in Farrell and neighboring New Castle and Youngstown, Ohio. Shown here are, from left to right, (first row) ? Sarangelis, Costas Talaganis, and Vassilios Tsimpidis; (second row) unidentified, Georgios Tsimpidis (George Pedas), Nikos and George Gianopoulos, Demetrious Talaganis, and Efstathios Tsimpidis (Steve Pedas) in 1920. (Courtesy of Marcy Pedas Sigler.)

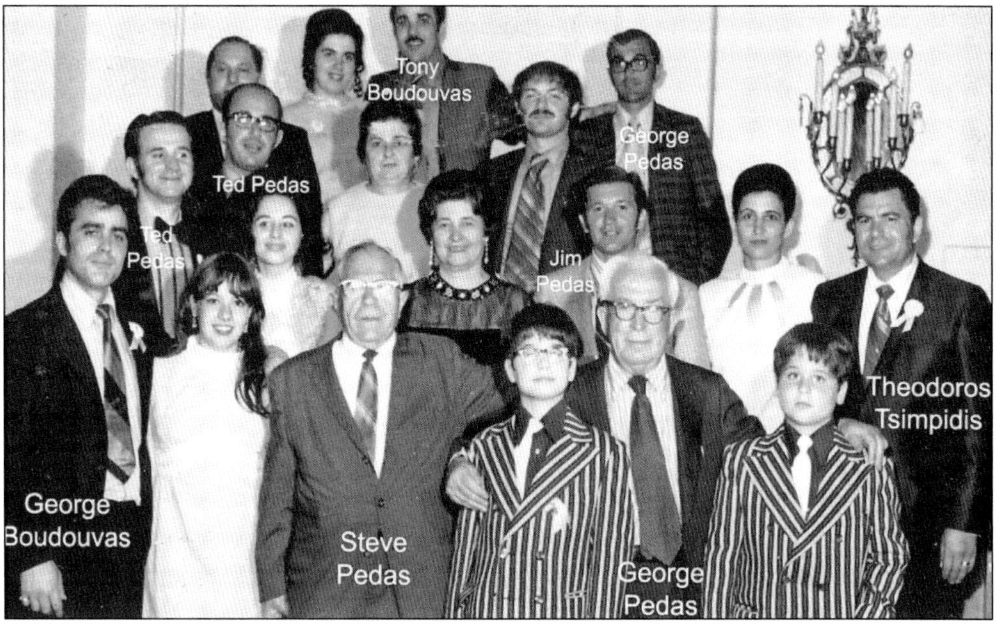

In the 1970s, some members of the extended Pedas family gathered for a photograph at a Greek wedding in Astoria while other family members were on the dance floor doing the Zorba dance. Steve Pedas owned the Broadway Cash Market, and at the same time George Pedas co-owned the Colonial Market on Broadway Avenue. The ranks of the second Pedas generation were filled with proud Farrell High School graduates. (Courtesy of Marcy Pedas Sigler.)

Former Greek shepherds achieved the American dream of establishing their own business. The Tsimpidis brothers, Vassilios and Georgios, along with Demetrious Talaganis, launched the Colonial Market at 611 Broadway Avenue, and Efstathios Tsimpidis (Steve Pedas) opened the Broadway Cash Market. In 1912, a 20-year-old Vassilios (seen here, holding his daughter) and 21-year-old Georgios migrated from Doriza, Greece, to Farrell. The young boy in the sailor suit is James Pedas. (Courtesy of Marcy Pedas Sigler.)

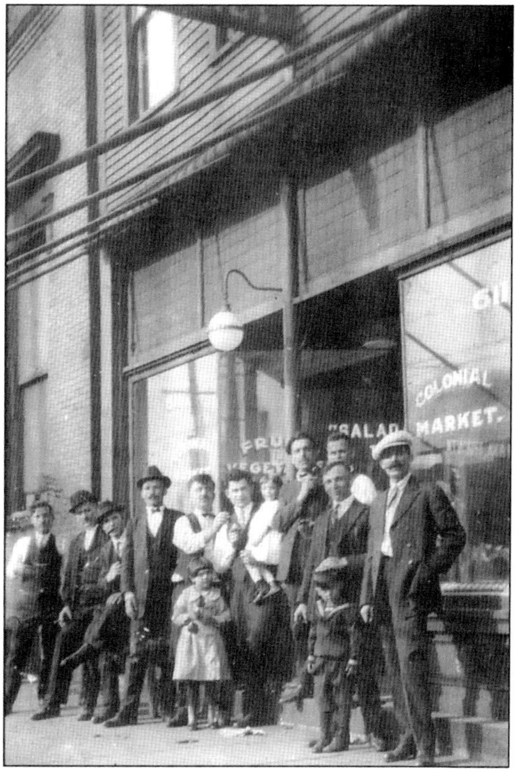

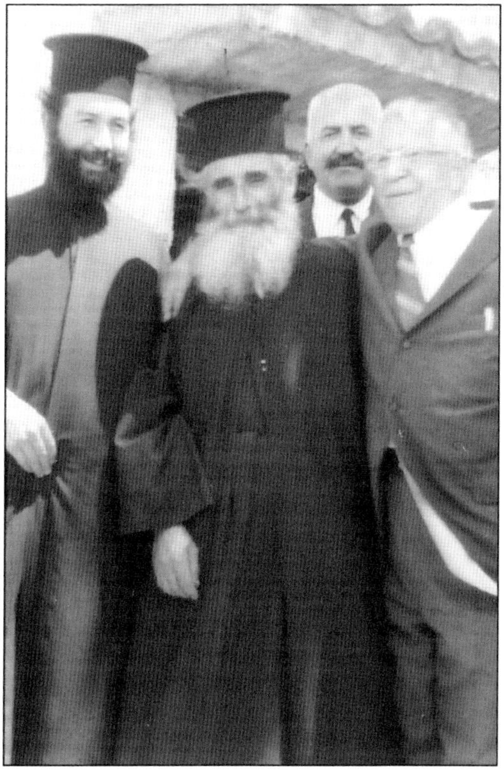

James Pedas and his brother Theodore were 2007 honorees on the Farrell High School Alumni Hall of Fame. Later in life, Steve Pedas (right) returned to his ancestral Greek village and church, which he last saw at age 12. Here, he stands with priests and gives thanks in front of a house—just one part of the dowry that he worked for and provided for his sister Stavroula Boudouvas. (Courtesy of Marcy Pedas Sigler.)

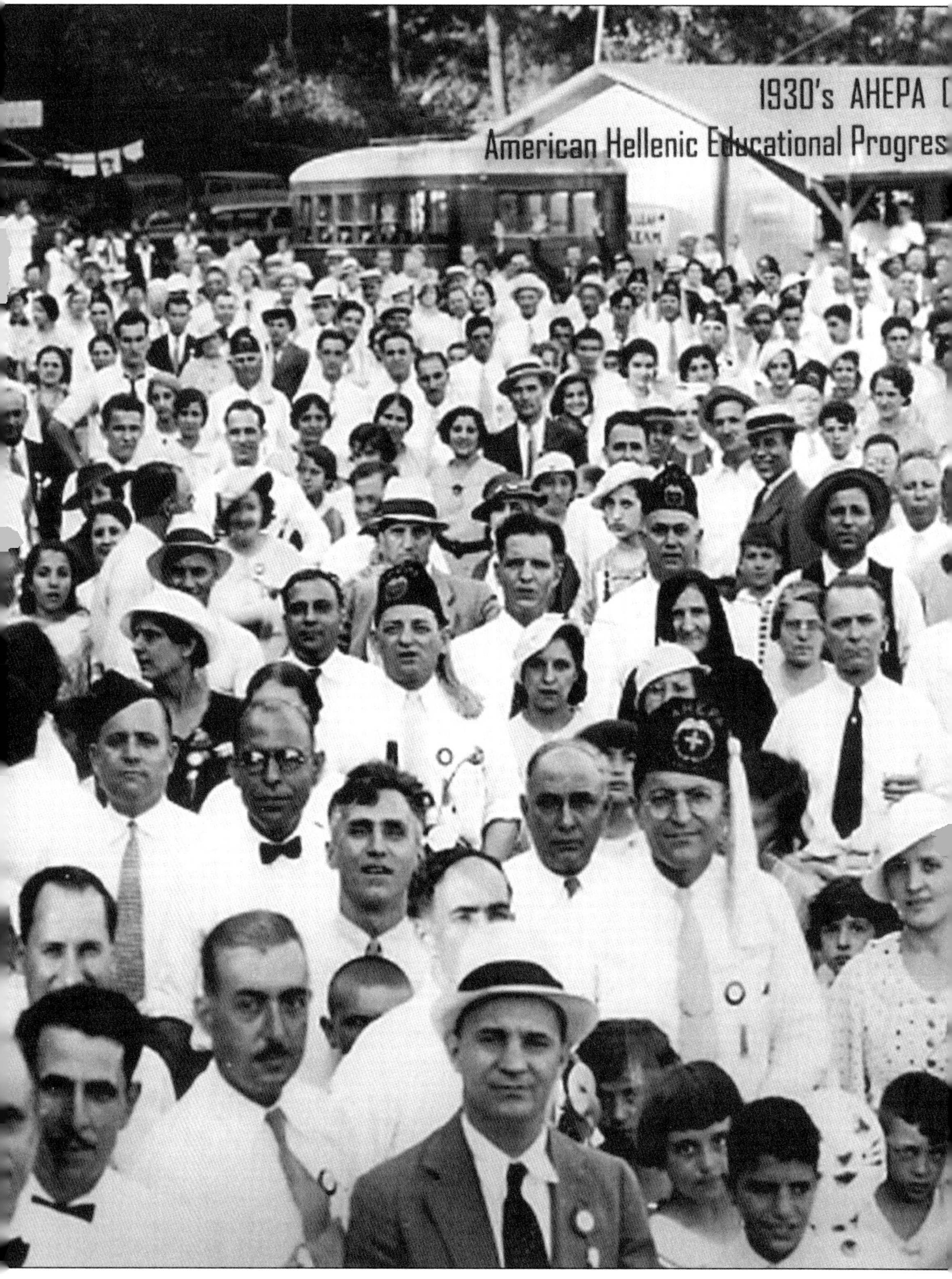
1930's AHEPA C
American Hellenic Educational Progres

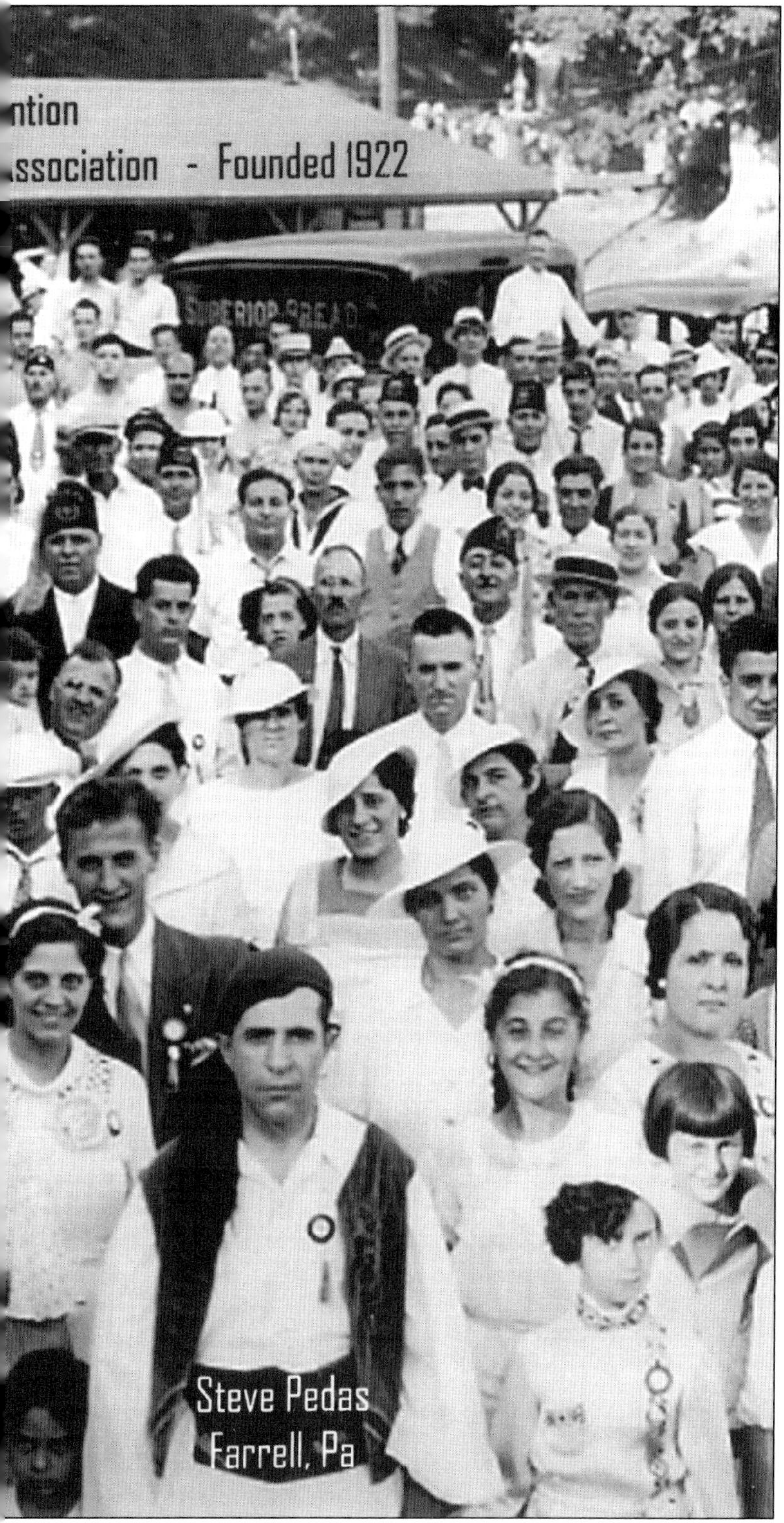

The community has been the proud beneficiary of values inculcated from the Hellenic world. In 2001, Ted Pedas, a lifelong Farrell resident, was the sole recipient of the Centurion Award during the city's 100th anniversary celebration. The honorees subcommittee selected Pedas because his "accomplishments and generosity have impacted our community to the highest degree." In 1969, he began his service as the planetarium director for Farrell High School. For 25 years, he was a planetarium and science education specialist at Youngstown State University. He has espoused Hellenic values of devotion, loyalty, and family, being passed down by his father, Steve Pedas, a Greek immigrant. The Pedas family was raised on Darr Avenue, where the city's oldest housing exists. Pictured at front right is Steve Pedas in traditional Greek costume at the American Hellenic Educational Progressive Association Convention in New Castle. (Courtesy of Marcy Pedas Sigler.)

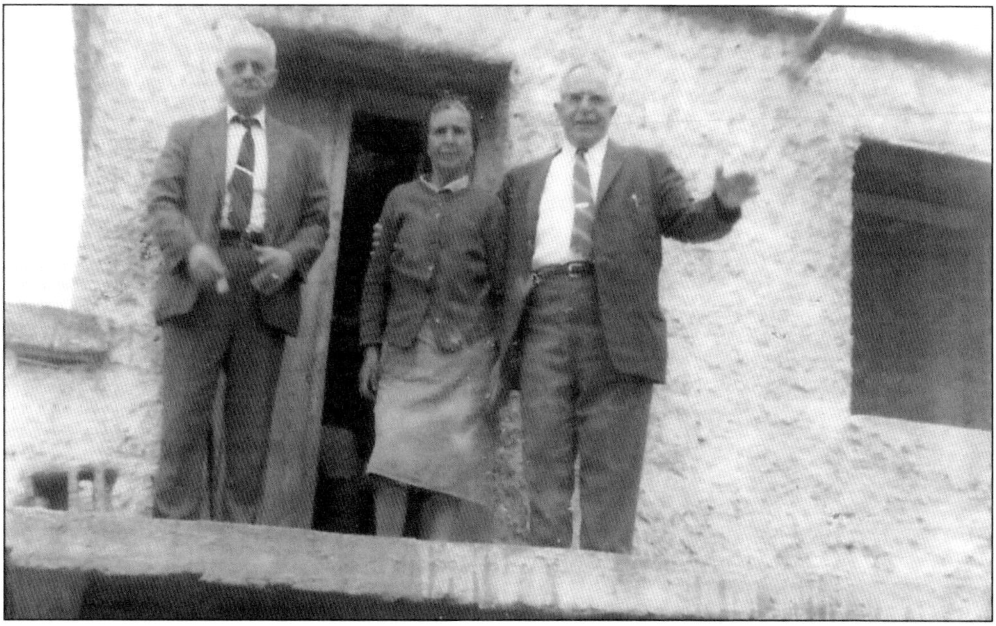

Steve Pedas worked hard and saved for years to provide a dowry for his sisters. The first time his money was lost when the banks collapsed during the Great Depression. He then returned, worked, and saved the money again. If he had not, his sisters back in Greece would be unable to marry. Here, Steve Pedas (right) stands with his sister Stavroula and his brother-in-law Panagiotis Boudouvas outside the house his dowry provided. (Courtesy of Marcy Pedas Sigler.)

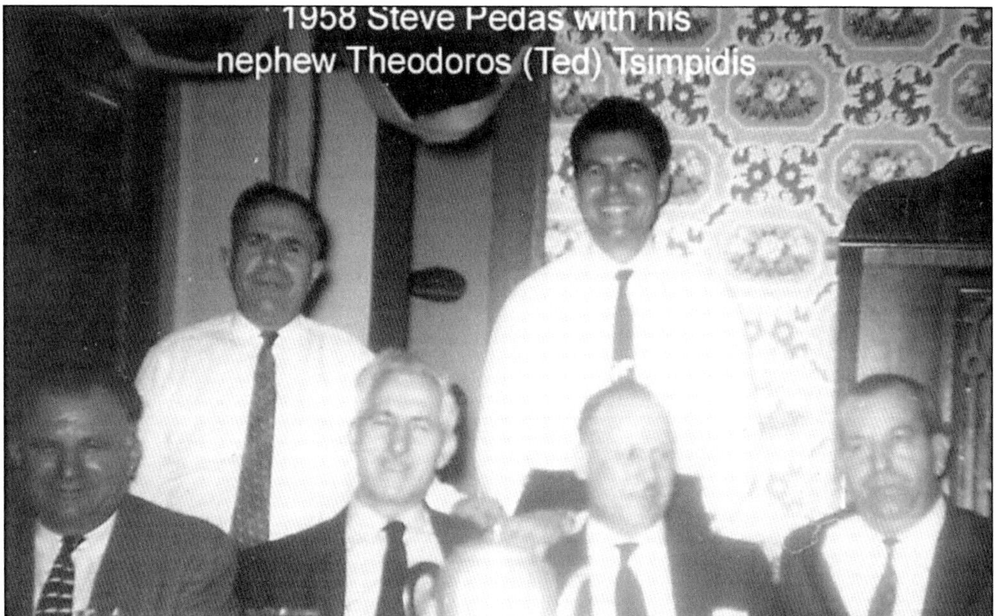

Brotherly love, loyalty, and faithfulness were core values in traditional Greek society. The first generation of eastern and southern European immigrants sought to pass on their business concerns, traditions, and values to the next generation, with mixed results. Steve Pedas gave many of his nephews their start in America. (Courtesy of Marcy Pedas Sigler.)

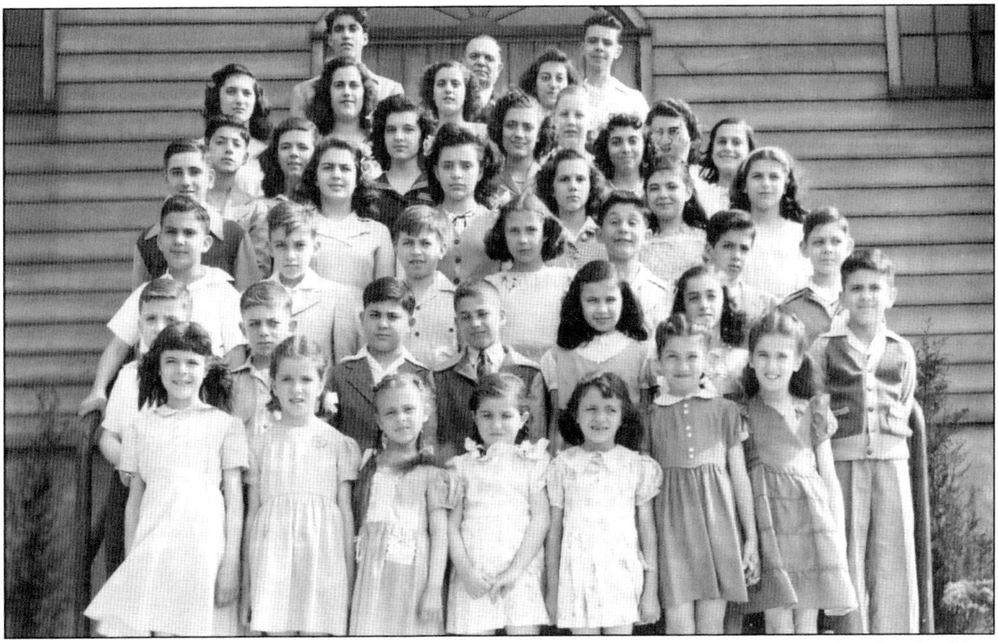

On the afternoon of April 27, 1948, Marcy Pedas returned home from Pargny School to find her mother crying. Angeline Havas Pedas had just learned that her devoted father, 58-year-old George Havas, had died at Sharon Steel of a massive heart attack. From left to right in the second row are Marcy's brother Ted Pedas, Sam Kartalis, and John Sava. The teacher at the Greek School, a Mr. Petridis, is in the center of the seventh row. (Courtesy of Marcy Pedas Sigler.)

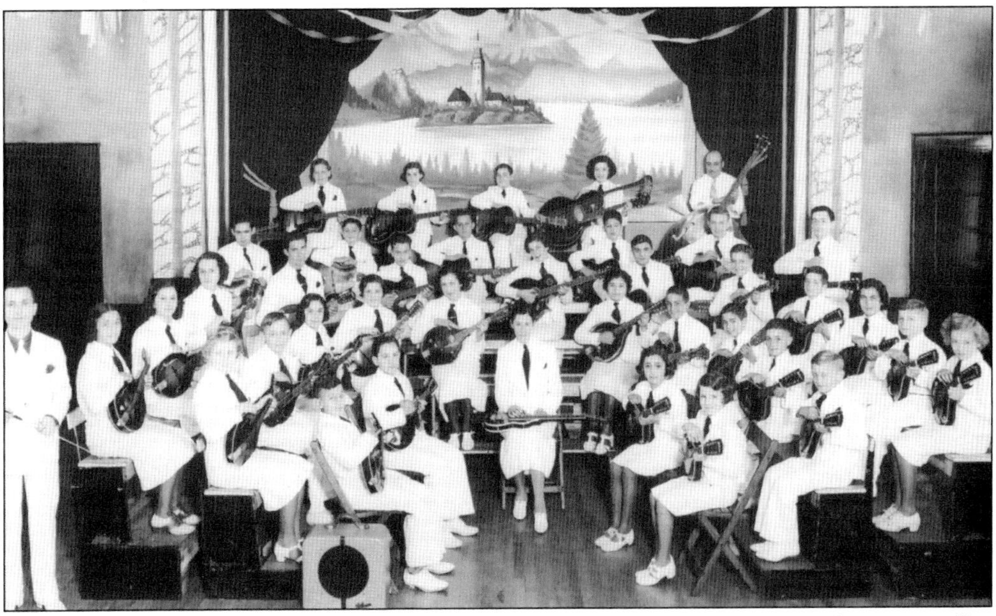

Nick Mavrapidos, a Pedas family friend who lived on Darr Avenue, played in the Shenango Valley Mandolin Orchestra. Greeks from the island of Rhodes congregated around Darr Avenue, where John Sava's family also owned their home. An important part of Greek culture, music, often accompanied by dance, permeated the homes of the first generation. Vincent Greco served as director of the Shenango Valley Mandolin Orchestra. (Courtesy of Marcy Pedas Sigler.)

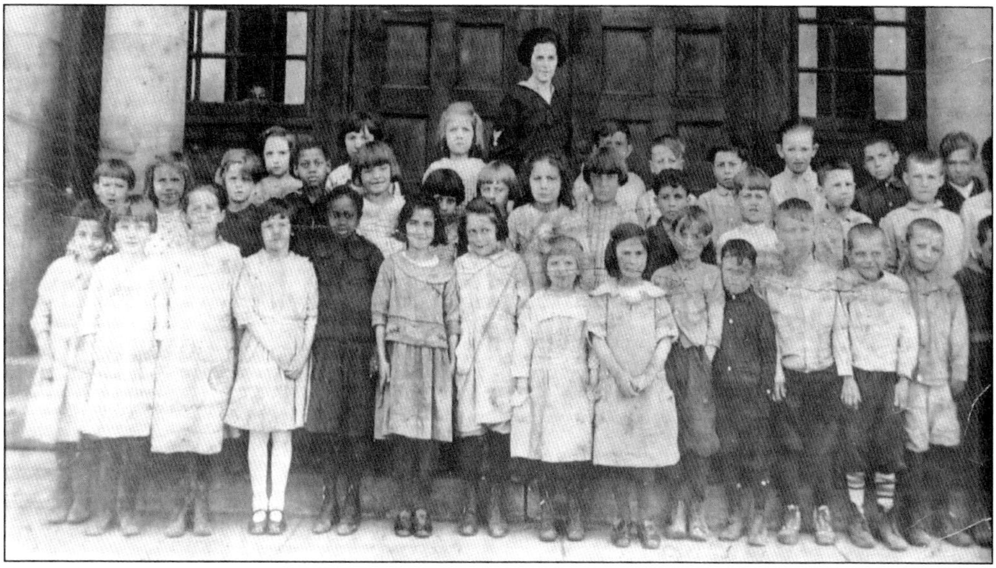

Anna Steverson (first row, fifth from left), a 1937 Farrell High School graduate, listed her aspiration as to attend Morris Brown College, a dream which she was unable to fulfill. As a single woman, Steverson saved, owned her own car, and purchased property, which was remarkable for a black woman at the time when many remained employed in private families in Farrell. Anna Steverson was one of two black students in her class at Pargny School in 1927. (Author's collection.)

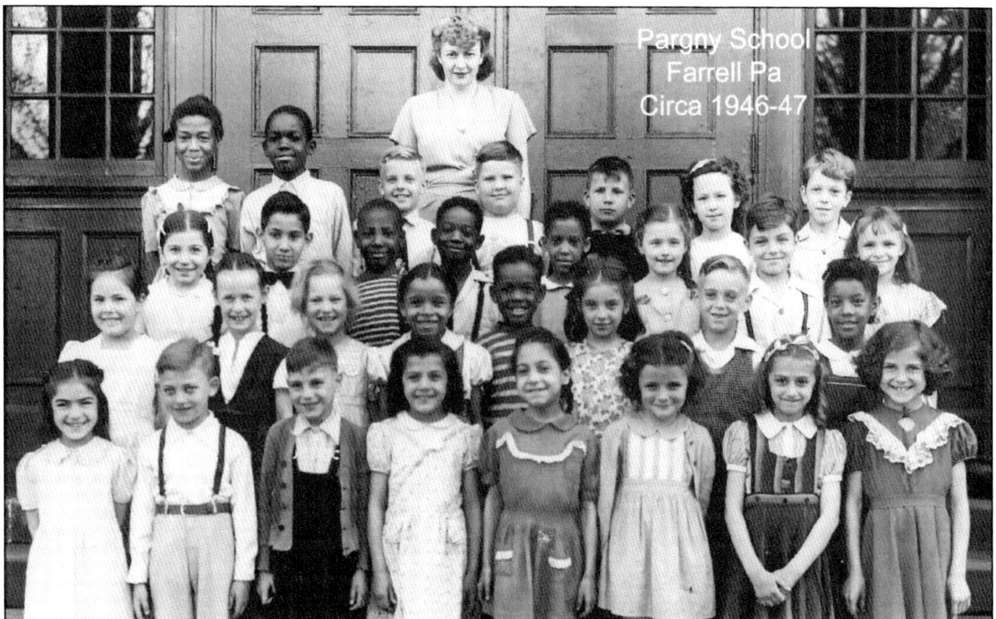

Marcy Pedas (third row, far left) was one of three Greek American girls in her class at Pargney in 1947; the other girls were Mary Kladitis (first row, far left) and Stella Caravolias (first row, fourth from left). By World War II, women's roles began to change. A 1956 graduate of Farrell High School, Marcy challenged women's roles in traditional Greek society. She moved to New York City and, with her brother Ted, developed tours around the world to sites of full solar eclipses. (Courtesy of Marcy Pedas Sigler.)

At the cramped but well used Farrell Public Library, located above the firehouse, Marcy Pedas found books that expanded her horizons. A love of reading was critical to her personal odyssey. She graduated from Youngstown State University and became a schoolteacher. Farrell schoolteacher and library board member Helen Stey (left) and librarian Barbara Lou Sullivan (right) provided assistance at the reference desk. (Courtesy of the SNPL.)

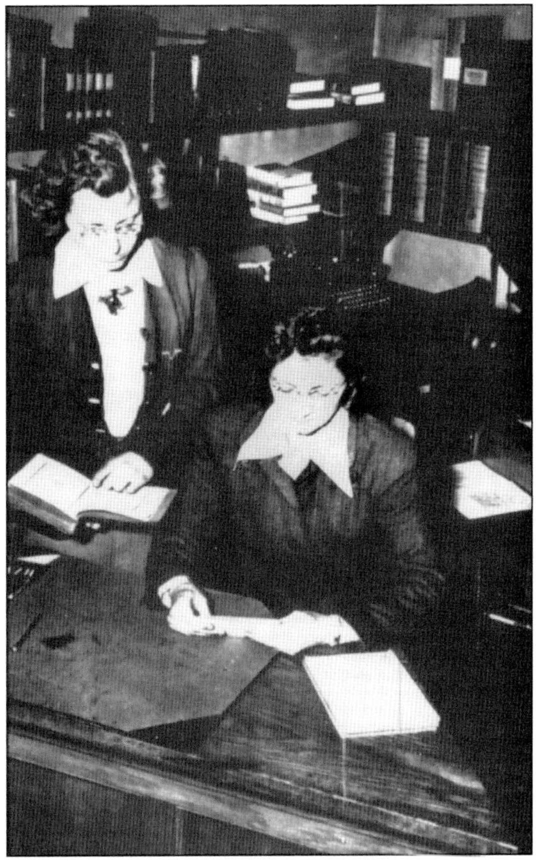

Greeks tended to congregate in Farrell with those from their own village. Farrell School District superintendent Dr. John Sava's "womb to the tomb" philosophy was studied in college textbooks. The Farrell Public Library, originally located on the second floor above the firehouse, outgrew the facility. Full-time crew for the fire department in the 1920s included Bill Miller, August Mason, Andrew Kaliney, Councilman John Krauss, Bates Grande, and George Duleba. (Courtesy of the SNPL.)

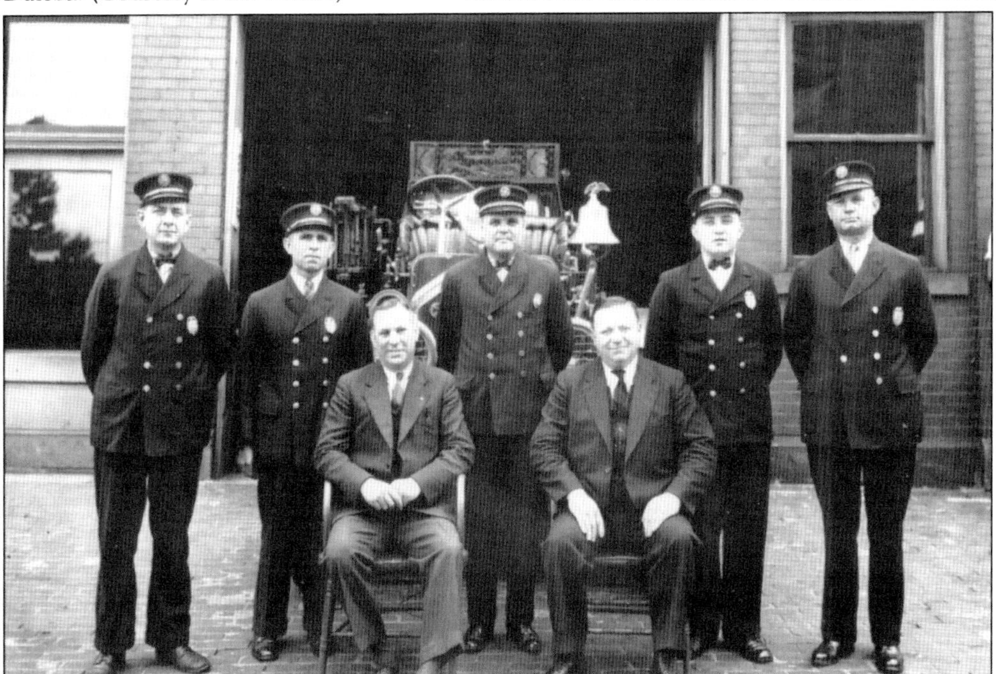

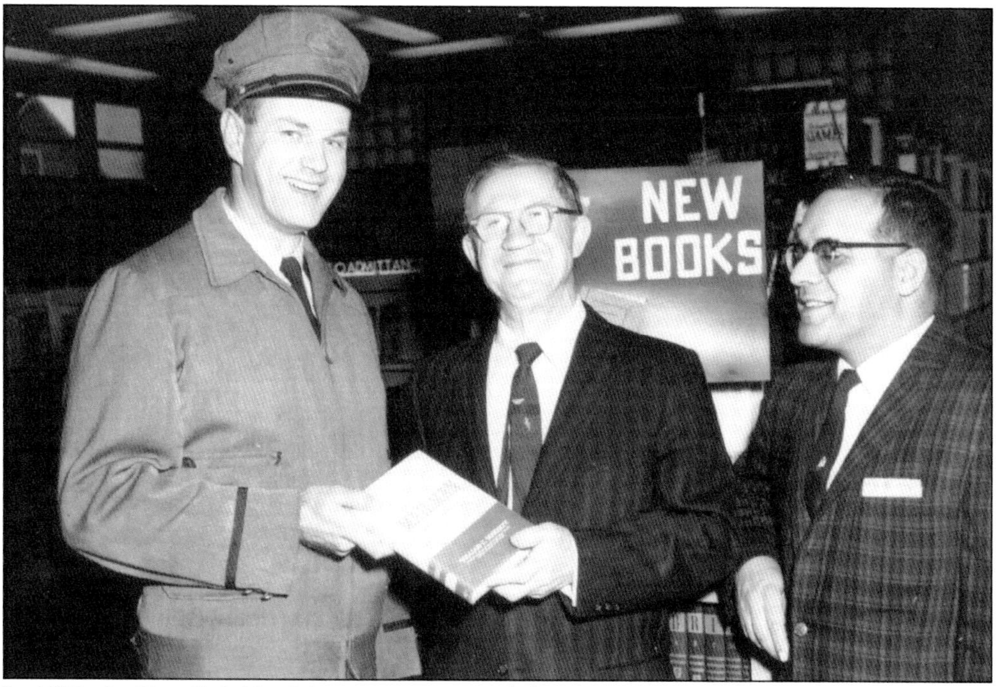

In 1977, the Farrell Public Library was renamed the Stey-Nevant Public Library. Adam Stey (center) is shown here. (Courtesy of SNPL.)

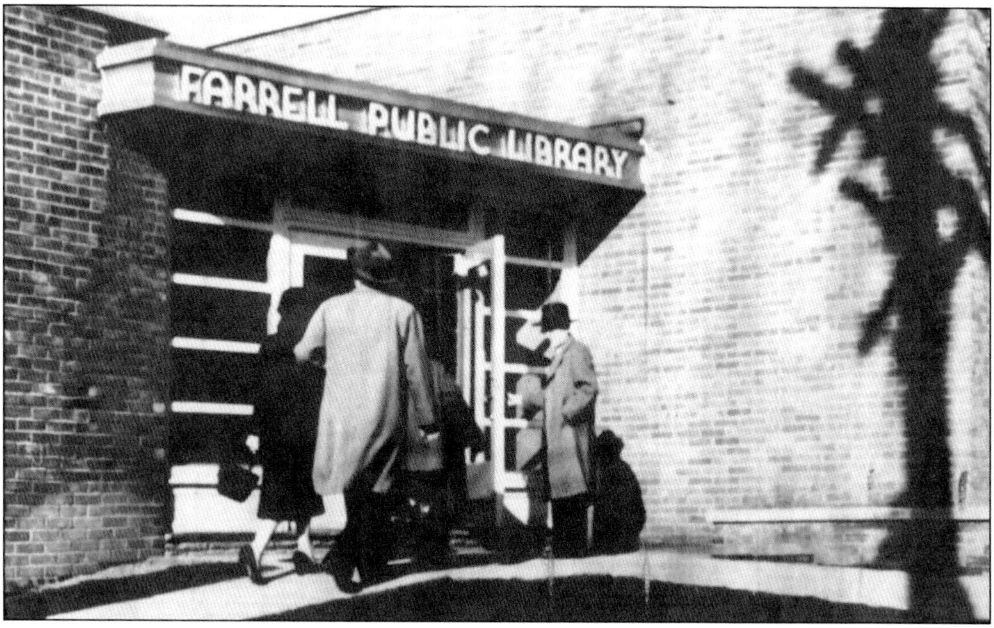

In the 1950s, the construction of the Farrell Public Library and Shenango Valley Osteopathic Hospital were significant advancements. Burt Moss, owner of Northside Furniture, and Lew Berger, publisher of the *Farrell Press*, both Jewish businessmen and civic leaders, enter the new Farrell Public Library for its grand opening. In 1960, the Shenango Valley Osteopathic Hospital opened near the Farrell City Park. In 1971, a new $1.2-million wing of the Shenango Valley Osteopathic Hospital is named in honor of Burton J. Moss. (Courtesy of SNPL.)

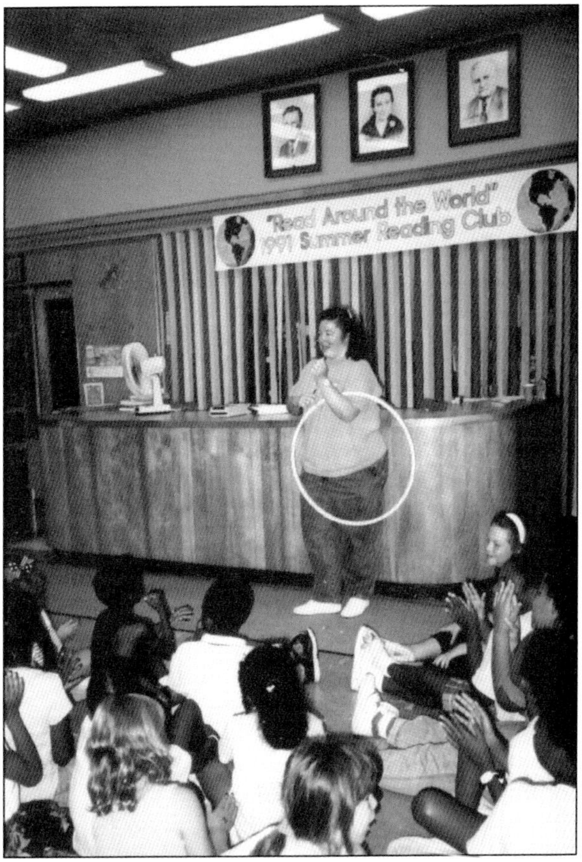

On March 12, 1952, a crowd of 1,500 people toured the new Farrell Public Library at 1000 Roemer Boulevard. In May 1977, the library's name changed to Stey-Nevant Public Library. In 1991, Margaret Orchard, the librarian, entertained youth during the summer reading club. In the background, portraits of the library's namesakes by Dan DeBonis and Ron Heath are, from left to right, Adam C. Stey, Helen Stey, and former mayor Michael Nevant. (Courtesy of SNPL.)

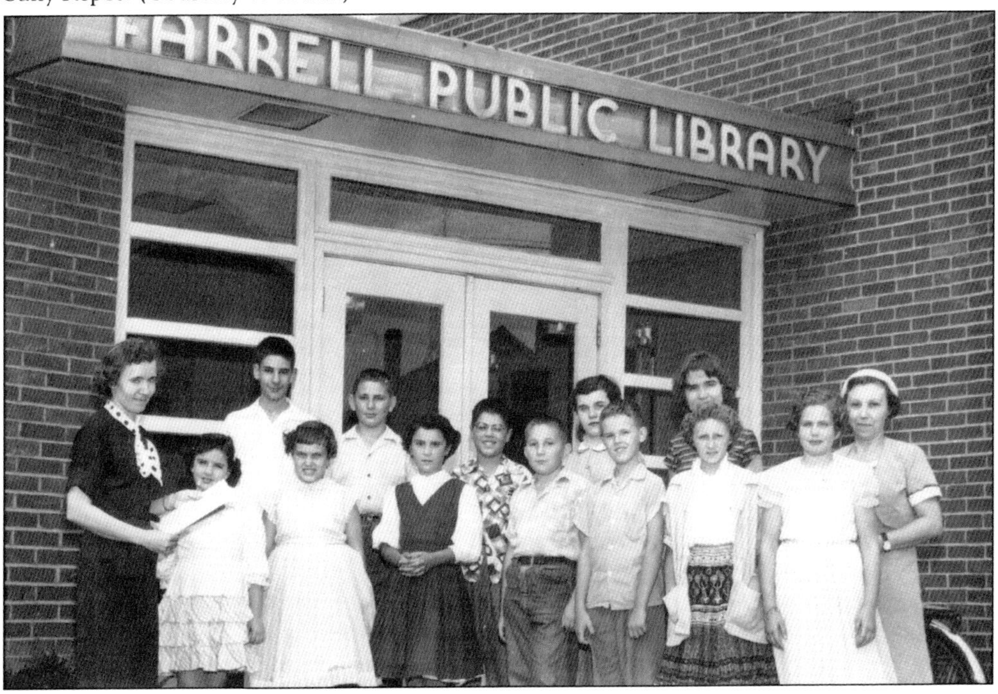

Summer reading club winners stand in front of the library in 1955 to receive awards. They are, from left to right, (first row) librarian Helen Roux, Bernadette Liscio, Rosaria Pugliese, Andrea Billak, Andrew Torok, Joseph Dyll Jr., Laura Pisko, Annette Pugliese, and library board member Helen Stey; (second row) Anthony Liscio, Steve Torok, Richard Grande, Donna Varro, and Sally Repos. (Courtesy of SNPL.)

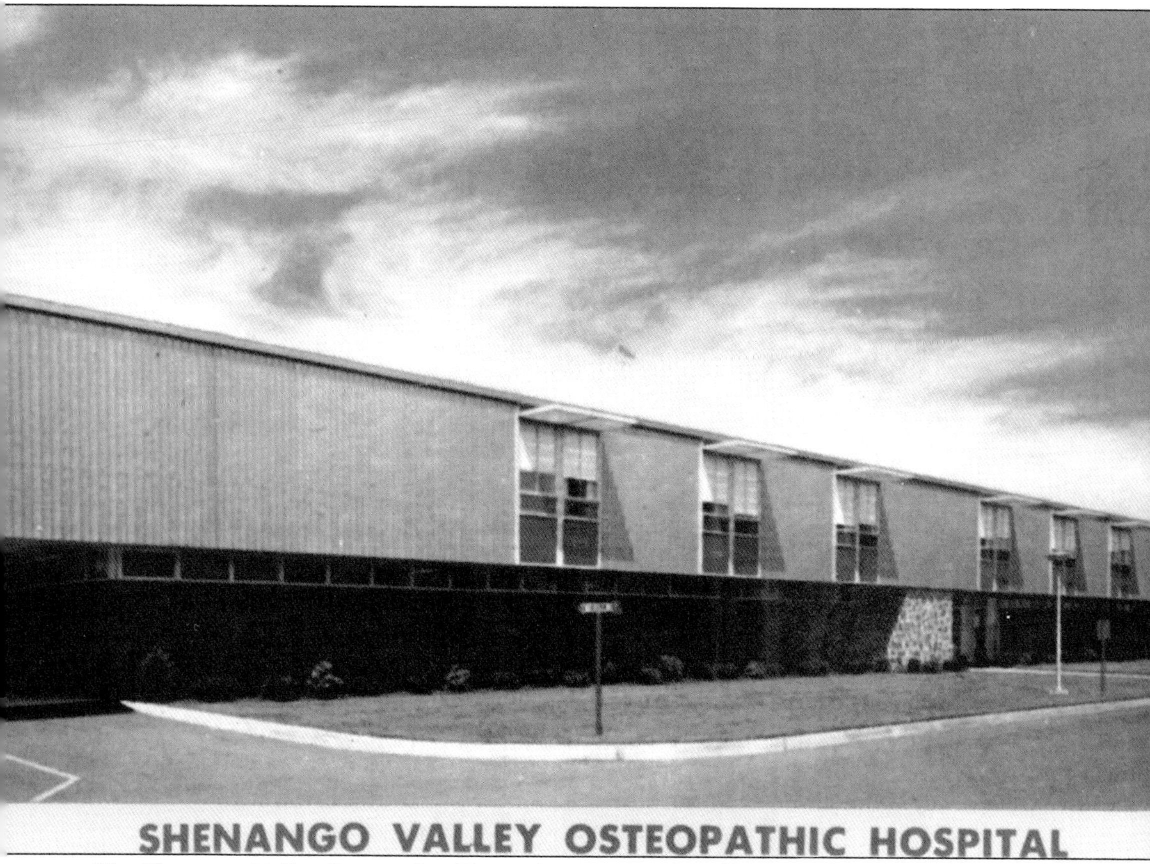

The Shenango Valley Osteopathic Hospital opens near Farrell City Park in 1960. In 1971, a new $1.2-million wing of the Shenango Valley Osteopathic Hospital is named in honor of Farrell businessman and Jewish philanthropist, Burton J. Moss. The completion of the Shenango Valley Osteopathic Hospital, today part of the University of Pittsburgh Horizon Hospitals System, is a major advancement in building and maintaining a healthy, livable community. (Courtesy of MCHS.)

Five

Farrell's Steelers
Got Team Spirit

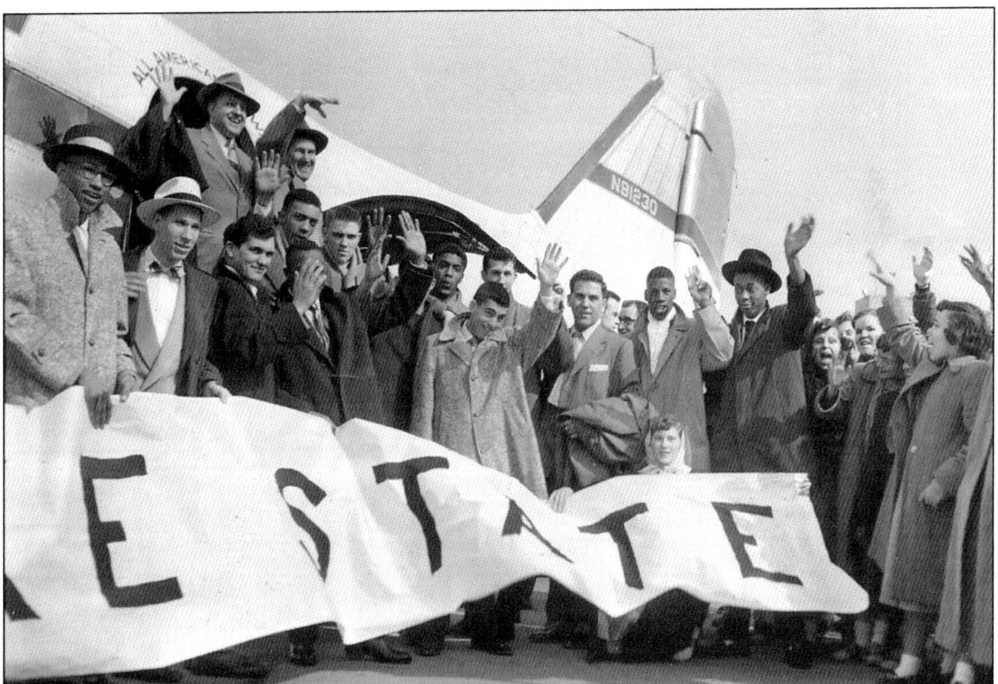

In 1952, the state champion basketball team poses with young fans upon their arrival back home. They are, from left to right, (first row) Julius McCoy, Russell DeCarmen, assistant coach Bob Trambacco, Paul Flint, Tony Decello, assistant coach Felix Bonadio, Ronald Crosby, and Wilbert Shannon; (second row) Sy Alli, Bob Hoffman, Bates Johnson, and assistant coach Bill Canterna; (third row) athletic director Ralph Dresch and coach Edward McCluskey. (Courtesy of William Jarrett.)

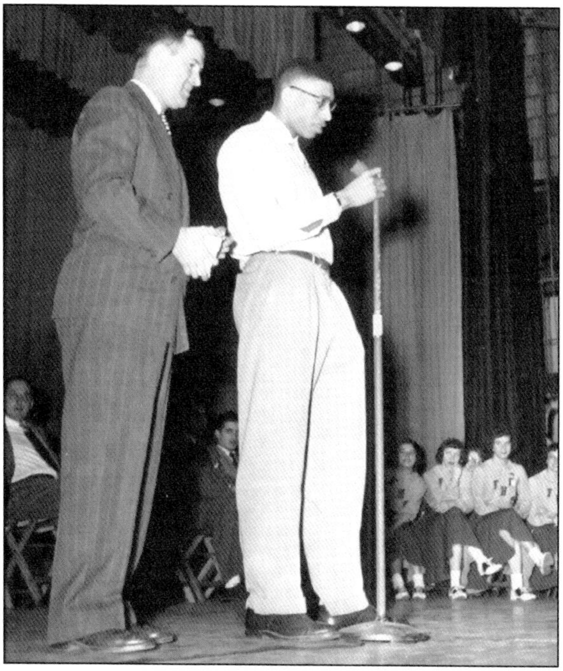

Julius "Hooks" McCoy (1932–2008) led the Farrell Steelers to the first of coach Edward "Eddie" McCluskey's seven Pennsylvania Interscholastic Athletic Association (PIAA) Championships. McCoy played professional ball with the Eastern Basketball Professional League and toured with the Harlem Globetrotters. His name was added to the Continental Basketball Association all-time team in 1996. Here, McCoy and Coach McCluskey speak at the state championship assembly. (Courtesy of William Jarrett.)

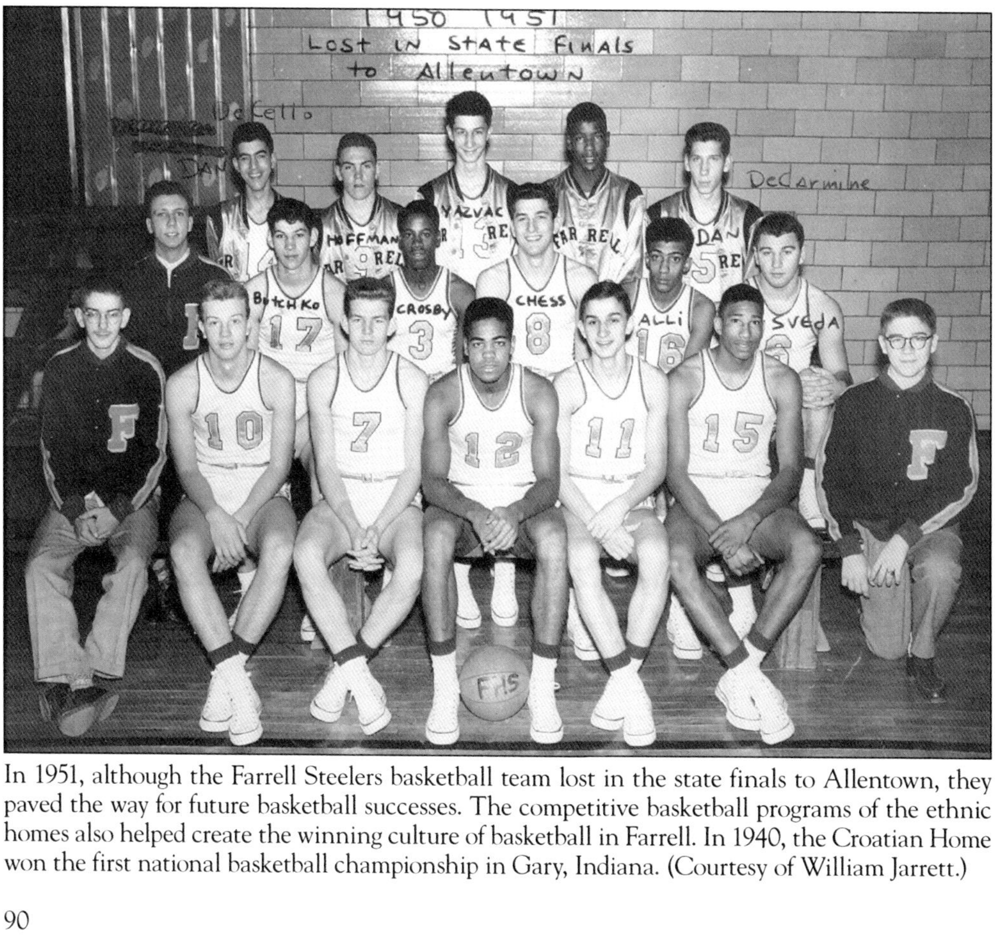

In 1951, although the Farrell Steelers basketball team lost in the state finals to Allentown, they paved the way for future basketball successes. The competitive basketball programs of the ethnic homes also helped create the winning culture of basketball in Farrell. In 1940, the Croatian Home won the first national basketball championship in Gary, Indiana. (Courtesy of William Jarrett.)

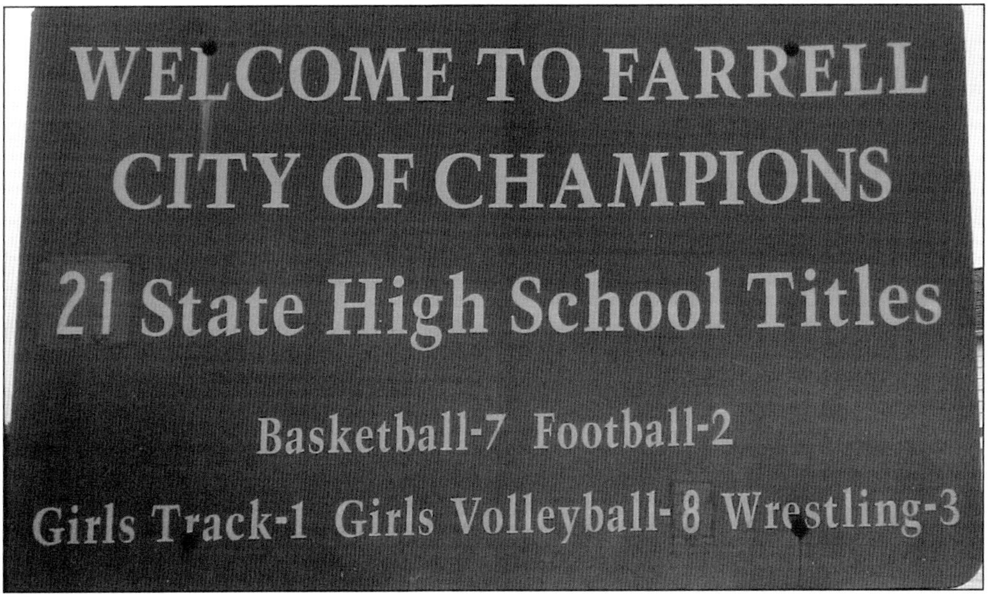

Farrell has established an enviable sports record and produced NFL standouts. Lorenzo Styles, a former linebacker for the Super Bowl champion St. Louis Rams, is one product of Farrell High School's sports program. Styles also played for the Atlanta Falcons. Signs on Martin Luther King Boulevard, the former Broadway Avenue, tout Farrell's winning record. The name change on the business corridor from Broadway Avenue to Martin Luther King Boulevard was due to Deacon Donald Wright of Bethlehem Baptist Church. (Author's collection.)

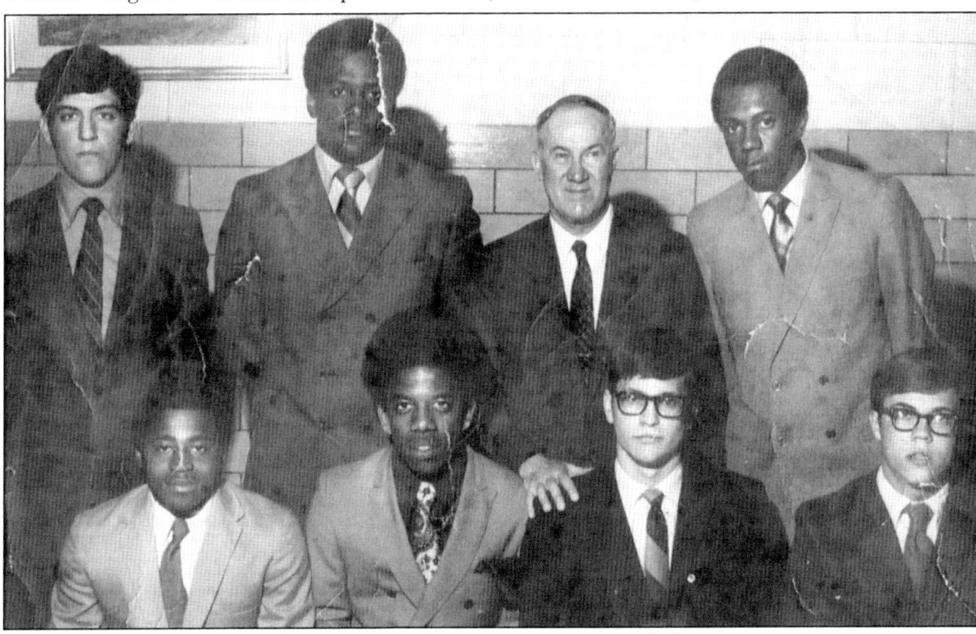

In New York City, Coach McCluskey and Julius McCoy attended the opening of the play *That Championship Season*, written by Jason Miller in 1972. The play was based on Farrell's 1952 championship and what transpired over the next two decades, culminating with the 1972 PIAA state championship. All-American tackle Randy Crowder (second row, second from left), who went on to play for the Miami Dolphins, is beside Coach McCluskey. (Courtesy of Martha Richards.)

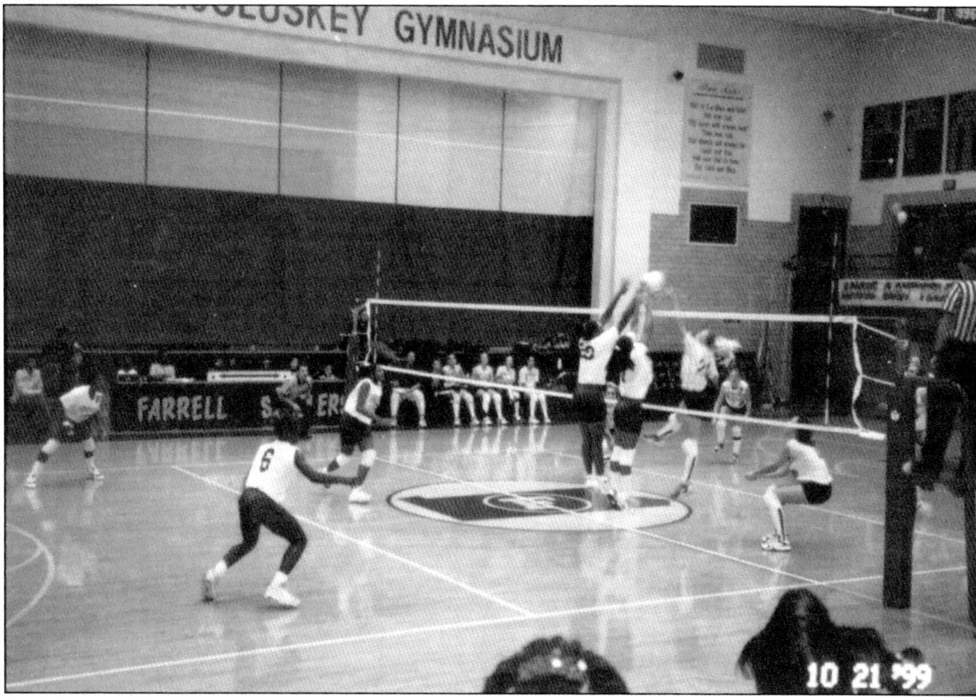

Coach Harriett Morrison won eight volleyball state championships. Below, the 1999 team included, from left to right, (first row) Aisha Weston, unidentified, Keturah Chambers, Angeline Santell, and Erin Houston; (second row) Lakia Gordon, Gena Elerby, unidentified, Flora Evette Harris, unidentified, Fontella Jones, Taneesha Williams, and unidentified; (third row) Alisha Jordan, unidentified, Jessica Brown, unidentified, S. Graham, unidentified, Magnolia Green, and unidentified. (Both, courtesy of Ronald Weston.)

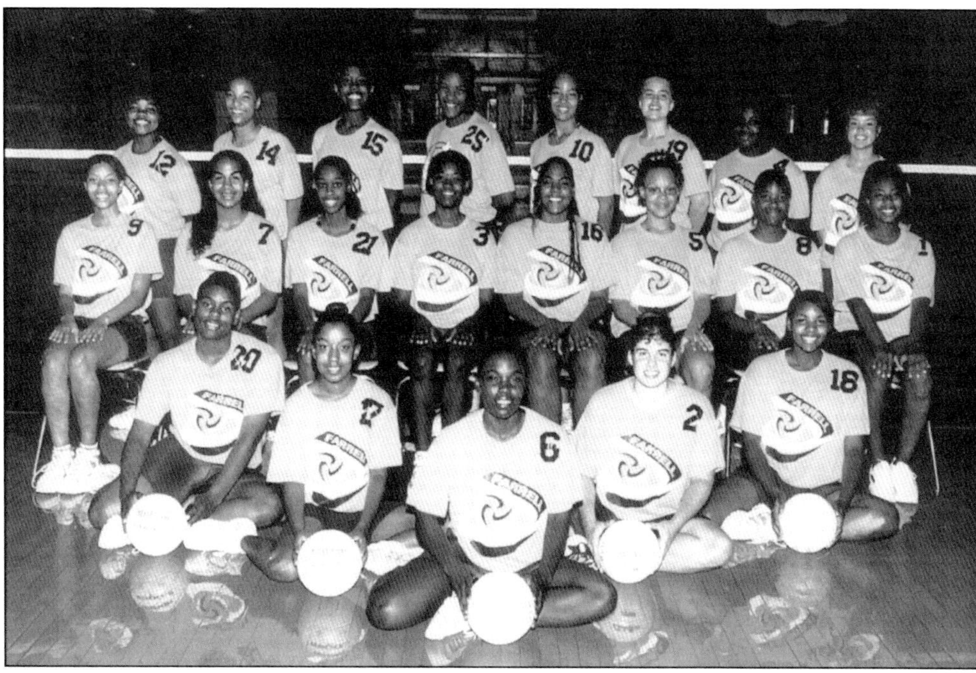

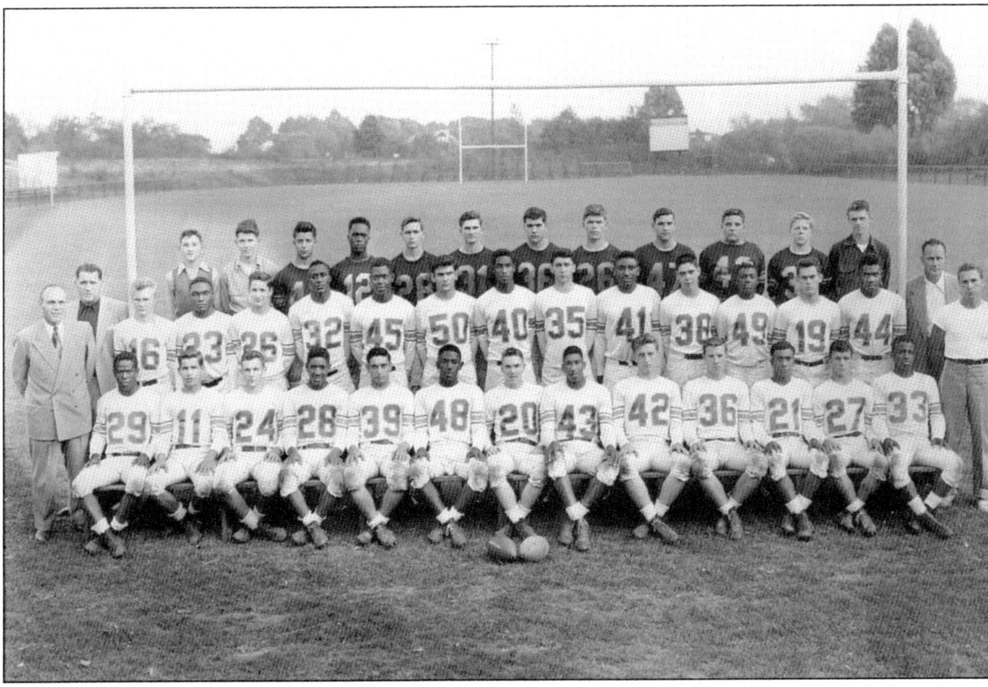

Farrell's football team was previously known as the Knight Riders. This team included, from left to right, (first row) Charles Sturdivant, Jack Scarvel, Alex Pustinger, Jim Johnson, Dick Santell, Bob Pegues, Bob Hoffman, Julius McCoy, Ted Smith, Joe Fronko, Si Alli, Max White, and Ellsworth Morgan; (second row) coach Anthony Paulekas, assistant coach John Papadak, Joe Staul, Norman Fuller, Tony Aiello, Paul Flint, Bill Kemp, Fred Sok, Bill Johnson, Jerry Rogan, William Wells, Fred Jones, Willie Allen, Joe Scarmack, Sidney McDonald, trainer Joe Tommins, and assistant coach John Gennock; (third row) manager Frank Egercic, Tom Cimoric, Christy Alter, Clarence Austin, Fred DeBonis, John Dufford, Richard Toskin, John Myers, Vic Zarella, Larry Chieffo, Stanley White, and manager John Fecik. The Farrell High School football stadium was later renamed Anthony J. Paulekas Stadium in the coach's honor. (Both, courtesy of William Jarrett.)

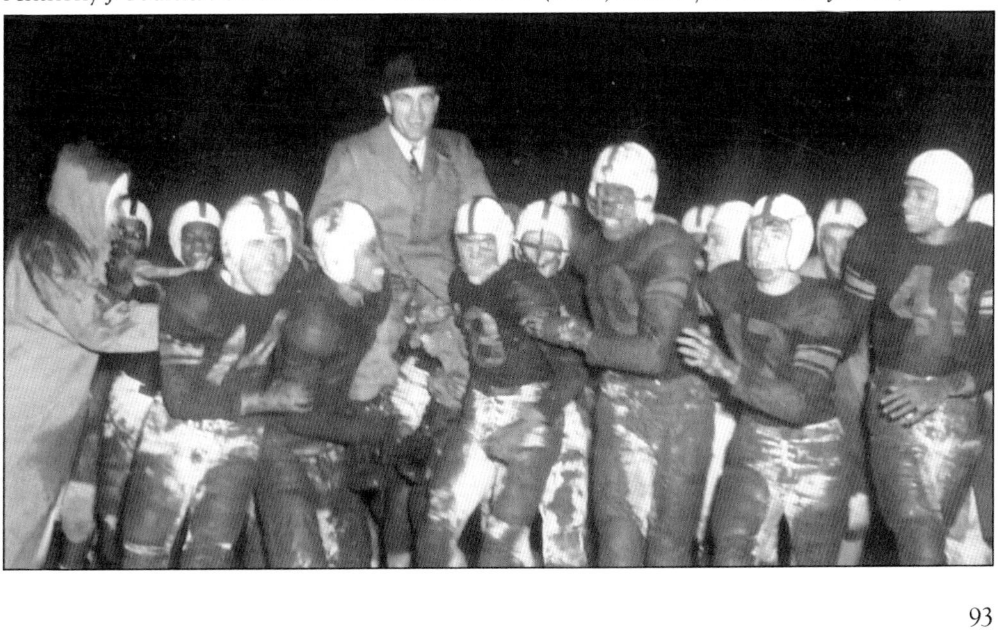

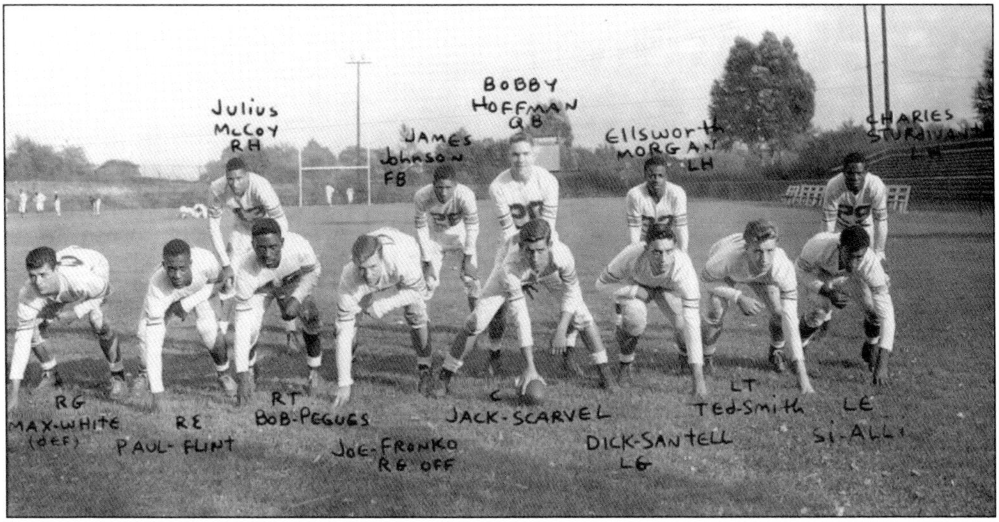

Seen above, Robert "Bob" Pegues helped lead the Knight Riders to a WPIAL Class AAAA Championship in 1951. Pegues played professional football for the Hamilton Canadian Cats in the Canadian League. Football coach Lou Falconi's Farrell Steelers brought home two consecutive state titles in 1995 and 1996. In 1996, Falconi was named Pennsylvania Football Coach of the Year. In 1965, Falconi (below, second row, far left) starred in football and was on the undefeated Farrell High School boys track team, seen below, coached by Russell Phillips. The assistant track coaches included Steve Karlovich and Dan Zipay. Pictured, from left to right, (first row) Bob Gasperec, Hasco Darden, Greg Jackson, Otha Hilton, Frank O'Stafy, Ron Capitol, Jim Sellers, Les Robinson, and "Sharkey" Flint; (second row) Lou Falconi, Dave Miller, Terry Williams, John Ostafy, Damun Gracenin, Bill Samuels, Willie Smith, Carl Basic, and Earl Adams; (third row) Rudy Jones, John Stey, Terry McCluskey, Bob DuMaire, Tom Latsco, Curt Hilton, Bob Jordan, Bill Wright, Mike Rococi, and Frank Smith; (fourth row) Pete Backo, Marty Andrusky, Mark Clayton, Joe Jarocki, Ray Wilson, Harlee, Campbell, John Hosey, Jon Ganzy, Charles Craig, and Chuck Drabick; (fifth row) Jerome Campbell, Robert Hughes, Adrian Capitol, Robert McLain, and Hugh McKinnis; (sixth row) managers Jack Lyden and Homer Dahringer. (Above, courtesy of William Jarrett; below, courtesy of Dorothy Jackson.)

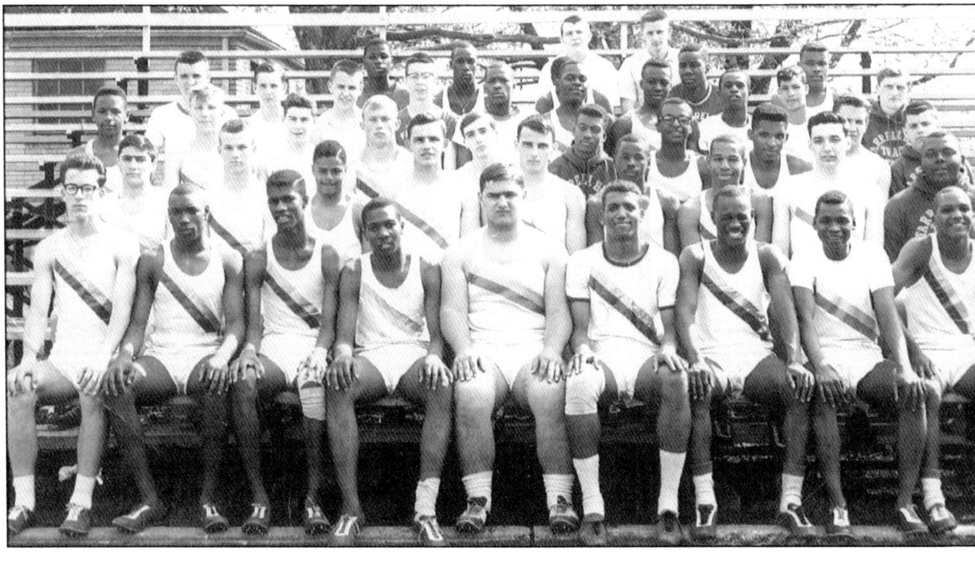

Six

In Service to Home and Country

Freedom's Journey

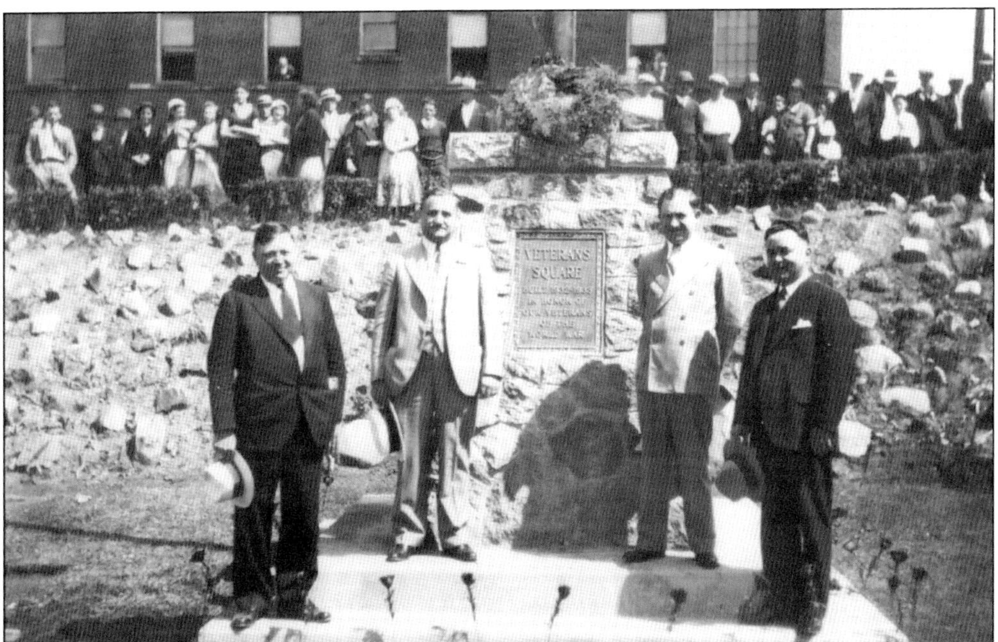

Veterans Square has been the site of many community events. Shown here are, from left to right, city councilmen John Krauss, Michael Nevant, and Lewis Levine and Mayor Joseph A. Franek at the dedication for Veterans Square in 1934. In the background is the Slovak Home located at the corner of Spearman Avenue and Federal Street. (Courtesy of SNPL.)

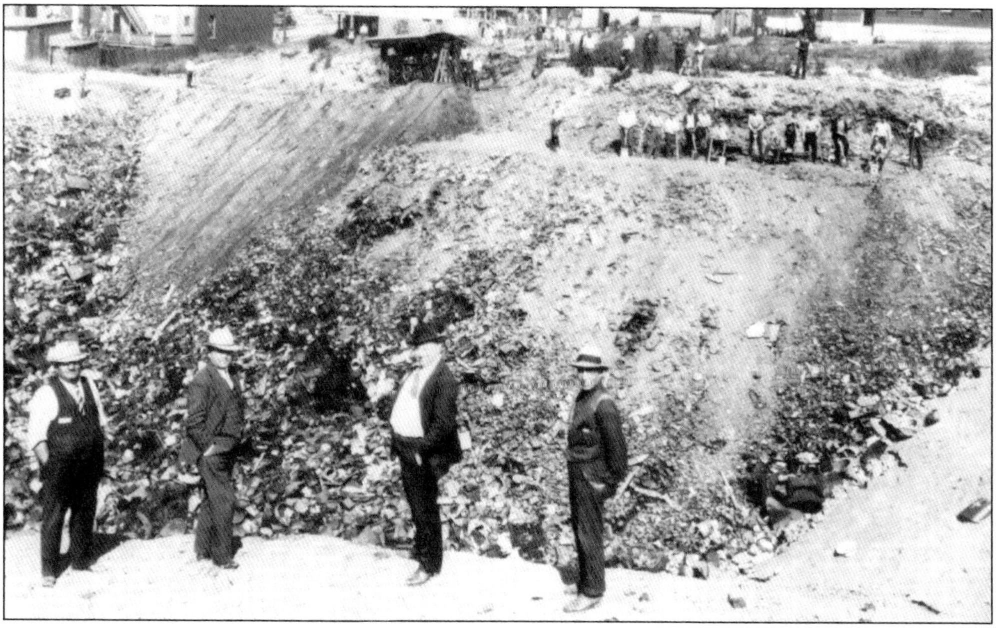

A decisive election held on November 5, 1929, changed the borough of Farrell to a third-class city. In 1932, Joseph A. Franek, a Slovak businessman, was sworn in as the city of Farrell's first mayor. During the Great Depression, from left to right, A.J. "Hook" Frank, Joseph A. Franek, John Krauss, and police chief John J. Sposito supervise the filling in of the massive hollow to become Veterans Square. (Courtesy of SNPL.)

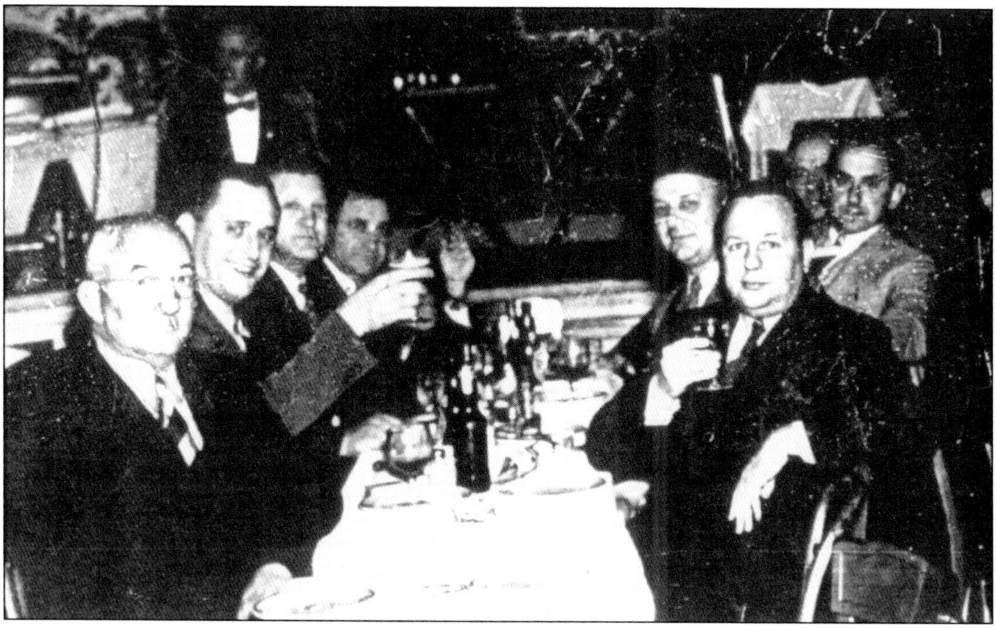

In 1936, Lewis Levine, a Jewish businessman, became the second mayor of the city of Farrell. Over 12 years, Levine served three consecutive terms. On September 12, 1940, from front to back, (left side of table) Mayor Lewis Levine, Councilman Roy DeBrakeleer, Councilman John W. Miller, and A.J. Frank; (right side of table) Councilman Arthur "Mac" E. McCarthy, Councilman Anthony J. Pintar, Joseph Broscoe, and Robert Davis meet over dinner. (Courtesy of Ann Yazvac.)

Benjamin H. Marks, Esq. Attorney at Law. Class of 1915. Sharon, Pa. A.B., Ohio State University; L.L.P., University of Pittsburgh. Practiced Law thirty years. Past City Solicitor for Farrell, and Mercer County Solicitor. Married to Miss Myrtle Speizer. Two sons, Mark Lincoln and Richard.

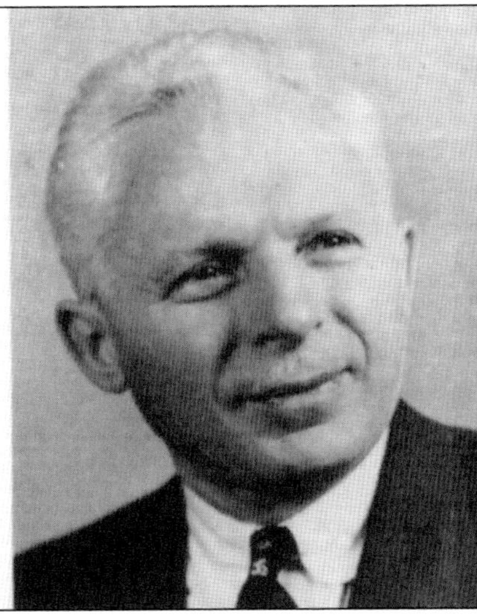

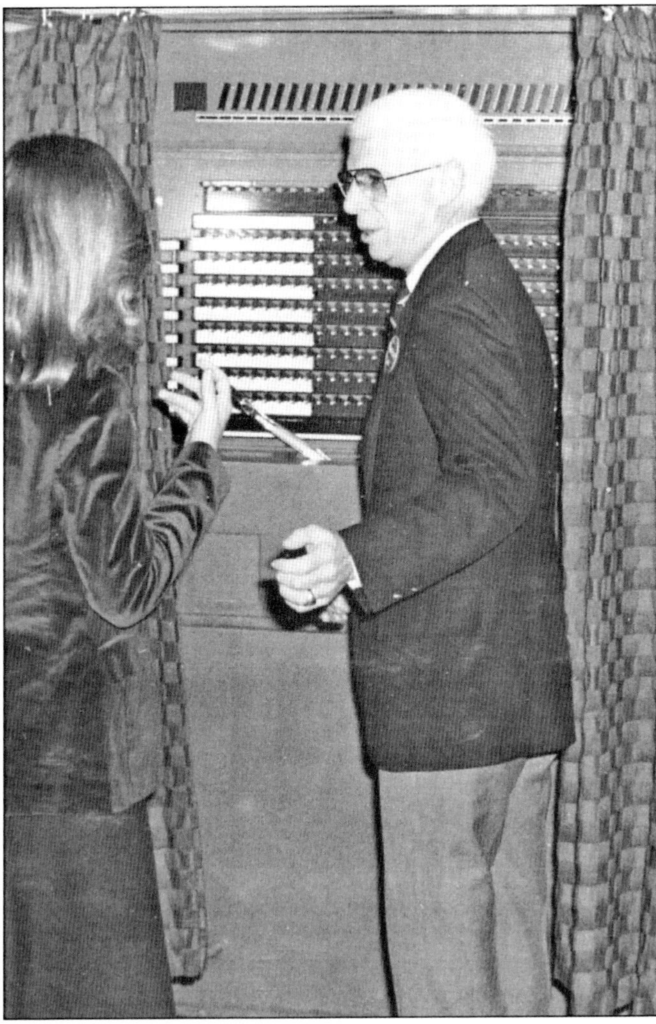

Jews held love for Farrell as "The Pearl." Farrell was a special place where the Jewish community lived amicably and thrived through full participation in government. Prominent Jewish civic leaders included Max Rosenberg, the first Jewish policeman on the South Sharon force in 1906, followed by Isadore Frankel, who served on the Farrell force for several years. Attorney Benjamin H. Marks, a 1915 Farrell High School graduate (seen above), was the first city solicitor, who served until World War II. His son Marc Lincoln Marks (b. 1927 in Farrell) served in the United States Congress from 1977 to 1983 and was featured in several national newspapers. At right, Marc Lincoln Marks enters a voting booth on Election Day. The Marks family's first American was a Hungarian immigrant, Morris Markovitz, a clothier on Broadway Avenue. (Above, courtesy of SNPL; right, courtesy of Ann Yazvac.)

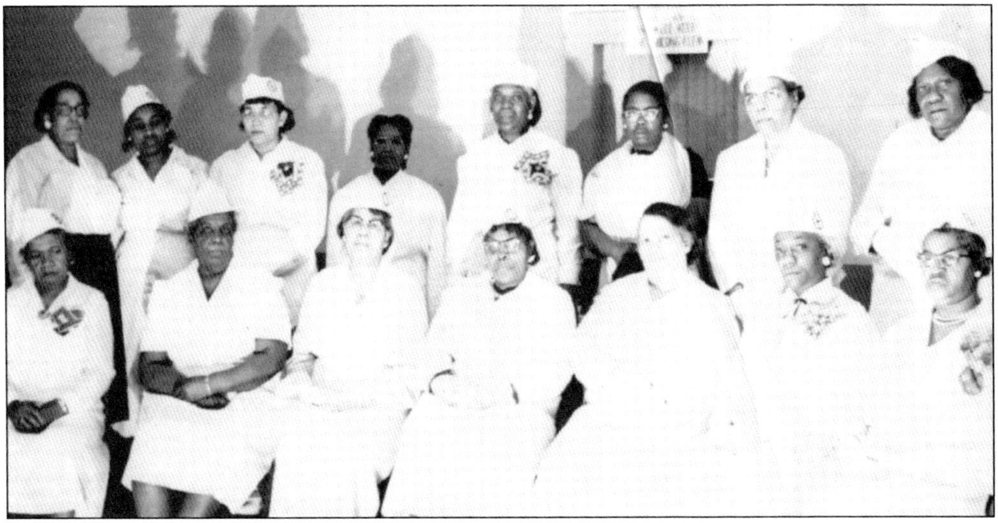

In 1946, the African American Crowder-Stewart No. 13 Blue Star Mothers of America, Inc., organized in the Farrell home of Mrs. Willie Atwood, who was elected first president. Charter members included, from left to right, (first row) Francis Hamm, Florence Stitt, Ruth Crowder, Della Stewart, Maude Hobbs, Onnie Alston, and Ocy Daniels; (second row) Henrietta Bowman, Lucretia Norman, Lorena Hill, Myrtle Preston, Dora Pegues, Mary Edwards, Willie Atwood, and Genetta Keys. (Courtesy of Martha Martin.)

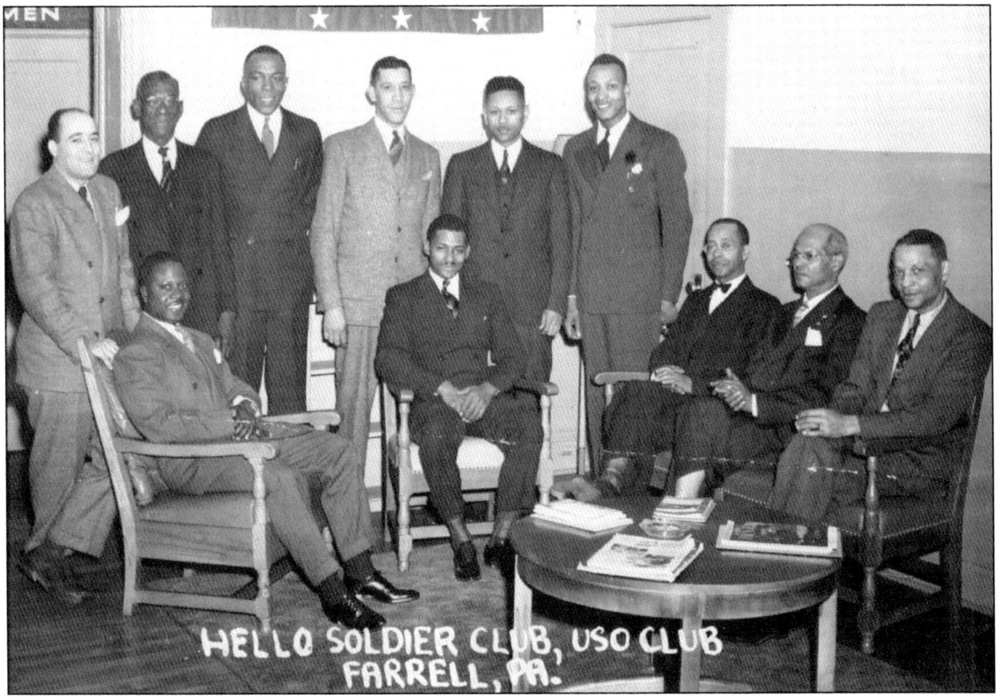

The Hello Soldier Club of the Farrell Colored United Service Organizations included, from left to right, (first row) Henry McCall, two unidentified people, Thomas Dillard, and unidentified; (second row) ? Mears, Herbert Paige, Raymond Johnson, Elmore Patterson, Harvey Satterwhite, and Lonnie Crawford. In 1943, the Farrell Colored USO, located at 809 Broadway Avenue, was considered one of the best in nation. (Courtesy of Renea Ingram.)

A *Sharon Herald* essay, "Survivor left horror behind, embraced love," written by Mark Schreiber, a 1968 Farrell High School alumnus, discusses his grandmother, Miriam Weiss, one of the oldest Holocaust survivors, who lived in Farrell from 1948 to 1981. Pictured here, Phillip Ellovich (1898–1986), a Jewish Romanian immigrant, and his wife, Miriam Gross Ellovich (1903–1989), were involved in fundraising to support Jews escaping Nazis. Miriam, born in South Sharon, is the youngest daughter of Jacob and Rosa Schreiber Gross. (Courtesy of SJHPRHC.)

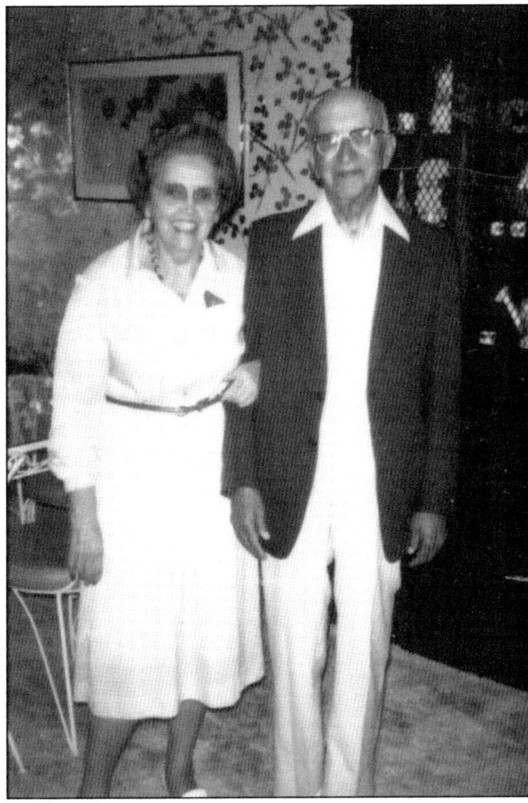

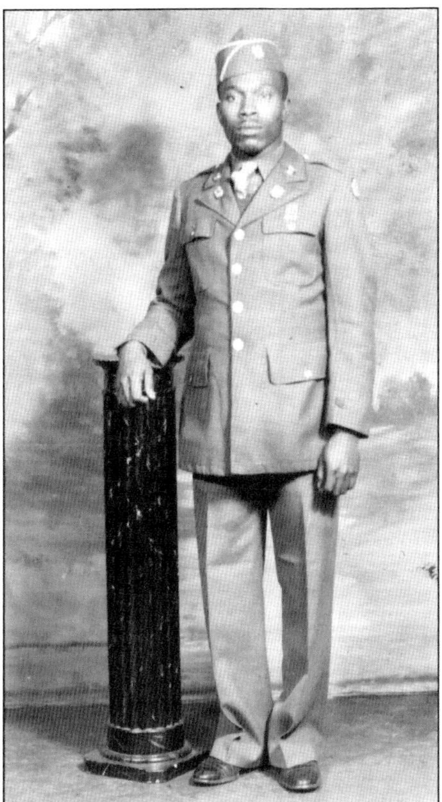

After World War II, Dillard Fielder (seen here) moved from Douglasville, Georgia, to Farrell for economic opportunity. Fielder served in a segregated unit where he survived sniper fire in the Philippines around 1943. At Sharon Steel, he suffered contusions and abrasions when a 3.5-ton plate fell 50 feet down into the blast furnace where he worked. He saw Graham Matthews and Gardner Birch being killed. It was a sight Fielder never forgot. (Author's collection.)

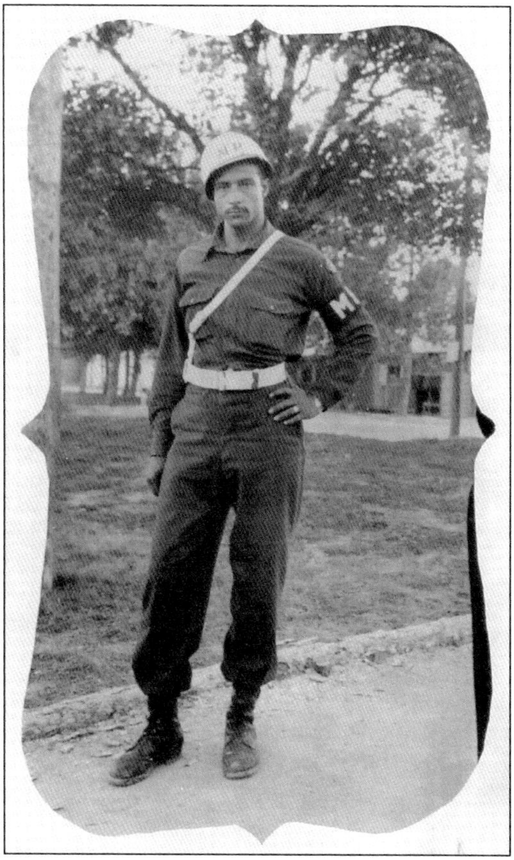

During World War II, African American soldiers stationed at Camp Reynolds frequented the Farrell Colored USO. Soldiers experienced racial tensions brought on by a segregated post exchange and theater. Questions still exist to the number of African American soldiers killed. Richard McClain (1921–1987) appears in uniform around 1942. At the Farrell Colored USO a few lucky girls met their future spouses. McClain married Ethel Jackson of Wheatland on July 4, 1943. (Courtesy of Ethel McClain.)

Serviceman often said that the Farrrell Colored USO certainly was "a home away from home." They frequently commented that it was "most hospitable" and one of the nicest organizations they had seen since entering the service. The site was at 809 Broadway Avenue in Farrell. Richard McClain is pictured fifth from the right, and Silas Askerneese (1916–2000) is standing in front of the door beside the lamp. (Courtesy of Ethel McClain.)

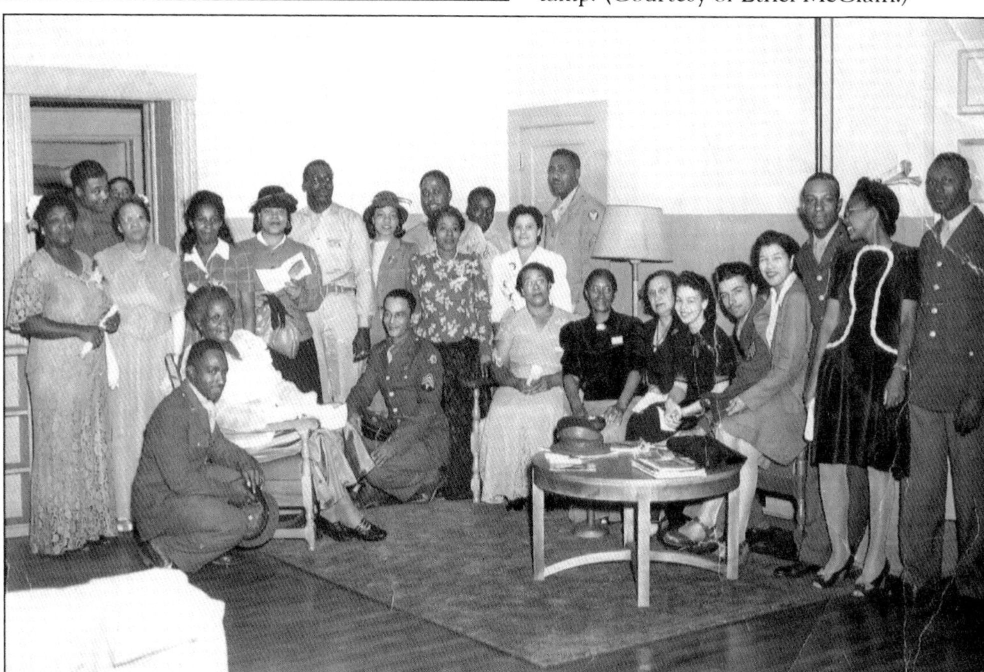

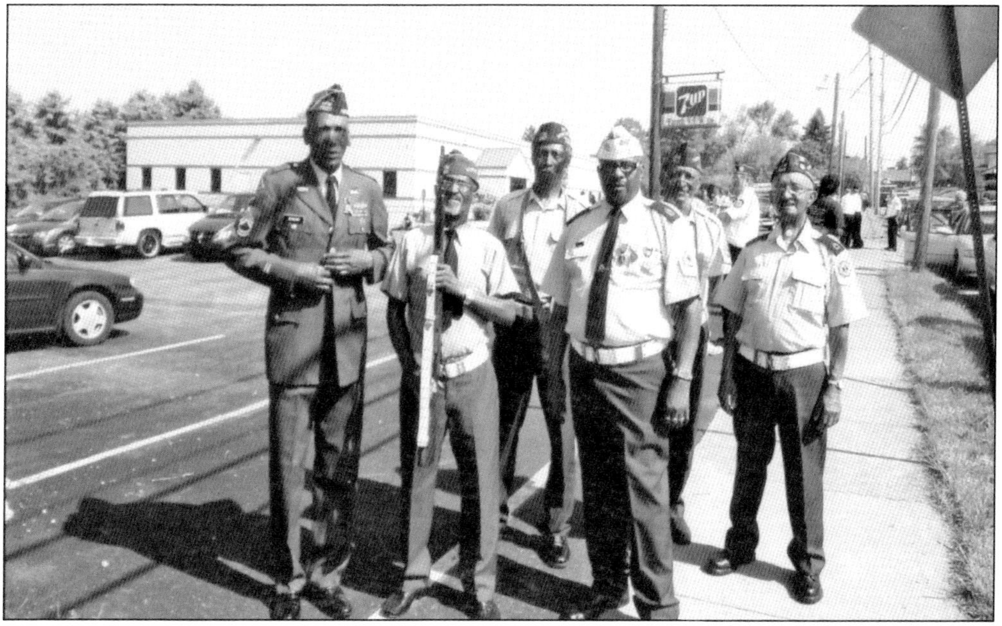

The New Bell Murray Post No. 7597 Veterans of Foreign War assemble at the staging area for the Farrell Wheatland Veterans Day parade in Farrell. Members include, from left to right, (first row) Vernon Jenkins, Dewey Gansy, and Jimmie Smith; (second row) Robert Wilkins, Earl Jones, and Douglass Smith. In the background, the Veterans of Foreign War Post No. 5286 on Indiana Avenue was rebuilt after a fire. (Author's collection.)

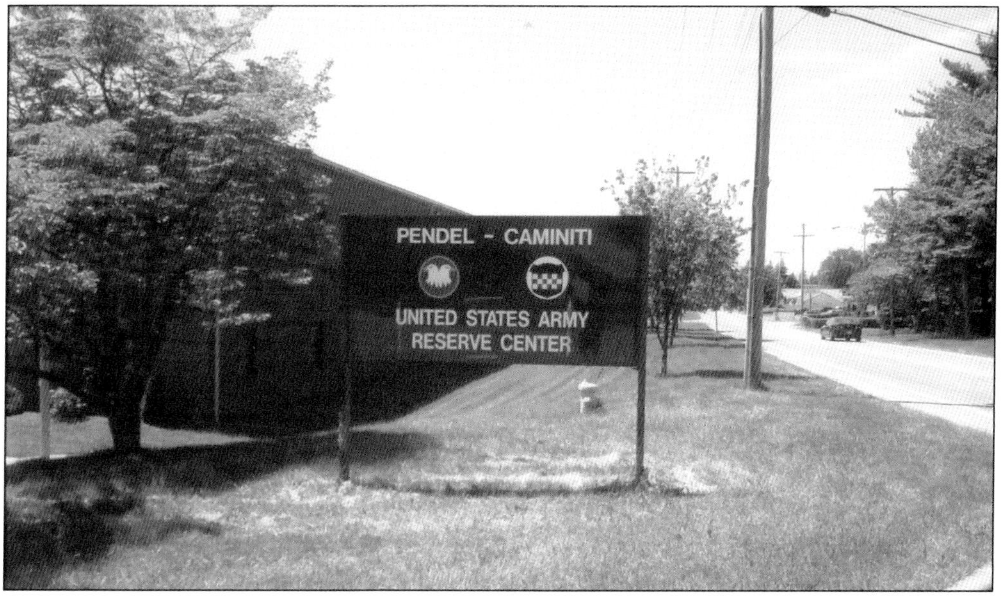

Farrell's Pendel-Caminiti US Army Reserve Center recognizes the patriotism of T.Sgt. Anthony G. Pendel, a descendant of Croatian immigrants who posthumously was presented the Distinguished Service Cross for his extraordinary heroism on March 22–23, 1945, at Waldreirbach, Germany, during World War II. S.Sgt. Harry W. Caminiti, a descendant of Italian immigrants, posthumously was presented the Distinguished Service Cross for his bravery on March 18, 1945, near Fraulautern, Germany. (Author's collection.)

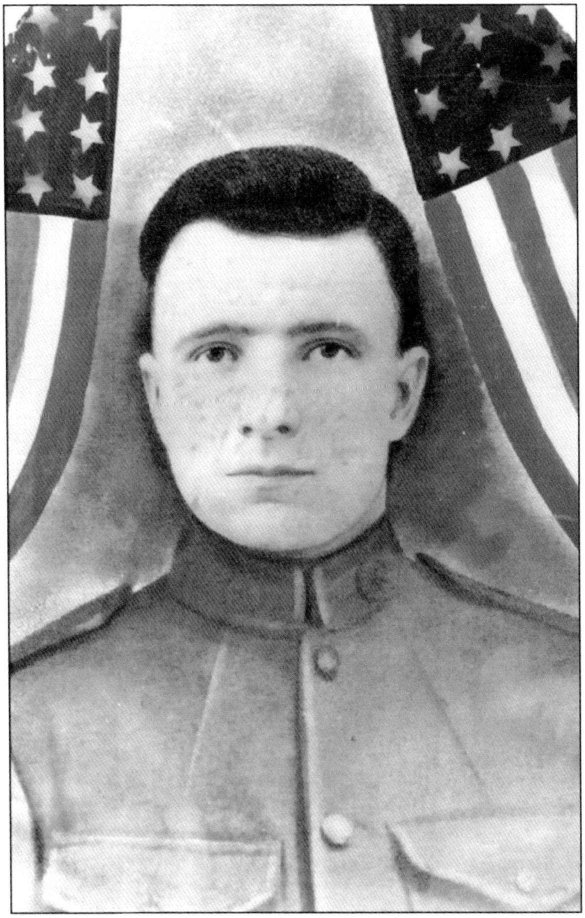

Fred Husnick Sr. arrived from Croatia in the United States in 1913. He served in the United States Army from September 6, 1919, to September 7, 1922. During his service, he was stationed in the Philippines, Hawaii, Japan, and Siberia. He was honorably discharged and received his citizenship papers for his military service. (Courtesy of Ann Yazvac.)

In 1917, the mill's whistle blew for 15 minutes when a group of African American recruits left for Camp Lee. Fred Lofton (second row, far left) appears as a flag bearer in the Masonic St. John's Day parade at the corner of Union Street and Greenfield Avenue in Farrell around 1927. The Russell L. Chinn Post of the American Legion was named in honor of the first African American soldier killed in battle during World War I. (Author's collection.)

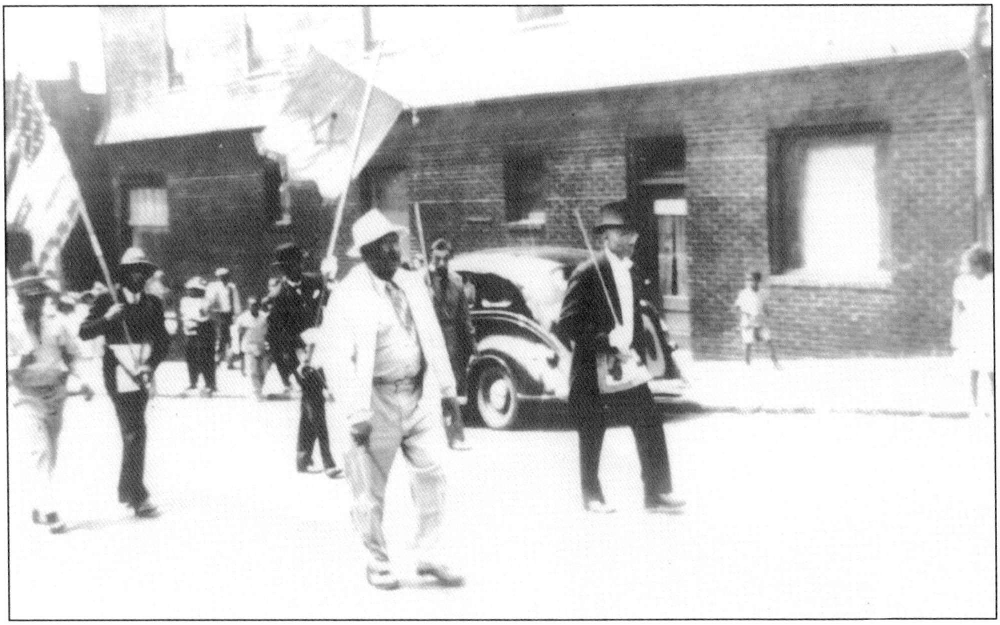

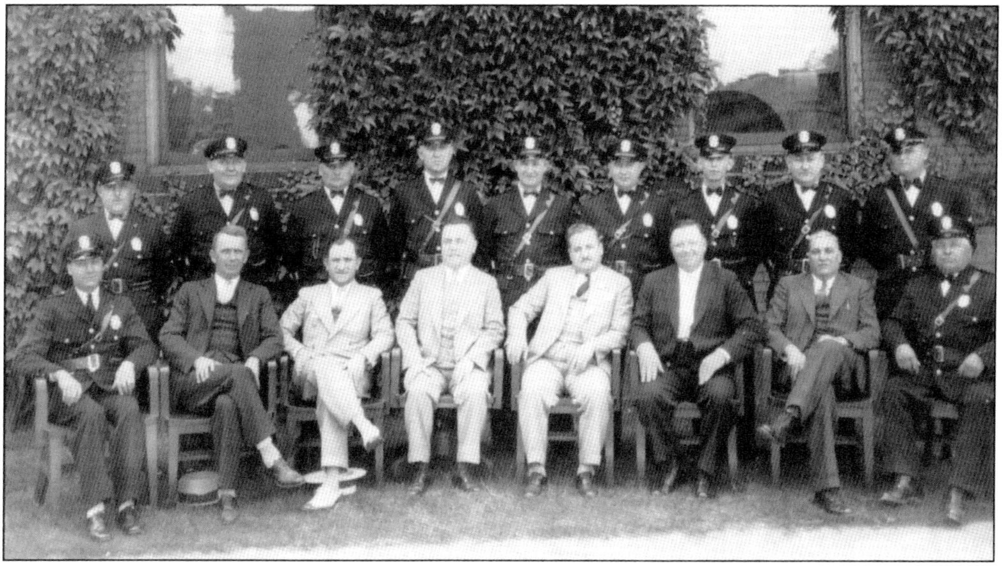

A long-serving policeman, Frank J. Egercic recorded the history of service. In the 1930s, the Farrell Department of Public Safety were, from left to right, (first row) Chief John J. Sposito, Councilman Harry Gerber, Councilman Lewis Levine, Mayor Joseph Franek, Councilman Michael Nevant, Councilman John Krauss, city treasurer Joseph Cantelupe, and Samuel Fleischer; (second row) ? Petrillo, ? Dorulla, ? Yershey, unidentified, Don Dignan, Frank Kowalski, ? Danilov, Isadore Frankel, and Joseph Volansky. (Courtesy of SNPL.)

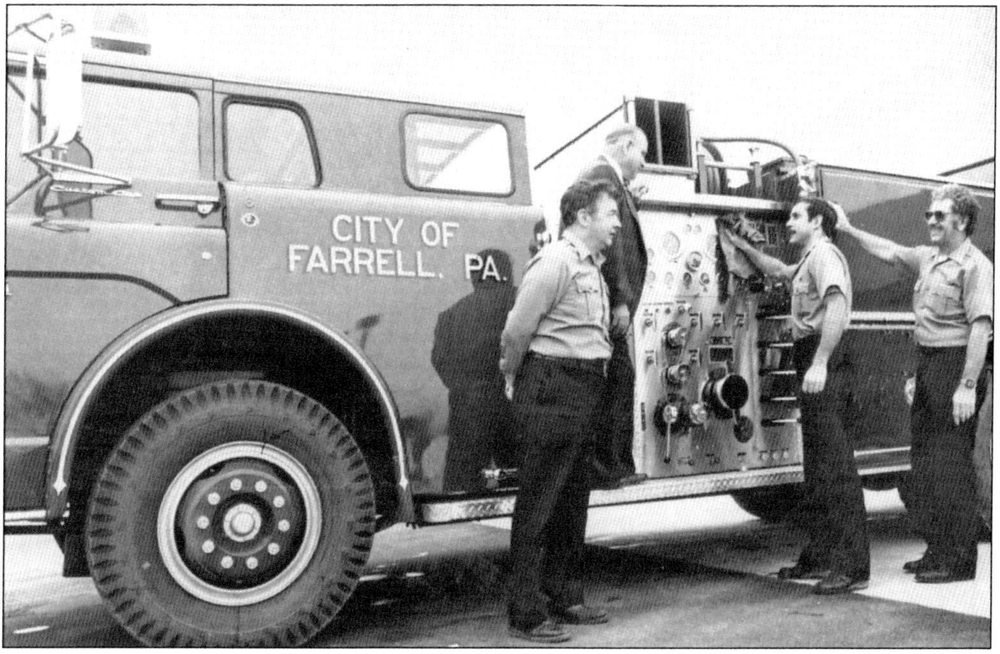

On August 24, 1940, the Farrell Fire Department hosted the convention of the Northern Firemen's Association of Pennsylvania. The mammoth parade of 75 companies, 50 bands, and some 150 pieces of equipment was the talk of the town. Richard M. Egercic (1953–2008, second from right) and Peter Yurcich (far right) served on the Farrell Fire Department. Both men belonged to the enterprising Husnick-Egercic-Yazvac clan. (Courtesy of Ann Yazvac.)

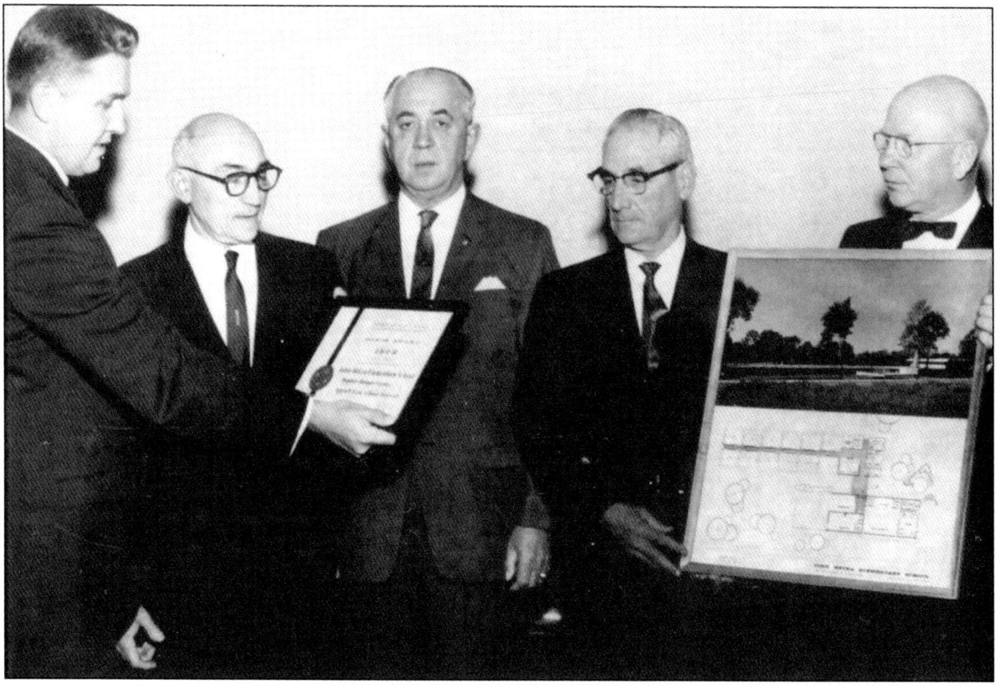

During World War II, Slav Days were held to promote the war effort. Former Farrell school superintendent John Hetra (center), a prominent Slovak leader, had an elementary school named in his honor. (Courtesy of MCHS.)

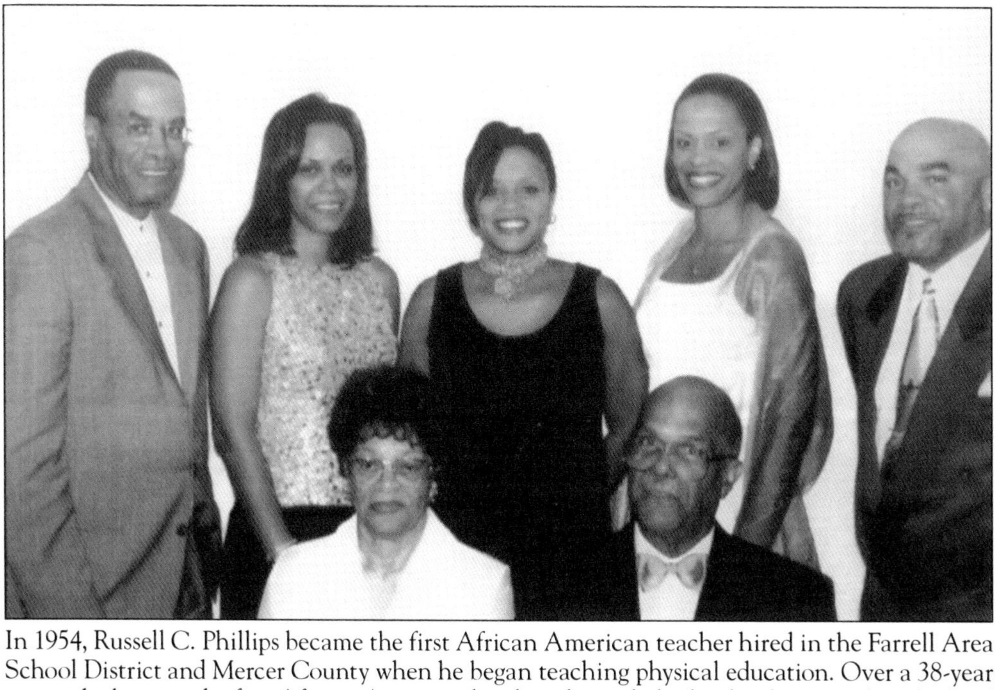

In 1954, Russell C. Phillips became the first African American teacher hired in the Farrell Area School District and Mercer County when he began teaching physical education. Over a 38-year tenure, he became the first African American head track coach, high school principal, and school administrator in the Farrell School District. Here, Russell Phillips (seated, right) and wife Mary Phillips (seated, left) are with family. (Courtesy of Russell Phillips.)

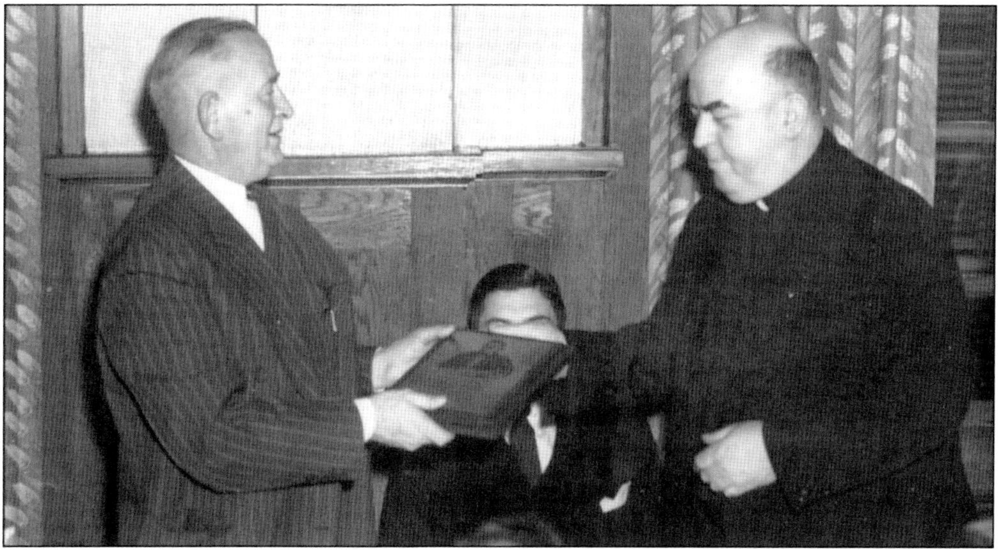

In 1957, at a dinner with more than 100 civic and business leaders, Rev. James F. Murphy, chairman of the War Problems Committee, presents a plaque to Henry A. Roemer, to mark Sharon Steel's purchase of the Farrell Works of the Carnegie Illinois Steel Corporation and to express to Roemer the community's appreciation of Sharon Steel's plans to keep that plant in operation. Some years earlier, Haywood Street was renamed Roemer Boulevard for his largesse in saving the city. Sharon Steel, with over 5,000 employees, was the major employer in the community until the 1980s, when it closed. (Courtesy of Ann Yazvac.)

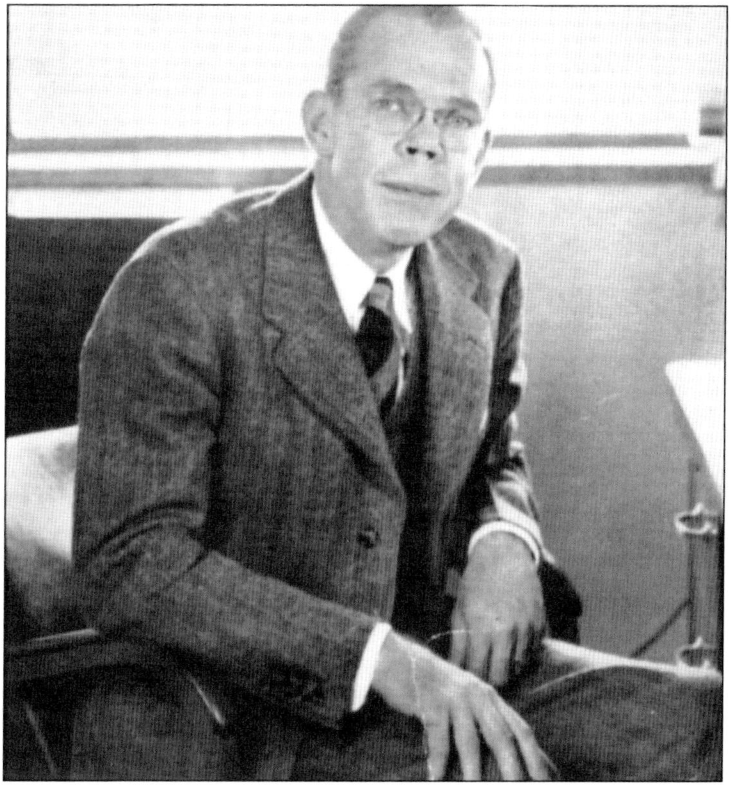

Carroll D. Kearns, who served as a United States Representative from 1947 to 1963, was an early advocate for reducing the voting age from 21 to 18. Here, Carroll D. Kearns, a Farrell resident, serves as Farrell school superintendent from 1941 to 1946, when he organized the Farrell Chamber of Commerce. Farrell mayor Michael A. Nevant and US Representative Carroll D. Kearns approached Henry A. Roemer about purchasing the closed Farrell Works Carnegie-Illinois Steel. (Courtesy of SNPL.)

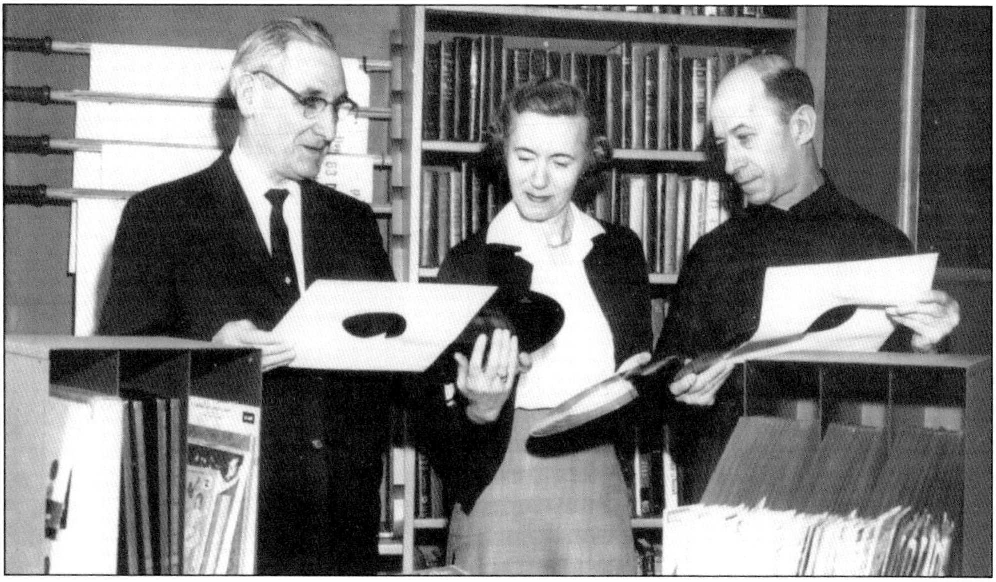

Service organizations have always supported the growth and development of the public library. Farrell's Lions Club is the oldest existing service organization in Farrell. Here, librarian Helen Roux (center) receives a donation of a record cabinet and records for a new audio-visual collection in commemoration of the library's 25th anniversary. Edward Flynn (left) and John Fart, both members of the Kiwanis Club of Farrell, help her sort the new records. (Courtesy of SNPL.)

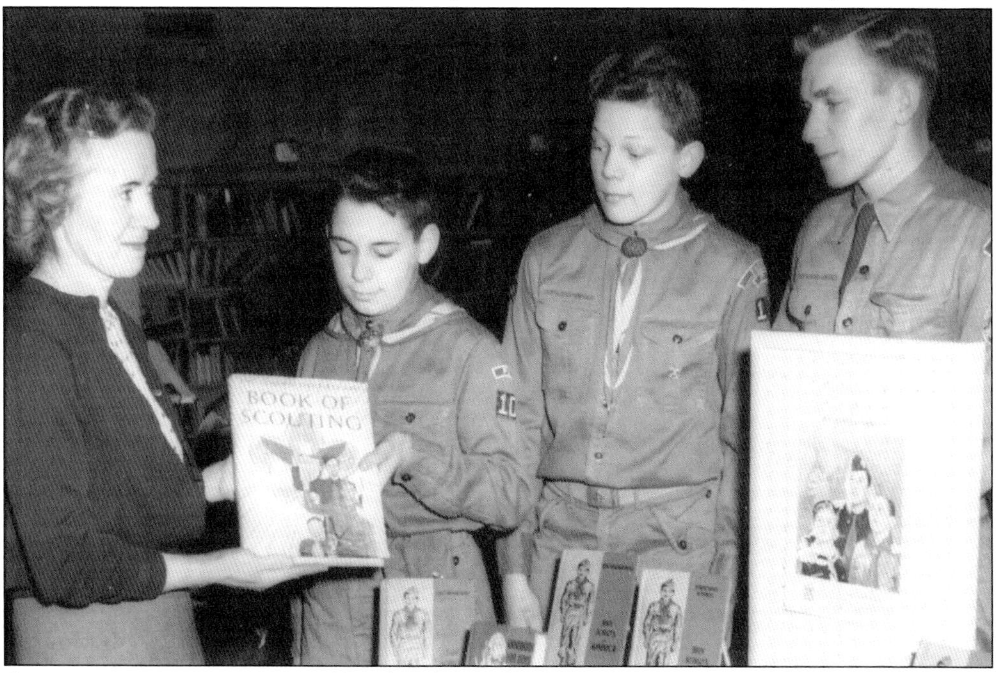

Scouting troops were sponsored by churches, schools, and community organizations and were numerous in Farrell. Librarian Helen Roux was presented with a donation, *Book of Scouting*, in commemoration of the 50th anniversary of Scouting by members of Farrell Boys Scout Troop No. 10, sponsored by the United Steelworker of America, Local No. 1193. From left to right, they are Roux, J. Iacino, Eric Murdock, and scoutmaster Tom Kovach. (Courtesy of SNPL.)

Seven

Struggles in Steel

Labor, Civil Rights, and Middle Class

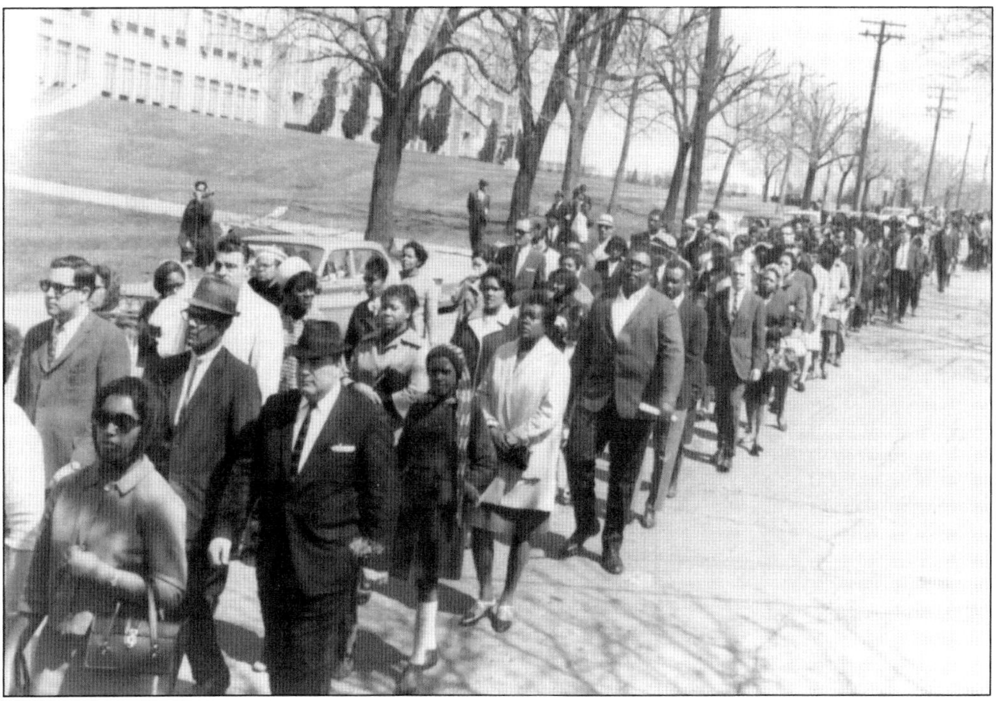

Prior to the beginnings of the civil rights movement, there was a rumbling going on. Here, protestors march for slain civil rights leader Dr. Martin Luther King Jr. in 1968. (Courtesy of Russell C. Phillips.)

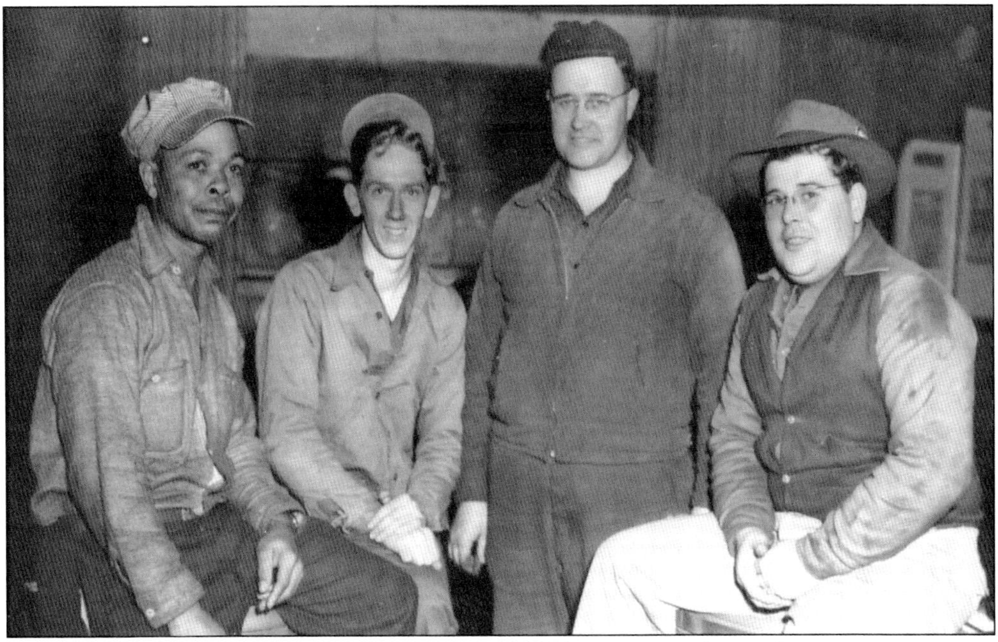

The Fair Employment Practice Commission (FEPC) was given the authority to investigate defense-related employers when President Roosevelt issued Executive Order 9346. In 1944, G. James Fleming, an FEPC examiner, replied to the grievances of the United Citizens Committee of Farrell concerning the "employment problem of the Negroes." At the hot mill, steelworkers are, from left to right, Gene Fifer, Raymond Coppage, William Alexander, and Richard Nuddy. (Courtesy of Ann Yazvac.)

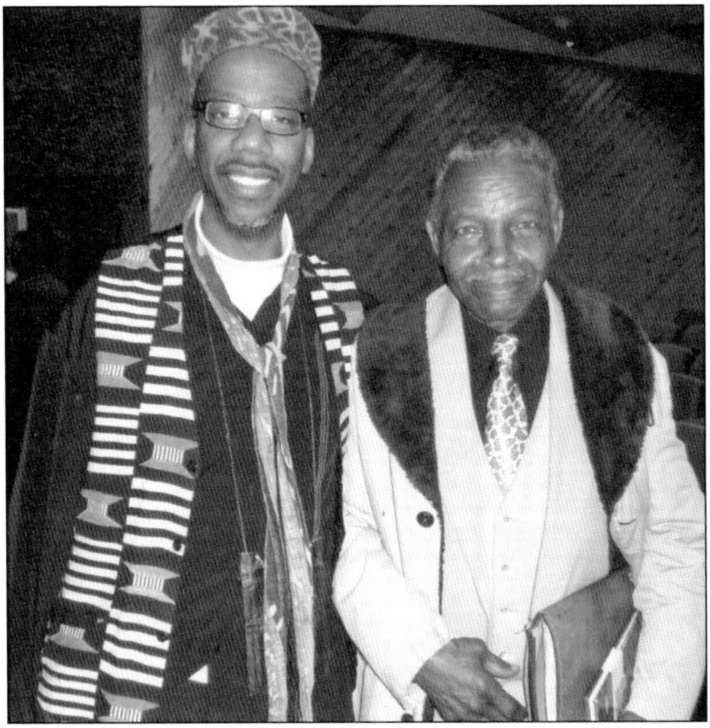

Rev. Robert Stewart, labor organizer, recalled how 13 departments at Sharon Steel did not employ minorities in the 1960s. Blacks were absent from good-paying positions in management because they worked "hot and dirty" jobs. Unresolved grievances led to a walkout, fomenting change. Here, Roland Barksdale-Hall, panelist (left), gives recognition to Reverend Stewart (right) at the forum on Labor, Civil Rights, and the Middle Class, held at Youngstown State University. (Author's collection.)

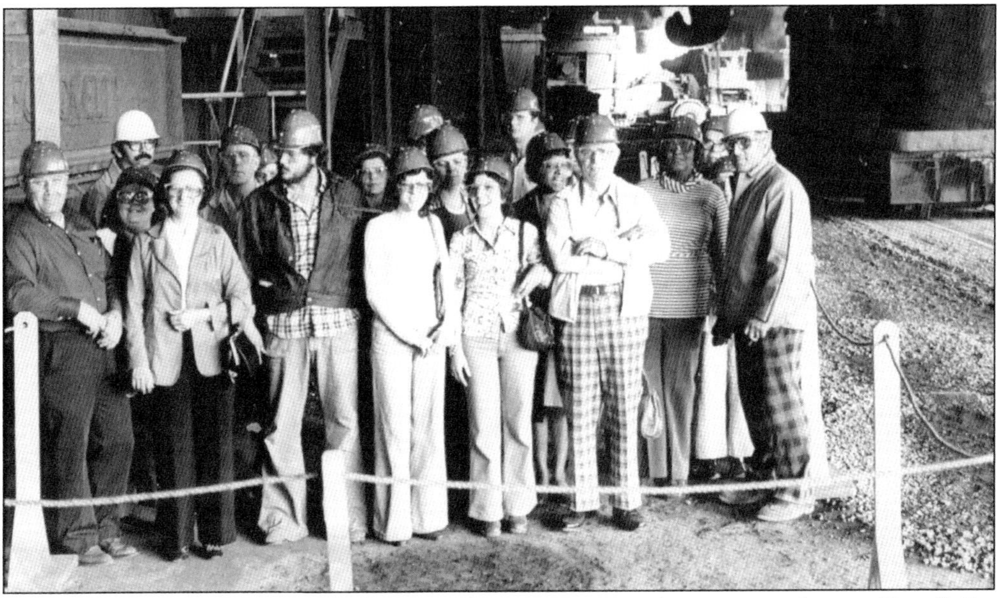

During World War II, Sharon Steel, seen in these images, was the major employer in Farrell. On July 31, 1942, in the *Farrell Press*, Henry W. Pelt, director of the Pennsylvania Bureau of Statistics of the Internal Affairs Department, noted the rise in the employment of African Americans in the heavy metal industries. In 1916, Frank Wilson Sr. had migrated from Cheraw, South Carolina, to Farrell and found employment at the Sharon Steel Hoop, the predecessor of Sharon Steel. People from Cheraw developed a reputation as good workers. Esther Brennam, the employee manager of Sharon Steel Hoop, hired anyone who said they were natives of Cheraw on the spot. Wilson heavily recruited others from Cheraw to Farrell and became an influential leader in the African American community. (Both, courtesy of Shirley Jean Matthews.)

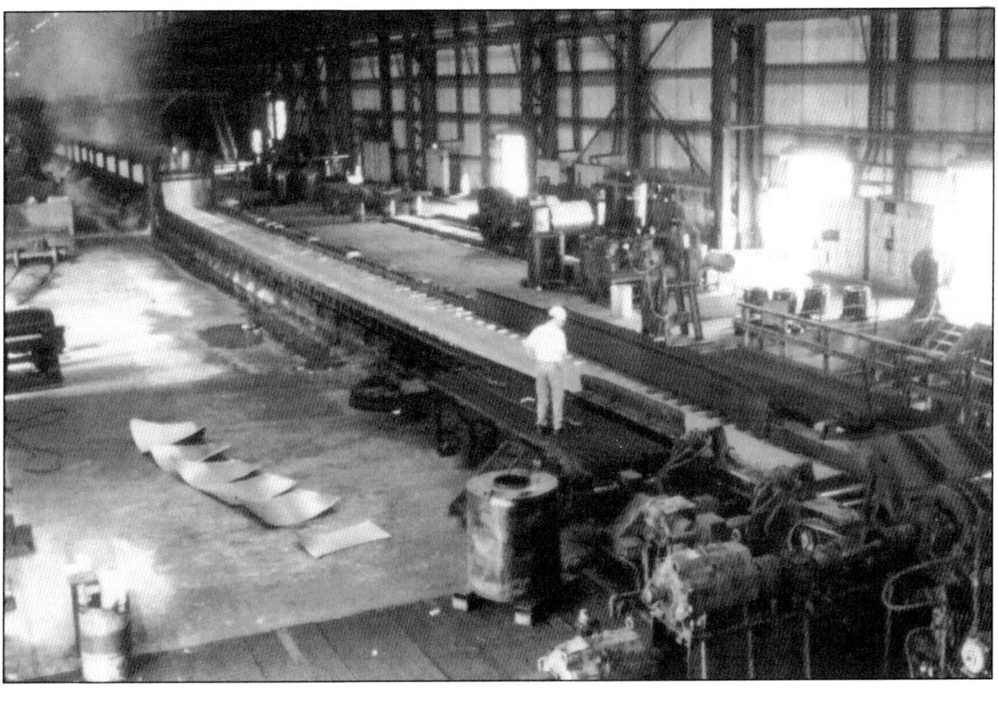

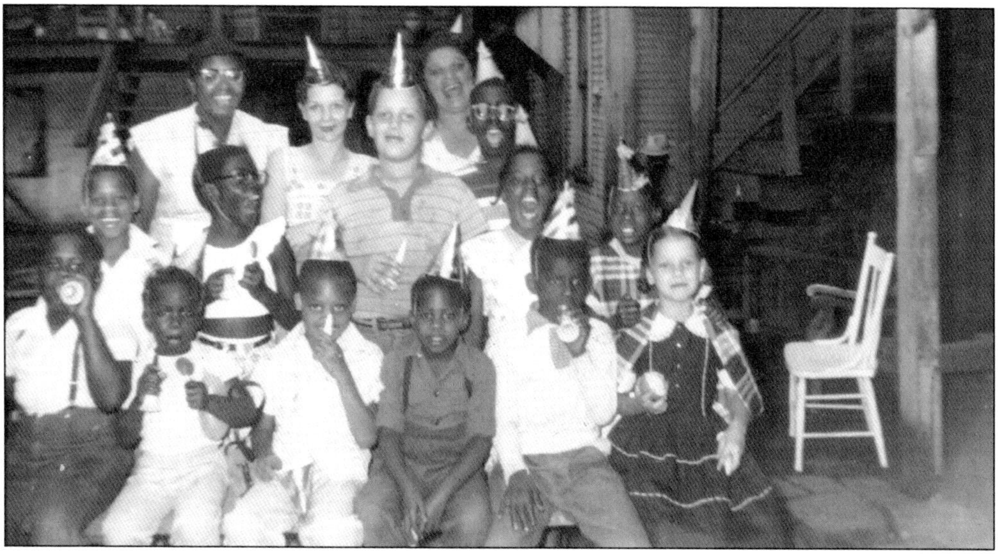

Tenements frequently did not have central heating, and the pipes would freeze during the winter. Above, Shirley Johnson and neighbors celebrate a nephew's birthday party in the dirt courtyard of a tenement on Darr Avenue. (Courtesy of Shirley J. Matthews.)

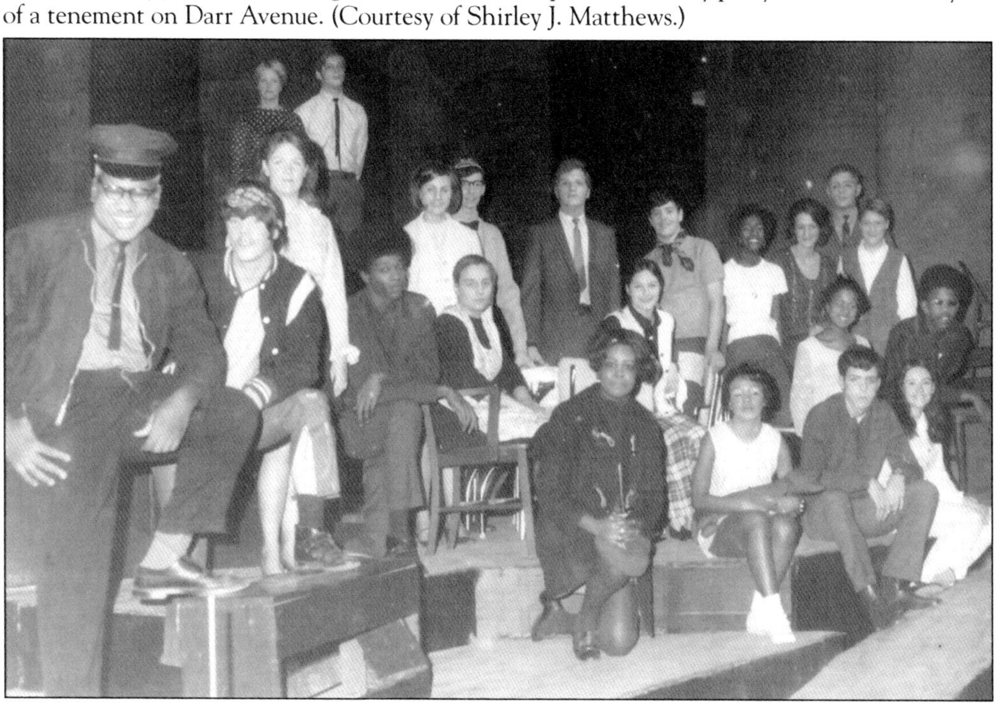

Farrell School superintendent Louis Morocco saw the arts as a way to bring people together. A theatrical production, *David and Lisa*, by James Reach, performed under the direction of Ronald Reed at Farrell School in the early 1970s, was complemented by a summer community playhouse. Pictured in the cast of *David and Lisa* are Bill Flowers, James Raykie, Patty McGrath, Georgiann Williams, Dave ?, Harry Capitol, Joy Churko, Mark Zolton, Maria Tamber, John Matsis, Veleter Mazyck, Marilyn Namey, Joe Raykie, Marion Ford, Dora Grace, Janet Bastide, Jacqueline Kennedy, Michael Skarica, Sam Monaco, Jane Leonetti, Paula Turosky, and George Richards. (Courtesy of Ronald Reed.)

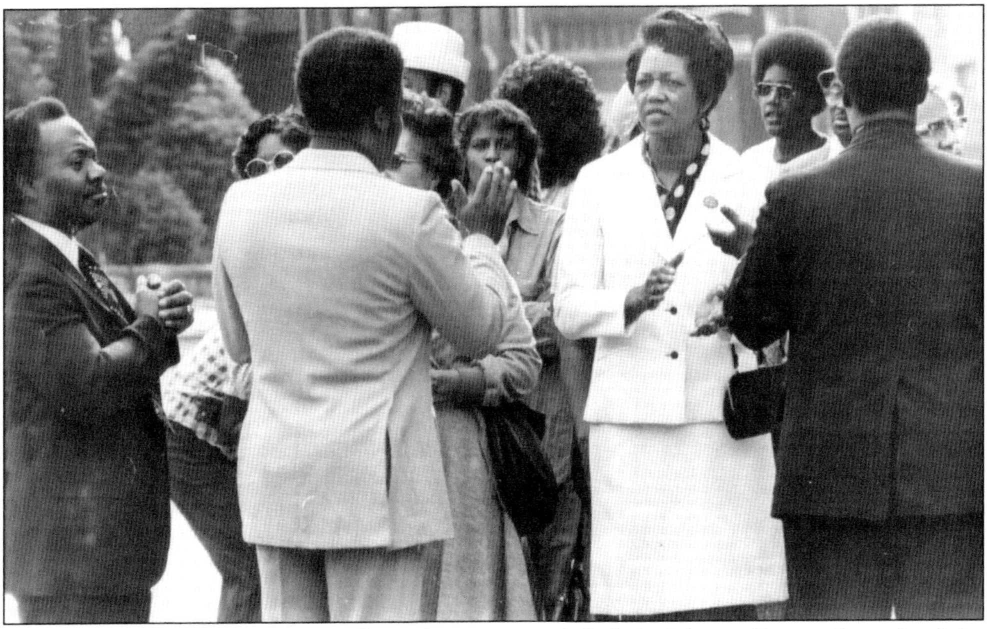

With their backs to the camera, these three reverends led the Mercer County branch of the NAACP in a rally in support of equal education. From left to right are Rev. W.M. Wingfield Jr., pastor of Second Baptist Missionary Church in Farrell; Rev. Walter Gillespie, pastor of Second Baptist Church in Sharpsville; and Rev. Clyde Crooks, pastor of Triumph Church of God in Christ in Farrell. The 1954 *Brown v. Board of Education* Supreme Court decision, which officially ended segregated public education, is still commemorated. (Courtesy of Martha Richards.)

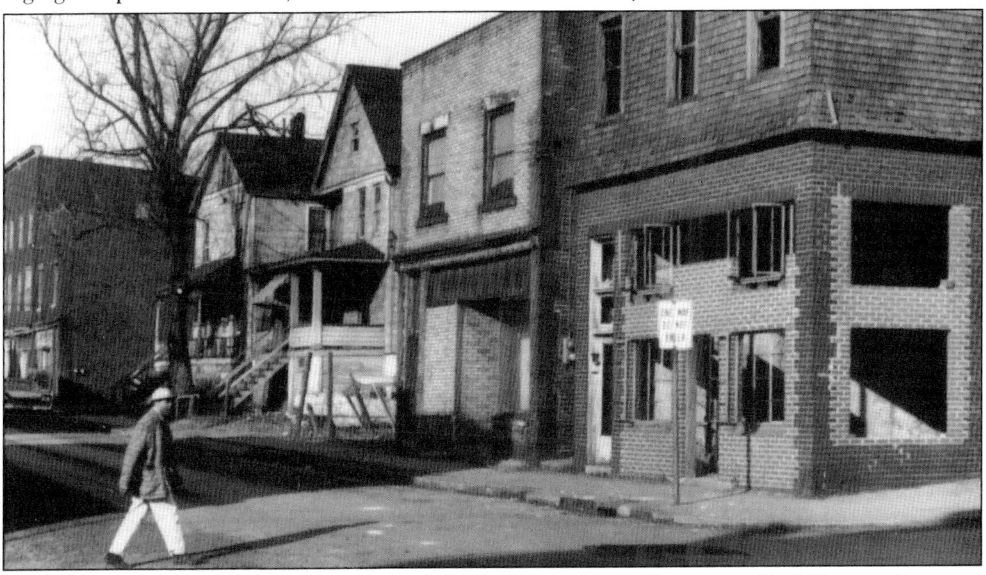

The Farrell Race Relations Project of the Youngstown State University Oral History Program focused upon the racial dynamic in community during the 1960s and 1970s. Interviews by Ronald Rice with James Edwards, Louis Morocco, Frank B. Donatelli, and William Samuels addressed poor housing, inadequate police, and community relations issues. Seen here is a representation of the neighborhoods from Wallis Avenue to Broadway near the mill, where the majority of African Americans live. (Courtesy of MCHS.)

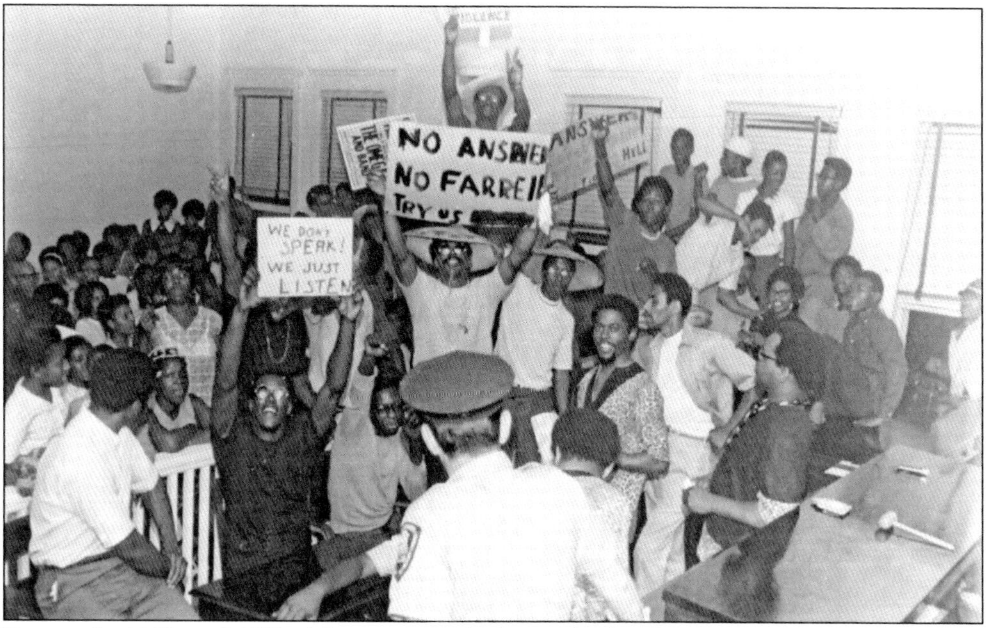

During the 1960s and 1970s, labor, civic, and religious leaders faced social upheaval. The black power movement arrived in Farrell in force. The *Wall Street Journal* explored what the root causes of rioting in towns like Farrell and York were in the 1960s. Historians still do not agree upon the root cause of rioting in towns. While in Farrell there was no loss of life, the city, which always prided itself on diversity, was damaged. Stores were destroyed. (Courtesy of Roger Winston.)

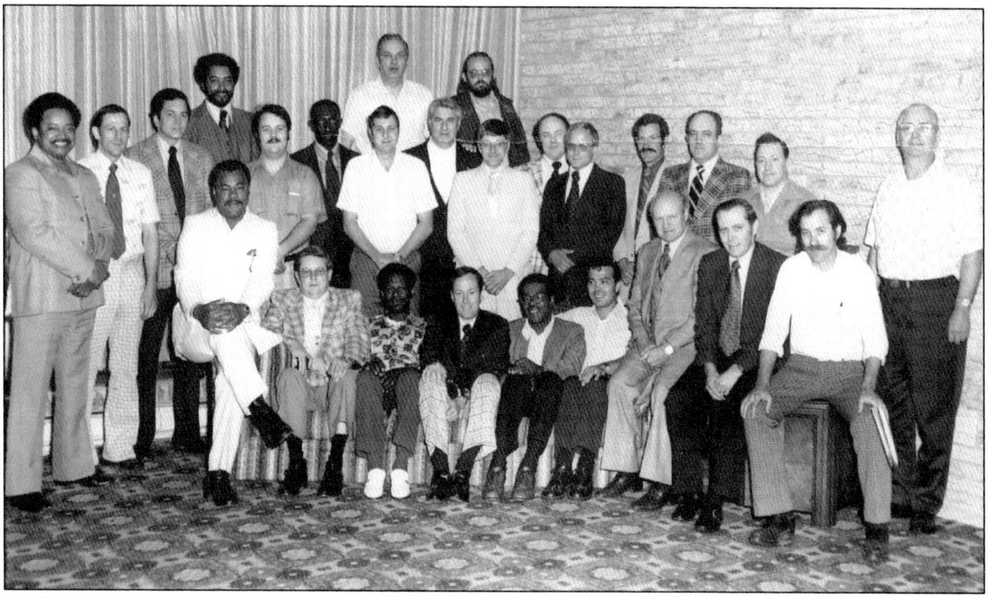

In the 1970s, prominent African Americans joined the middle class. For protection from unfair employment practices and to make better lives for their families, African Americans assumed more responsible positions in union locals. Larry Austin (far left rear, by curtain) became president of Union Local 1477 of the United Steelworkers of American, and Clarence Barksdale Hall Sr. (seated, fifth from right) was chairman of the Grievance Committeemen in the 1970s. (Author's collection.)

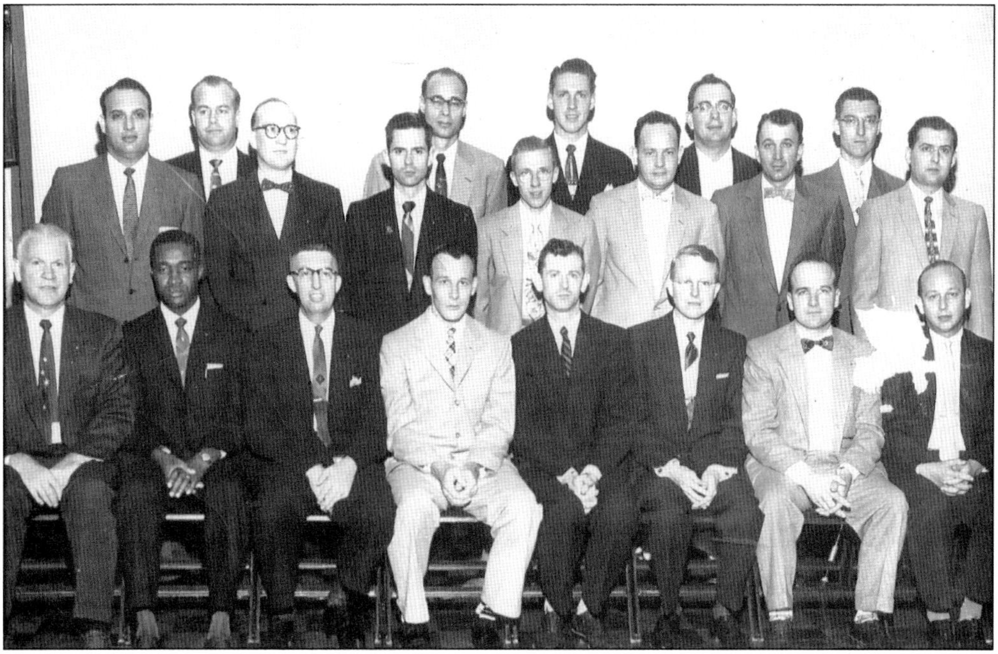

Ernest Robinson, a civil rights organizer, noted participation in government as an outcome from protests during civil rights. In 1970, William R. Hyatt, boys' supervisor at the F.H. Buhl Memorial Centre, becomes a Farrell councilman. In 1972, Toby Jackson becomes the first African American on the Farrell School Board. Here, Toby Jackson is the only African American member of Wiseman that organized the YMCA in Hermitage. (Courtesy of Dorothy Jackson.)

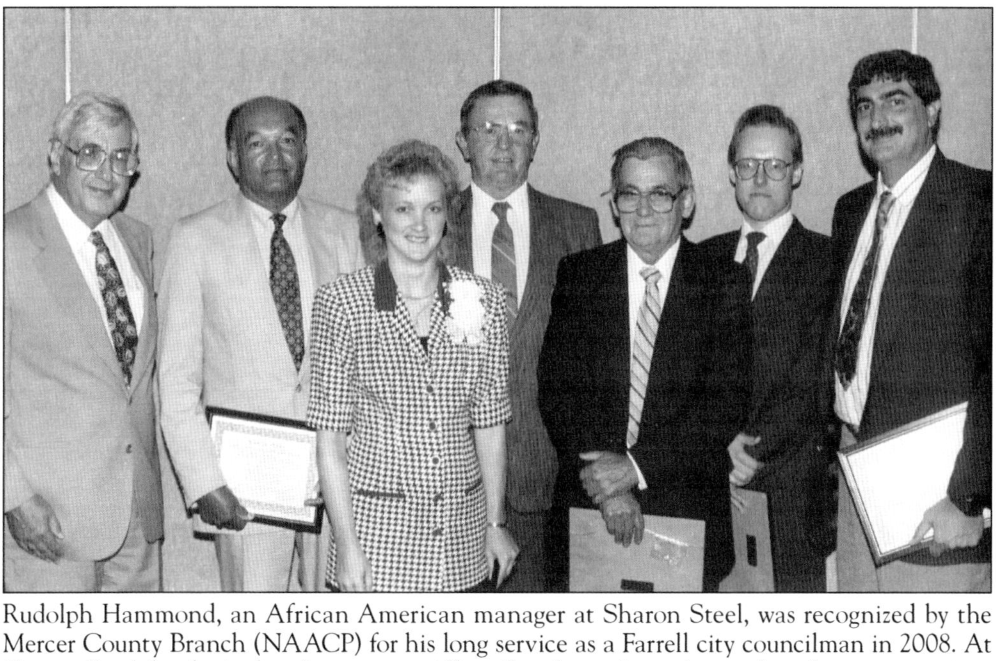

Rudolph Hammond, an African American manager at Sharon Steel, was recognized by the Mercer County Branch (NAACP) for his long service as a Farrell city councilman in 2008. At Sharon Steel, he devised a plan to move idle railroad cars from the stockyard at a cost savings of $200,000 per month. Here, Hammond (second from left) receives the Sharon Steel Chief Executive Officer's Award from the CEO. (Courtesy of Rudolph Hammond.)

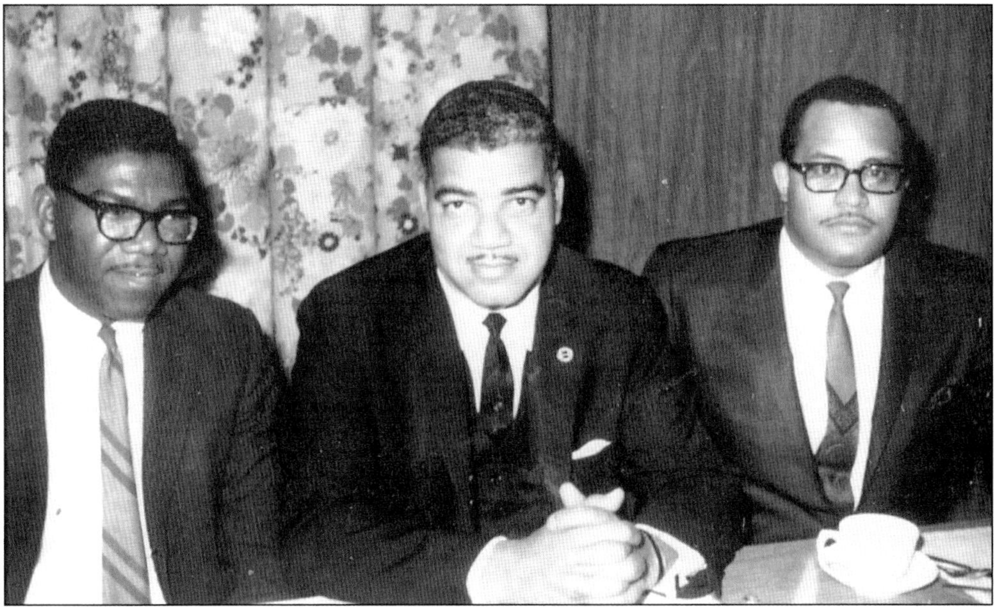

On April 26, 1968, local NAACP members discussed the need for a local Urban League. The Shenango Valley Urban League (SVUL), organized on May 28, 1968, became operational in just eight months; it was called the Instant Urban League. Theodore L. Yarboro, MD, then president of the local affiliate, received the charter from Whitney Young Jr., executive director of the National Urban League, at a banquet in Hermitage. Other organizers included George Pickett, Walter E. Matthews, Wilbert L. Shannon Sr., and William J. White. Shown above are, from left to right, Dr. Theodore Yarboro, Whitney Young, and Ernest Prince. "Working Together" was the theme for the 1995 Kwanzaa. Shown below, Mike McNair (standing), publisher of the *Buckeye Review* newspaper, addresses cooperative economics in the SVUL public meeting room. (Above, courtesy of Theodore L. Yarboro, below, author's collection.)

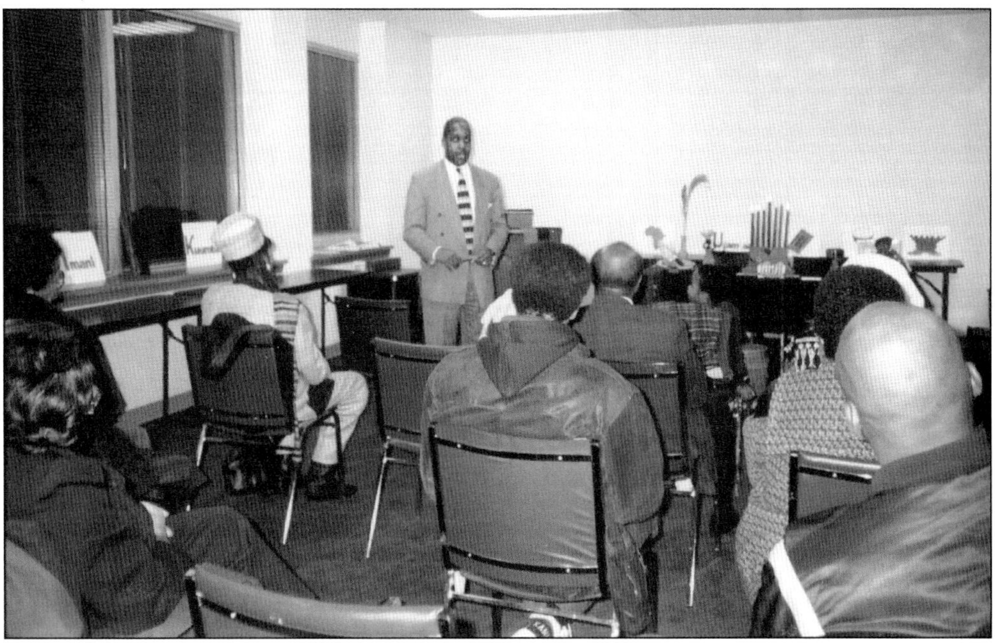

Eight

Coming Home
Community Reunions

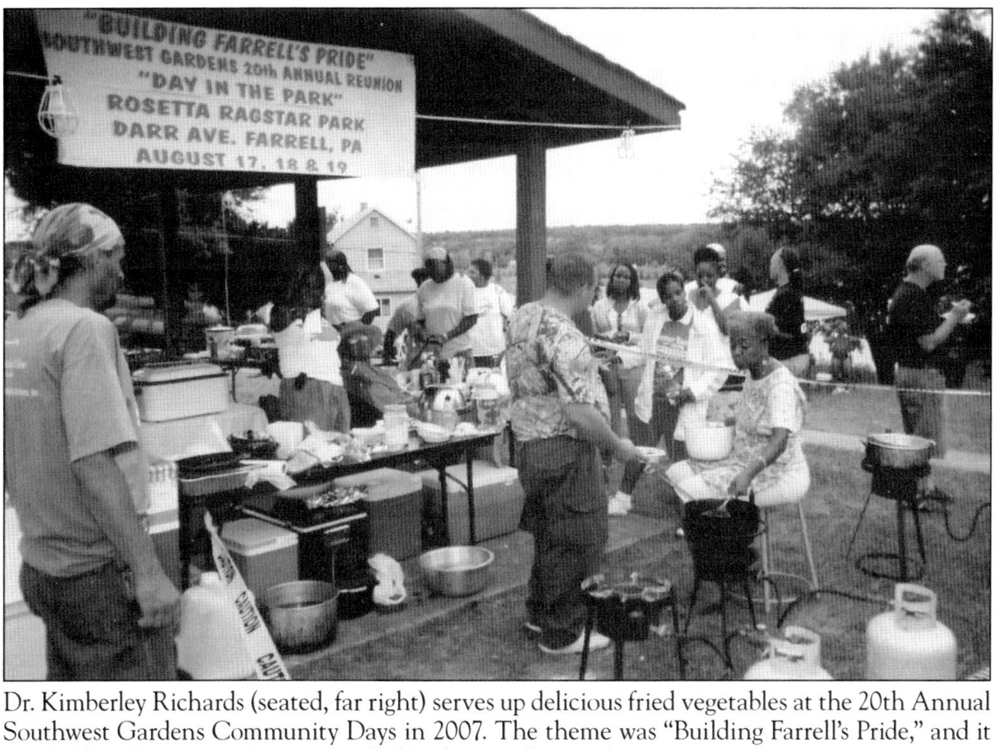

Dr. Kimberley Richards (seated, far right) serves up delicious fried vegetables at the 20th Annual Southwest Gardens Community Days in 2007. The theme was "Building Farrell's Pride," and it was held at the Rosetta Ragster Park. (Author's collection.)

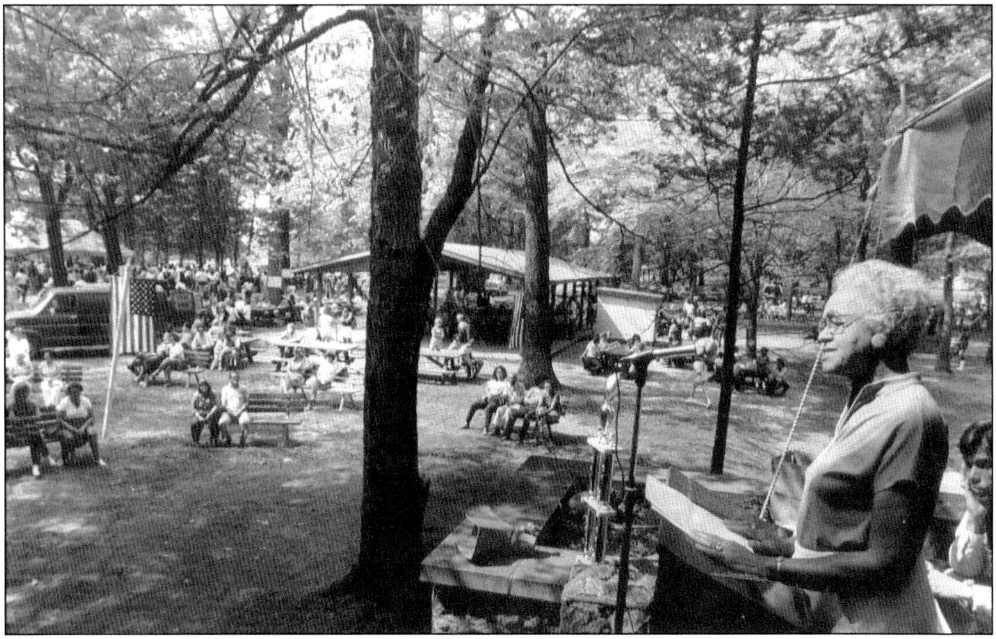

The annual Southwest Gardens Community Days helps guests reminisce about the Farrell Homecoming celebrations, held at Farrell City Park in the late 1970s. Shown here is Louise Ponder reading a celebratory poem at Farrell's Homecoming celebration, held in the former Farrell City Park. (Courtesy of Martha Richards.)

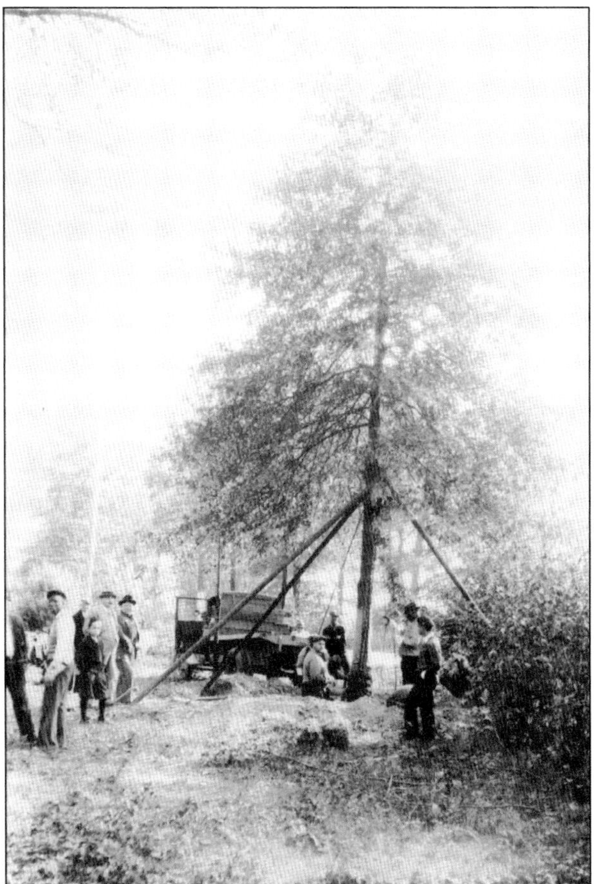

The 10.5-acre Farrell City Park was designed as a recreational center. Picnics and highly contested baseball games were played there. Children had their first pony ride there, too. Pictured is tree planting in the Farrell City Park in the early 1930s. (Courtesy of SNPL.)

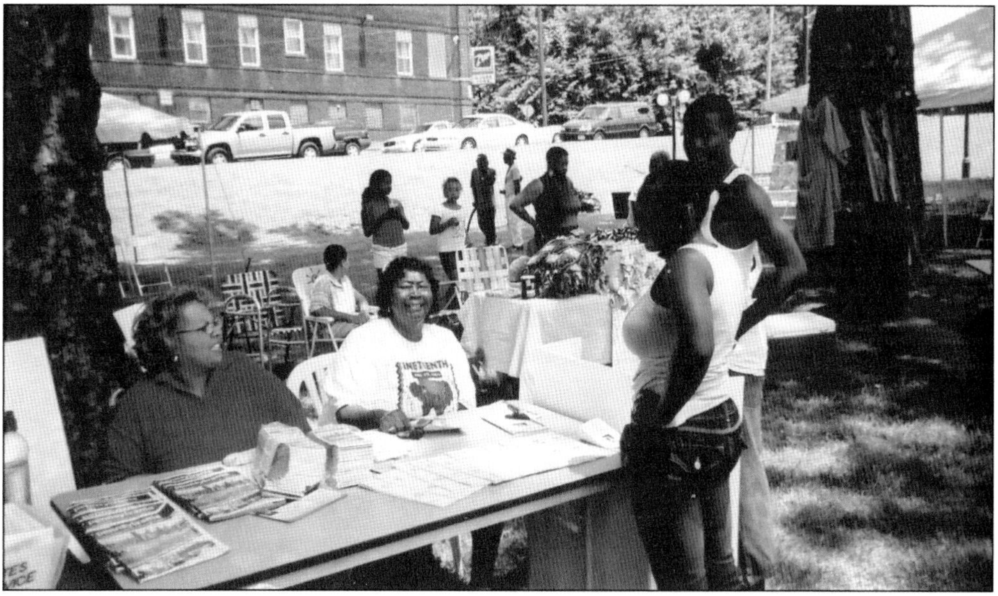

Current Farrell mayor Olive McKeithan has said, "We need houses. We need our community cleaned up . . . We're not afraid to walk down our streets at night. We want others to feel the same way." Miss Ollie has been a longtime advocate for revitalization, and under her leadership, new housing is being planned in Farrell once again. She is both the first African American and first female mayor of Farrell, a city fast approaching a 50-percent African American population. (Author's collection.)

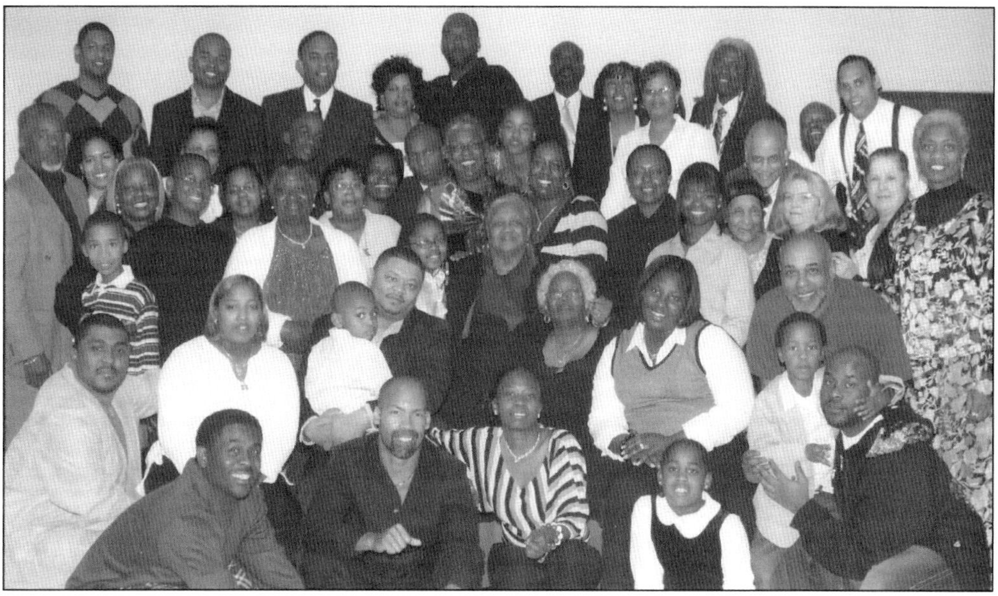

Longtime community organizer Martha Richards began by knocking on doors and picking up trash, which led to a block club and later the development of Southwest Gardens. She is affectionately known as "Ma Richards" to the community. Richards (third row, center), founder and director emeritus of Southwest Gardens, poses with a large group at a birthday celebration held at the Veterans of Foreign War Post 5286 at 1233 Idaho Street. (Photograph by Guy Gibbs; courtesy of Martha Richards.)

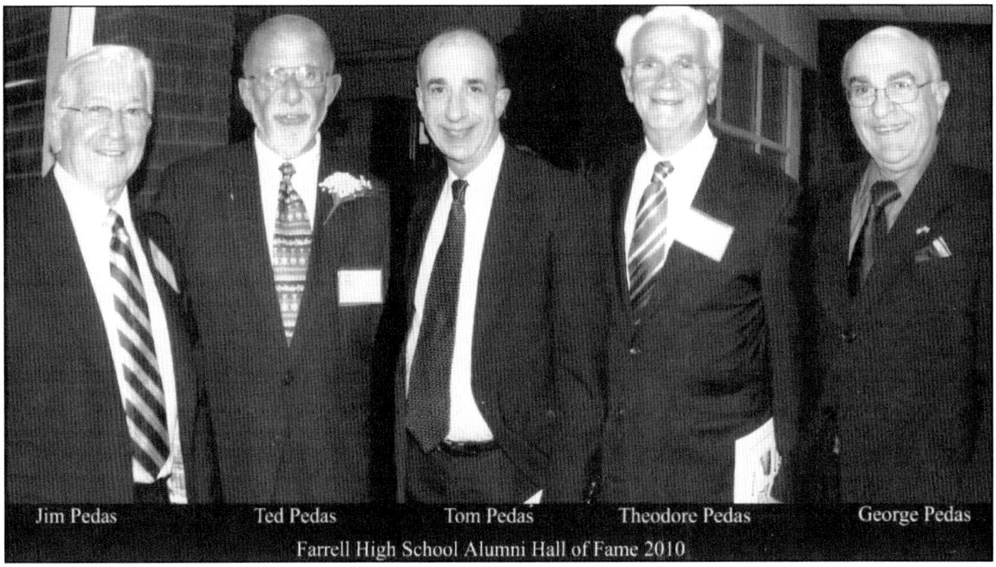

The Farrell High School Alumni Hall of Fame is the mastermind of local philanthropist Ted Pedas, who generously provided seed money and continues to make annual contributions along with family and friends. The Alumni Hall of Fame recognizes the achievements of alumni and retired school staff. Ted is shown here (second from left) with his brothers George and Tom and their cousins Theodore and James Pedas from Washington, DC, at the 2010 Alumni Hall of Fame banquet. (Courtesy of Marcy Pedas Sigler.)

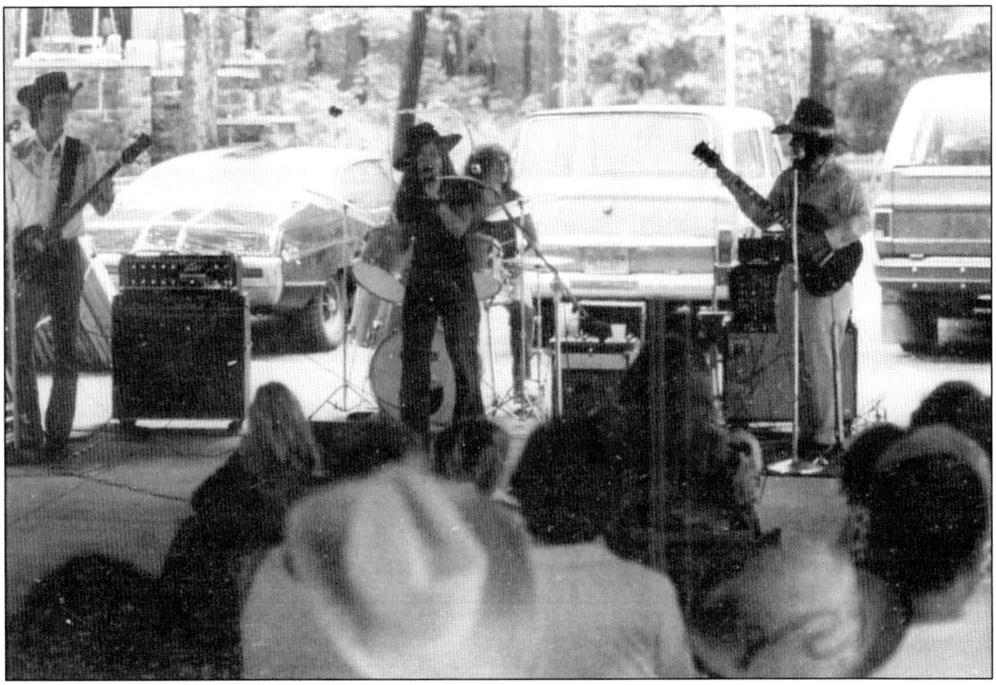

Farrell's Homecoming has been like a down-home barbecue or family reunion, where guests were treated to a sweet atmosphere complete with parade, tasty aromas, pop music, and plenty of well-wishers. Shown here is a concert under the pavilion at a Farrell Homecoming celebration on August 3, 1980. (Courtesy of Ann Yazvac.)

In 2010, the author of this book developed a summer enrichment program to increase civic pride. Youth expressed surprise that Elaine Lobl Konisburg, seen here, winner of coveted book awards and author of *From the Mixed-up Files of Mrs. Basil E. Frankweiler*, was the 1947 Farrell High School valedictorian. The book, which explored her Jewish heritage, was turned into a movie, *The Runaways*, starring Ingrid Bergman. (Courtesy of SNPL.)

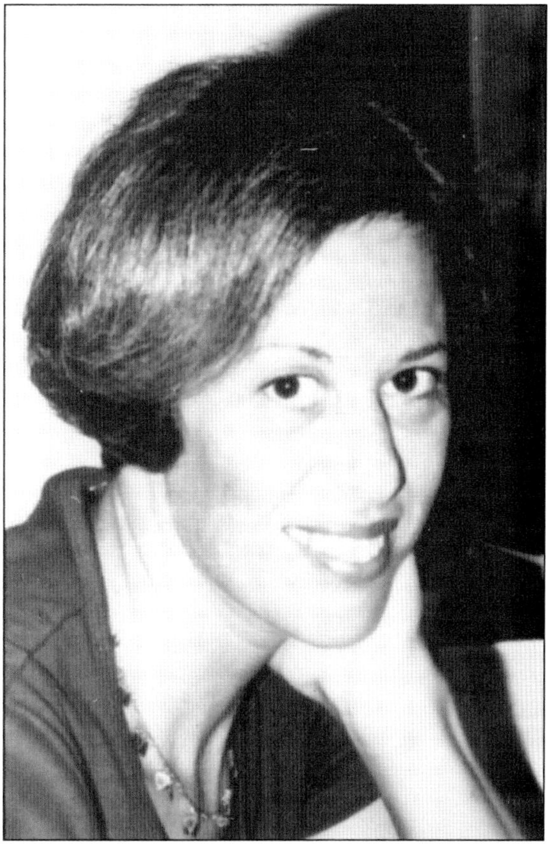

Youth at the summer enrichment program were asked to find out where Farrell got its name. Children searched the Internet for the answer, and their exit ticket had to name James A. Farrell as the city's namesake and provide his occupation as either an industrialist or president of United States Steel. Treats were provided in return for their exit ticket. Here, local parent Annette Manilla is holding her son while her daughter (first row, far right) and other children listen to story time at the public library. (Courtesy of SNPL.)

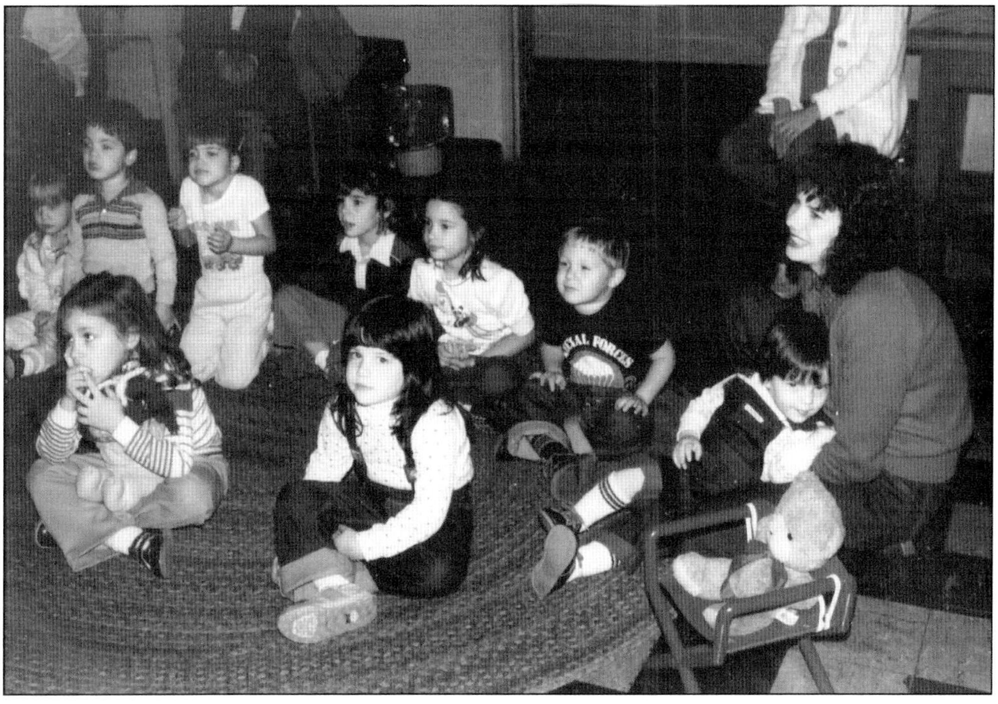

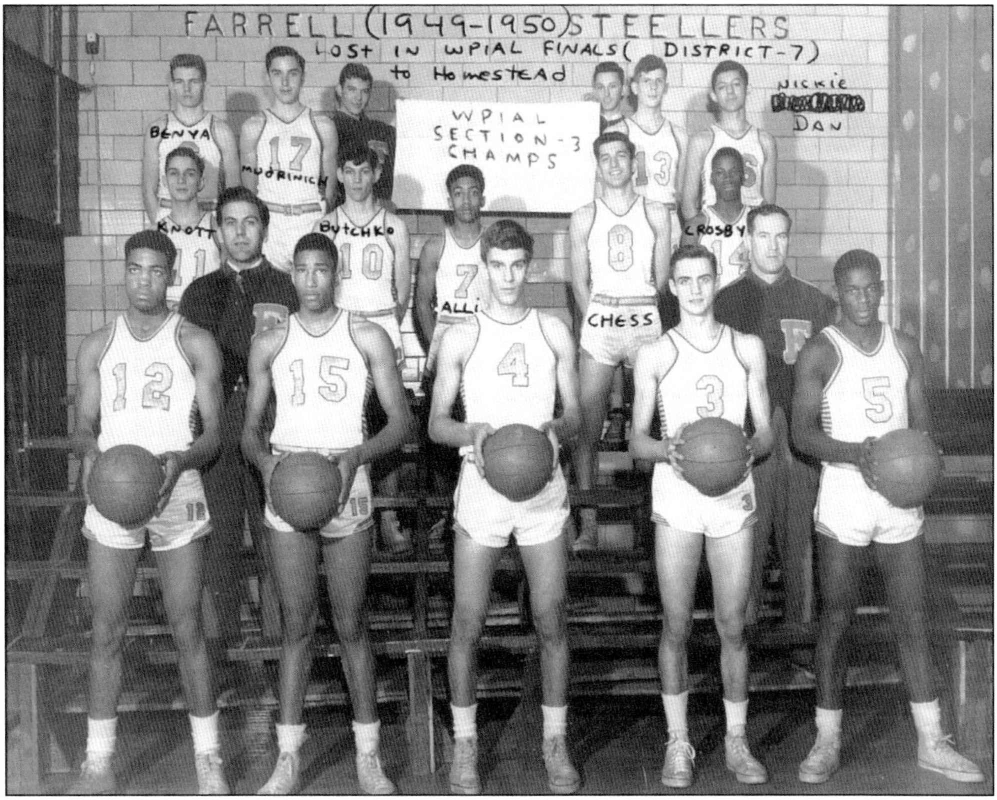

Youth were enthralled to find men of valor in their town's history. Herbert "Herbie" Williams, a 1950 Farrell High School graduate, was an all-around athlete as well as a decorated Vietnam veteran and retired lieutenant colonel. He returned home where he unselfishly served his community as a councilman. He is buried in Arlington National Cemetery. Coach Edward McCluskey's basketball program molded men of valor. Both Herbert Williams (first row, far right) and Edward McCluskey (second row, far right) are seen in this team photograph. (Courtesy of William Jarrett.)

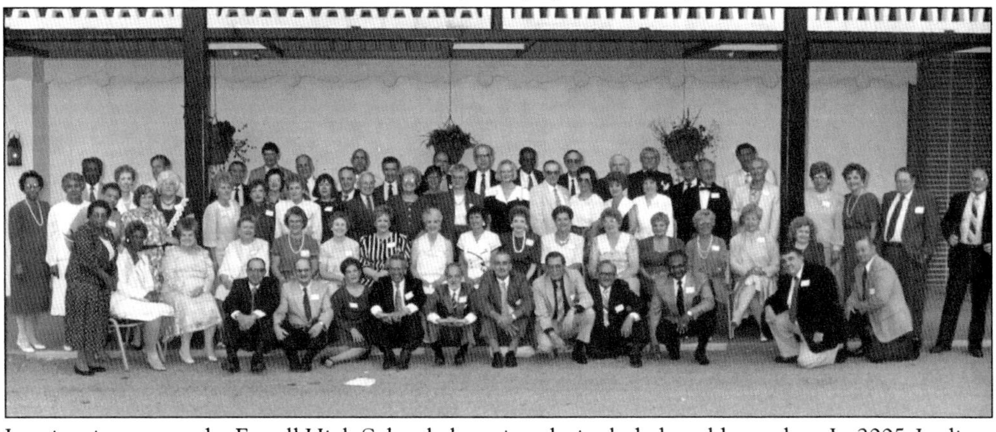

Luminaries among the Farrell High School alumni ranks included world travelers. In 2005, Ludima Gus Burton, a romance writer who draws on her Polish heritage, was inducted into the inaugural hall of fame class. Dr. Martha Bruce, a world traveler and Farrell High School Alumni Hall of Fame honoree, writes children's books about Africa. Shown here is the 40th reunion of the Farrell High School class of 1950. (Photograph by Gene Paulson; courtesy of Shirley Matthews.)

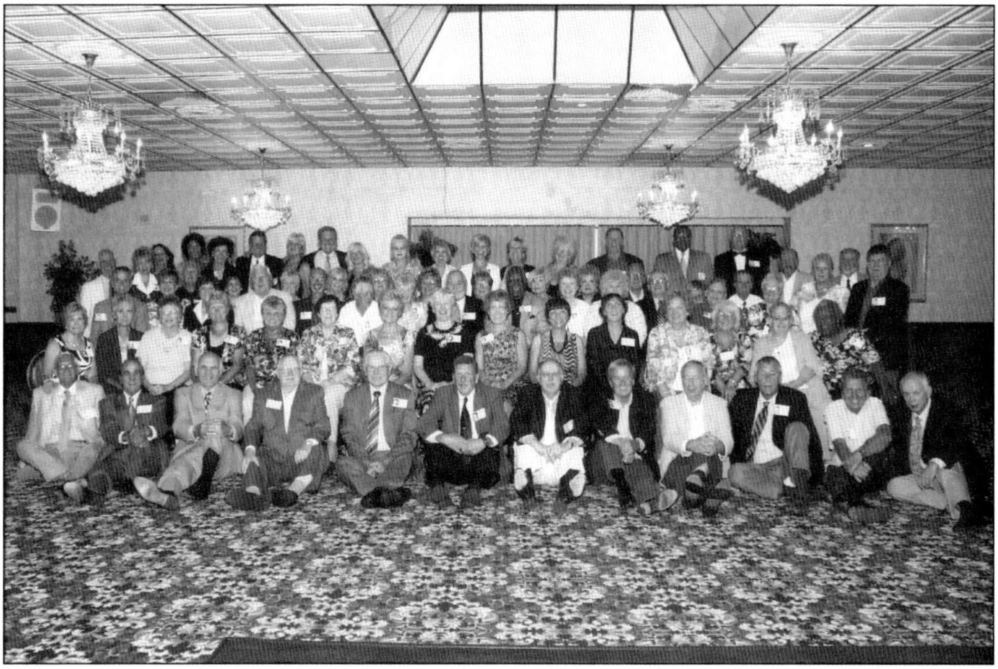

Youth researched and wrote about the lives of Farrell High School Alumni Hall of Fame honorees and their major accomplishments and cheered for distinguished Farrell alumni who were doctors, architects, and school superintendents. For some, Farrell High School class reunions are a time to reflect upon life lessons learned. Everybody agrees that Farrell provided a quality education and work ethic with no sense of entitlement. Above, Vince Cardamon (first row, far left) poses for a group shot at the 50th reunion for the class of 1960. Invariably at reunions, the conversation turns to past magic on the basketball court. Below, former Farrell High School seniors from the 1960 state basketball team are, from left to right, Willie Somerset, Dr. Paul Kudelko, Dr. Louis Mastrian, and Dr. Brian Generalovich. (Both, photograph by Kerry Lapcevich and Brandy King.)

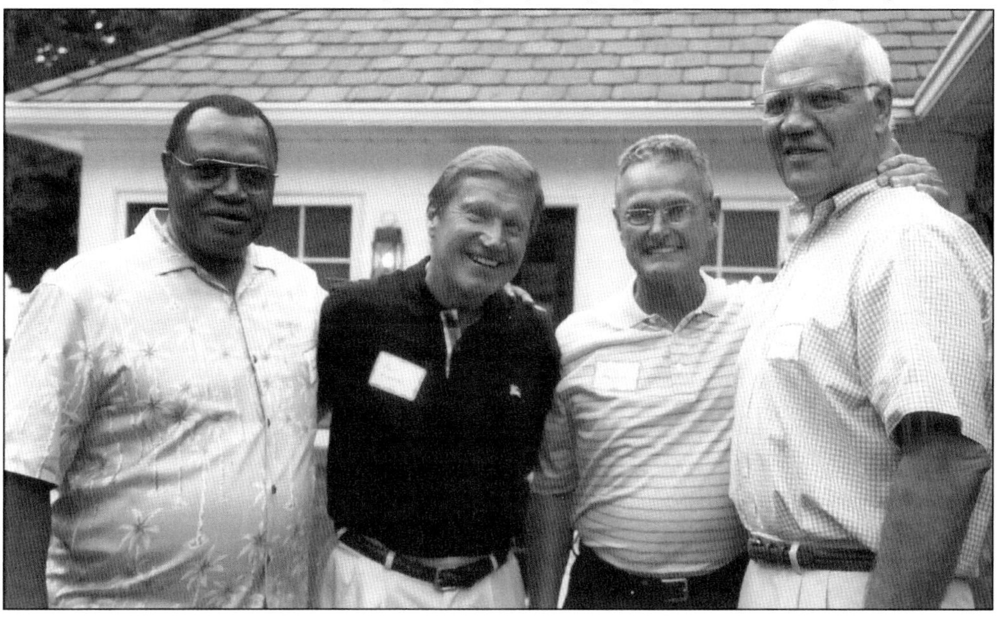

Attorney Daryl Winston, a 2008 Farrell High School Alumni Hall of Fame inductee, was the alumnus speaker for the 2011 commencement. Winston is a descendant of restaurateurs Elizabeth Alford and her daughter Jessie, who migrated to Farrell during the Great Depression. Shown here at another event the Mercer County Frontiers Club scholar recognition luncheon are, from left to right, (seated) keynote speaker Daryl Winston and Roland Barksdale-Hall, author of this book; (standing) Ronald Weston, Amanda Nogay, Tymmesha Brown, James E. Shephard, Jordan T. Garner, and FHS valedictorian Jackson Jones. (Courtesy of Veral Adair.)

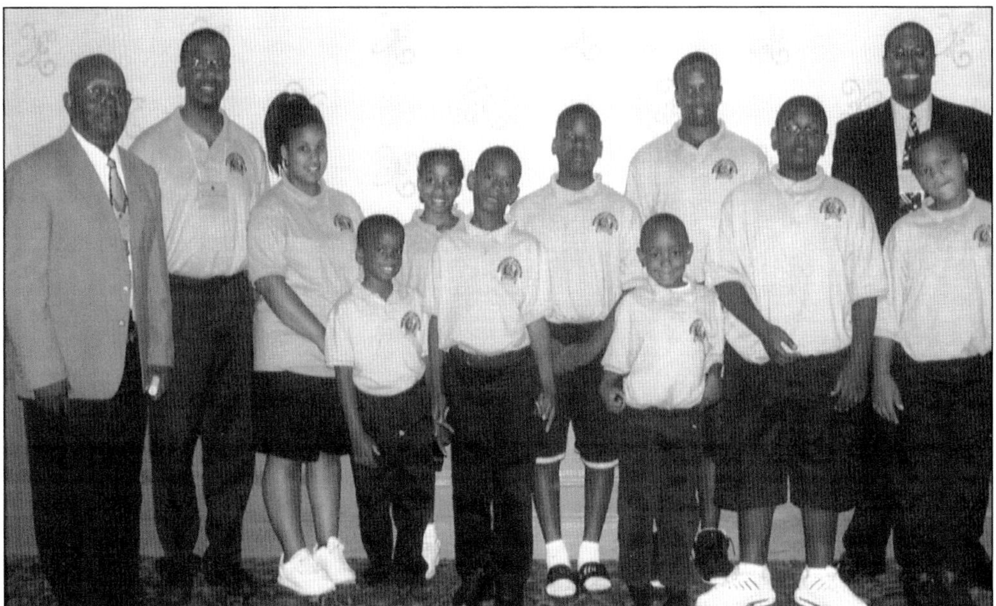

In 2005, youth from the Mercer County Frontiers Club were delegates to the 64th annual Frontiers International Convention, held in Columbus, Ohio. Delegates are, from left to right, (first row) Imanuel Hall, Robert Wood, Charles Barron, Keith Brown, and Darin Barnes; (second row) David Myers, club treasurer; Roland Barksdale-Hall, club youth advisor; Martha Howell, Vonita Hall, Shawn Howell, Drew Barksdale Hall, and attorney Jawwaad A. Rasheed, Frontiers International national youth director. (Author's collection.)

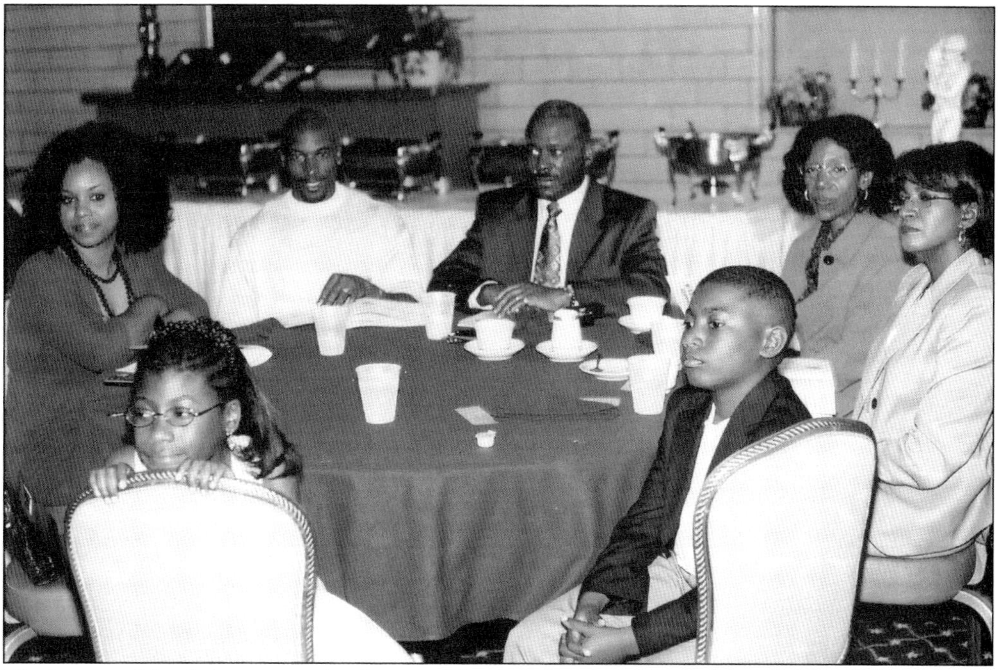

The hearts of the fathers turned to listen to the sons. Roger Winston listens to his son's address at the Mercer County Frontiers Club awards luncheon. Shown here are, from left to right, (seated, bottom left) Jaina Winston, Monique Winston, Kennya Winston, Roger Winston (father of Daryl Winston), Betty Winston (mother of Daryl Winston), Jo Ann Winston, and Dawson Winston. (Courtesy of Veral Adair.)

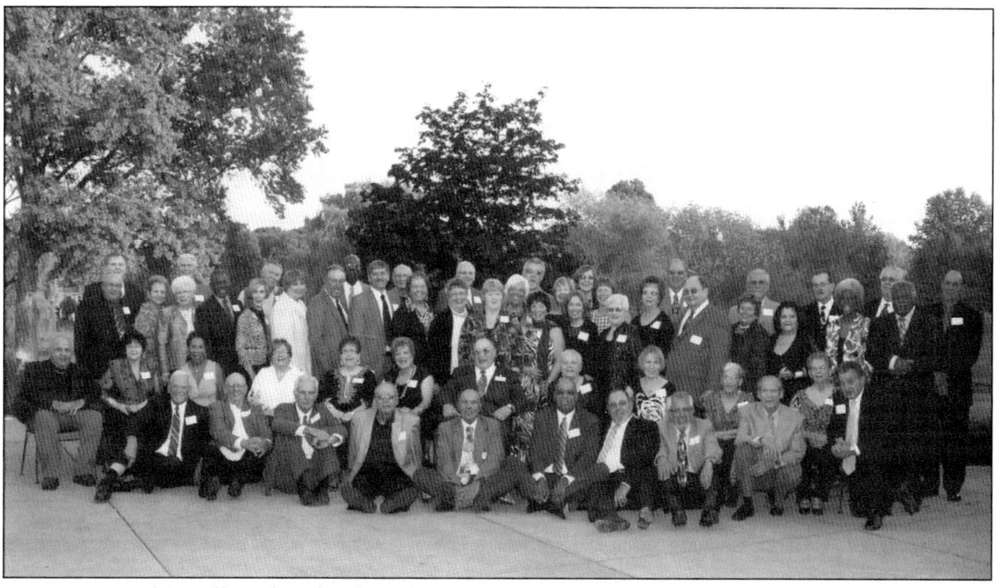

Generations of Farrell High School graduates and their families have gone on to make their mark in the world. At a 50th Farrell High School class reunion, attendees kiss, hug, and reminisce about their lives. The class reunions are much like a family reunion. Roger Winston (third row, fourth from left) poses with his 1961 high school class. (Photograph by Kerry Lapcevich and Brandy King; courtesy of Roger Winston.)

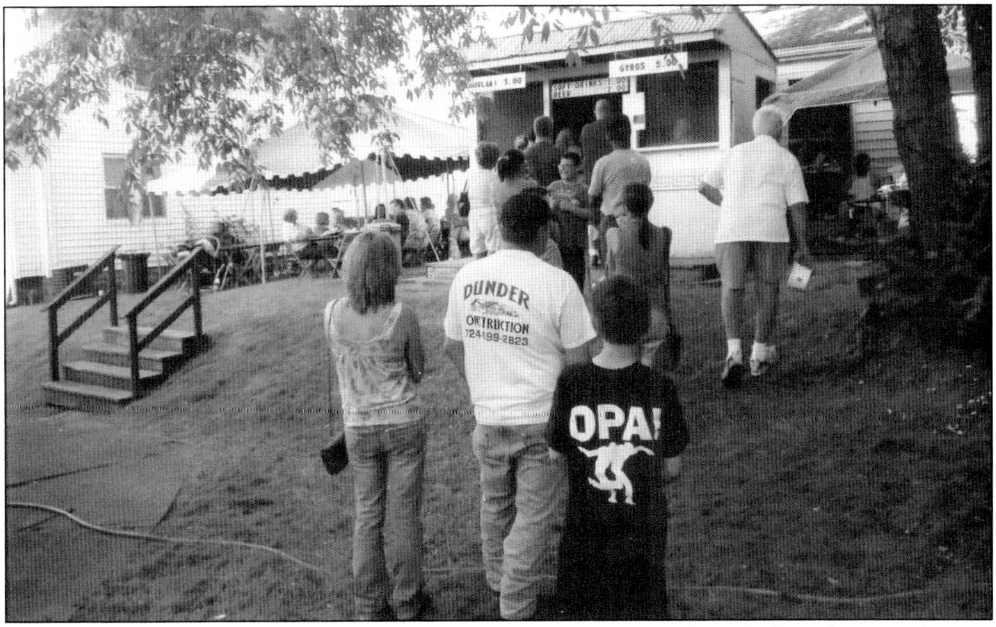

Roland Barksdale-Hall highlighted Farrell's summer cultural festivals and ethnic heritage for area youth. The youth learned about the life of Ted Pedas, a Farrell alumnus, who provided cash awards for the student of the month. Youth learners talked about Greek heritage and food. Several had tasted gyros. They were asked about the ingredients that go into gyros. Shown here is the waiting line for gyros at the 18th Annual Greek Food Festival on the grounds of the Annunciation Greek Orthodox Church located at 1007 Washington Street. (Author's collection.)

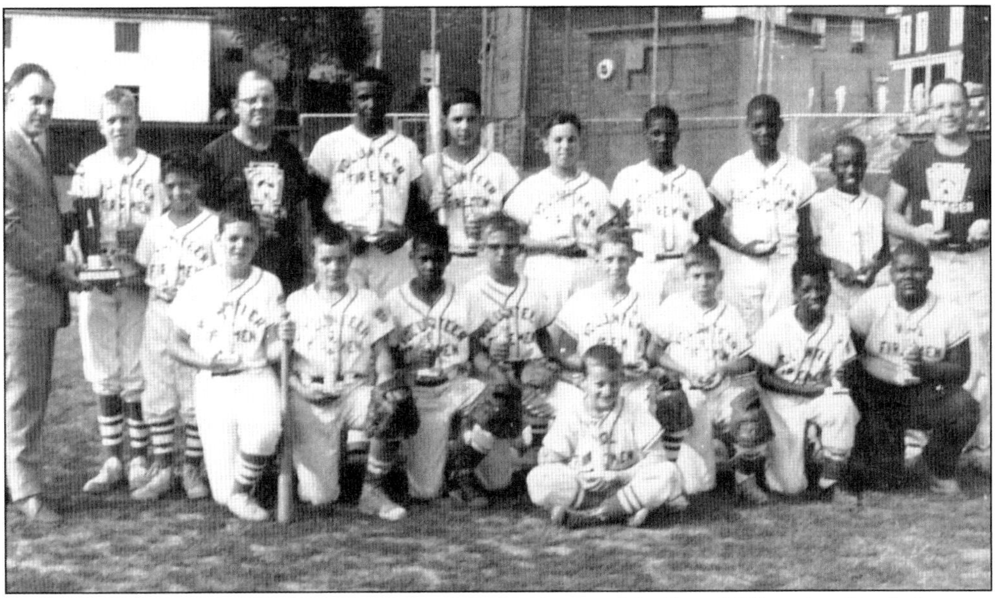

Youth were thrilled to learn the Recreation Complex, home of the Farrell-Wheatland Little League, was once part of a hollow that Farrell's courageous pioneers with a can-do spirit worked to fill in, remaking the city. Fireman Little League Champion of Mercer in 1962 include manager John Stan, Dennis Staul, Larry Long, Bob Donatello, Mark Brysh, Don Dionsio, Forest Underwood, Ernie Somerset, Larry Stinson, R. Richards, and D. Defazio. (Courtesy of Martha Richards.)

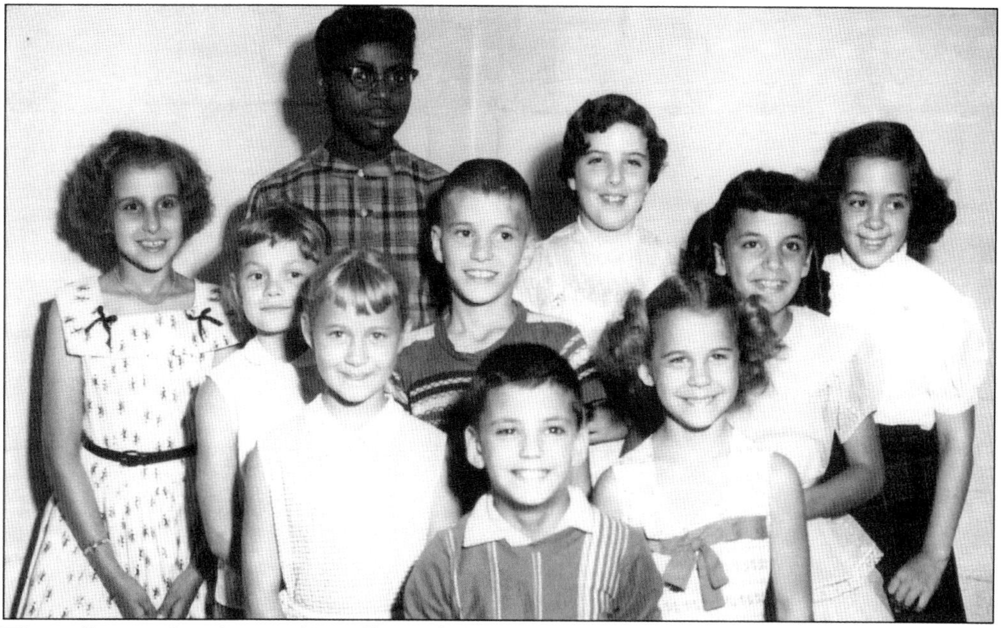

The walking cultural tour of Farrell concluded at the Stey-Nevant Public Library. Generations have viewed the library as a fun place. On August 25, 1958, top winners at the summer reading club party included, from left to right (first row) Joseph Salatino; (second row) Rebecca and Mary Beth Suchy; (third row) Louise Sveda, Joseph Sveda, and Kathleen Andree; (fourth row) Joanne Belcik, Karen E. Johnson, Bernadette Liscio, and Mary Frances Mosky. (Courtesy of SNPL.)

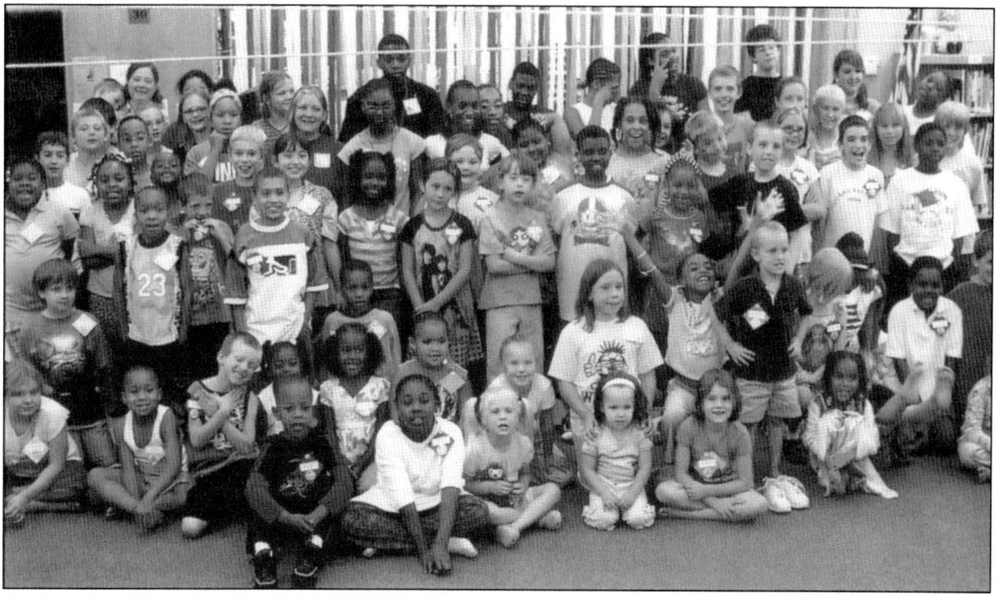

A 1938 Farrell High School graduate, Irene Johnson graduated with honors from nursing school. Her daughter Karen Johnson Weston, a 1964 Farrell High School graduate and former Farrell Elementary School teacher, benefitted from the library's summer reading as a youth and now serves on the library advisory board. A festive sleepover culminates the summer reading program. Here, in the fourth row, far left, is Karen Weston 's granddaughter Niyah M. Darzey at the summer celebration. (Courtesy of SNPL.)

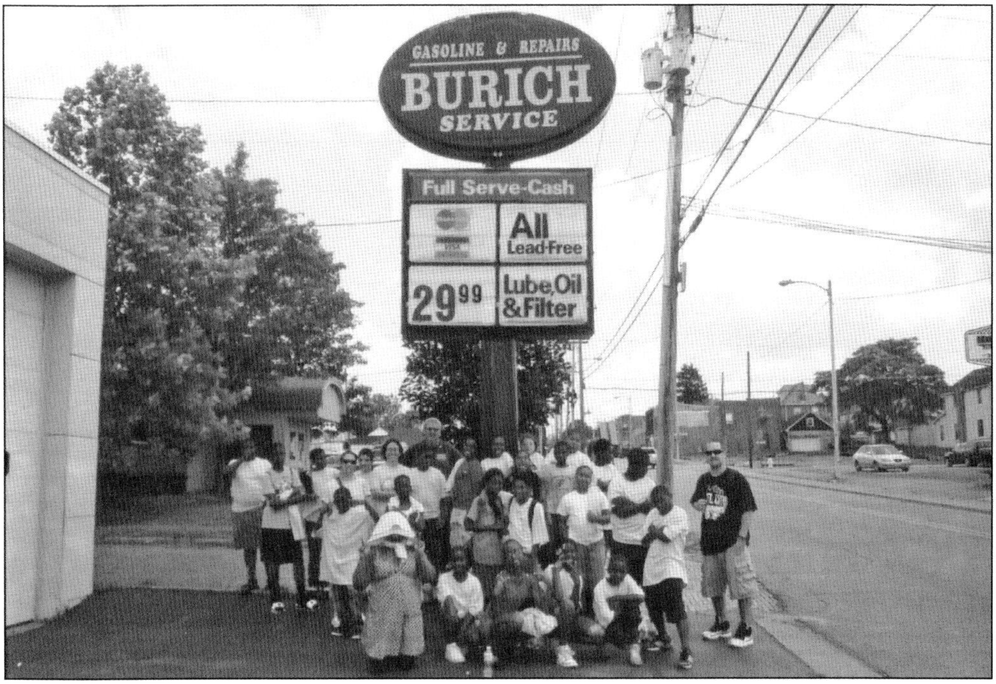

Over a century ago, the bulk of Farrell's pioneer hailed from eastern and southern Europe and the American South. There was restlessness in peasants' feet as they carried themselves away to make their mark in the world. Shown here is a descendant of Croatian immigrants, former Farrell councilman Robert Burich (back row, tall man), who now operates Burich full service gas station on Roemer Boulevard. He talks with youth group on walking cultural tour. (Author's collection.)

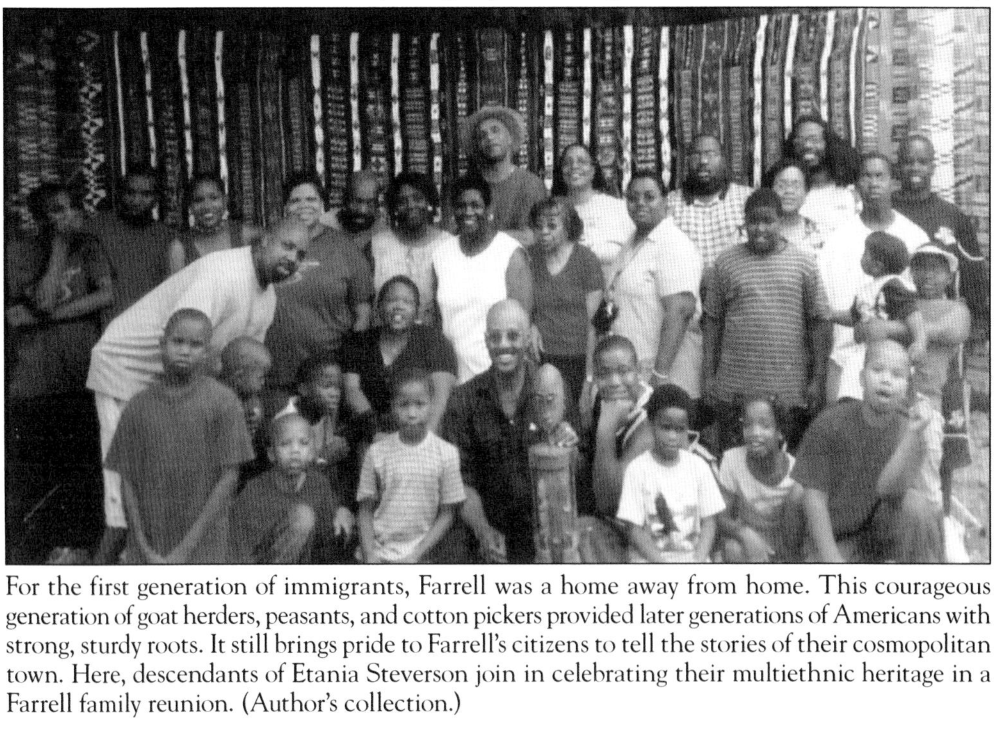

For the first generation of immigrants, Farrell was a home away from home. This courageous generation of goat herders, peasants, and cotton pickers provided later generations of Americans with strong, sturdy roots. It still brings pride to Farrell's citizens to tell the stories of their cosmopolitan town. Here, descendants of Etania Steverson join in celebrating their multiethnic heritage in a Farrell family reunion. (Author's collection.)

Many chatted and stood in long lines when nostalgic pricing was brought back during Farrell's Homecoming. More than 1,500 hot dogs sold in four hours at 10¢ each. Frank J. Egercic served as chairman of the nostalgic pricing committee. Shown here, a vintage car rides in parade at a Farrell Homecoming celebration on August 3, 1980. Today, Harakal's Lowery Notary Service is located on Roemer Boulevard. (Courtesy of Ann Yazvac.)

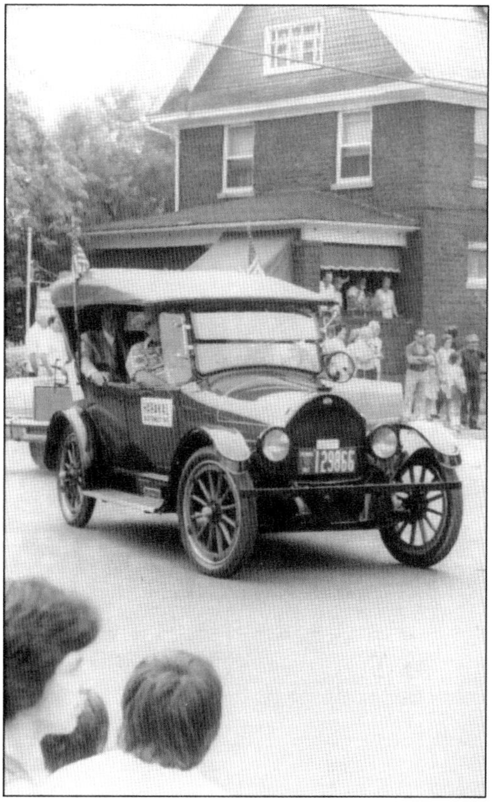

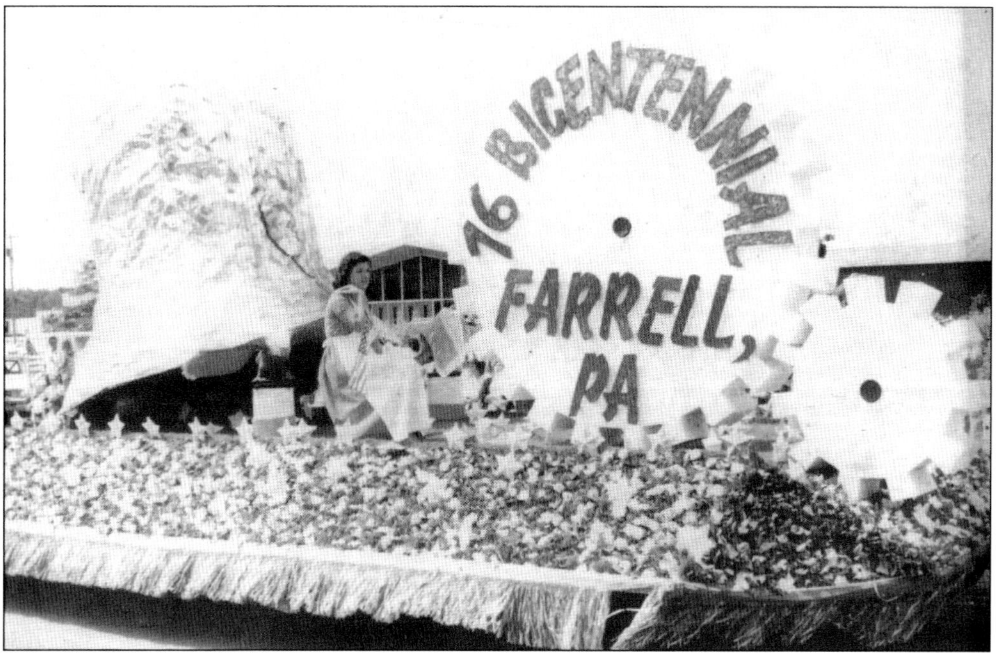

In 1976, Farrell's float in America's bicentennial celebration celebrates a shared multiethnic heritage. Farrell's rich mosaic has sealed strong and enduring bonds of loyalty and friendship. Can I get a witness? (Courtesy of Ann Yazvac.)